W9-DEV-492

DISCARDED

SOUL BABIES

SOUL BABIES

Black Popular Culture and
the Post-Soul Aesthetic

Mark Anthony Neal

ROUTLEDGE
New York • London

Published in 2002 by
Routledge
29 West 35th Street
New York, NY 10001

Published in Great Britain by
Routledge
11 New Fetter Lane
London EC4P 4EE

Routledge is an imprint of the Taylor & Francis Group.

10 9 8 7 6 5 4 3 2 1

Library of Congress Cataloging-in-Publication Data
Neal, Mark Anthony.
    Soul babies : Black culture and the post-soul aesthetic / Mark Anthony Neal.
        p. cm.
    Includes bibliographical references and index.
    ISBN 0-415-92657-2 (alk. paper) — ISBN 0-415-92658-0 (pbk.)
1. African American—Intellectual life. 2. African Americans in popular culture. 3. Popular culture—United States. 4. African Americans—Social life and customs. 5. Soul music—History and criticism. 6. African Americans—Race identity. I. Title.
    E185.615 .N35 2001
    305.896'073--dc21   2001020490

Dedicated to

my parents, Arthur Cleveland Neal and Elsie Eleanor Neal,

my wife, Gloria Taylor-Neal,

and my daughter and "Soul Sista,"

Misha Gabrielle Neal (the Baby-Girl Diva)

And in memory of

Frankie "the Chief Rocker" Crocker
Helen Martin
Beah Richards
Curtis Mayfield
Grover Washington Jr.
Roebuck "Pops" Staples
Stanley Turrentine
Whitman "Grady" Mayo

Contents

Preface

The SUNY-Albany campus where I teach is roughly a twenty-minute drive from my home in Schenectady, New York. As my daughter's preschool is a scant three minutes away from the campus, I basically carry the bulk of day-care duty. The daily drives have allowed my daughter and me a kind of one-sided sharing, as she is subjected to my diverse listening taste and my need for daily doses of *Tom Joyner in the Morning*, a nationally syndicated drive-time program hosted by the self-described "fly-jock" jock and featuring a host of characters like newswoman Sybil Wilks, comedians J. Anthony Brown and Myra J, and Tavis Smiley, with his twice-weekly commentary. Because my home life over the last two years has essentially been taken over by this now-two-and-a-half-year-old girl, who we affectionately, and on more than few occasions derisively, call "the baby-girl diva," the time that I spend in my ten-year-old Honda, with or without my daughter, is special; it's almost the only time I get to listen to *my* music. As I shuttle back and forth from day care to campus and the local Starbucks, where I do much of my writing and reading, my car has become my second home base. So as I got deep into this project, it was not unusual to find stacks of books, CDs, and videotapes sprawled across the backseat, along with box juices, stray Fig Newtons, and an army of children's toys and books, ranging from the Nathan's hot-dog man (yes, there is such a thing) to a toy cell phone (absolutely a necessity for a small child with a particular affinity for *your* cell phone) and board books written by quilter Faith Ringgold.

It was during one of these morning sojourns that my daughter, who already has distinct taste in shoes, music (she prefers Ray Charles to Stevie Wonder), and reading material, reached over into my book bag and pulled out my copy of Fred Jameson's *Postmodernism; or, The Cultural Logic of Late Capitalism*, opened it and proceeded to read aloud, "Blah, blah, blah, blah." Now my daughter, who was three months short of two years at the time, obviously couldn't read yet, though she had already begun to refer to writing, be it in her favorite *Hand, Hand, Finger, Thumb* book or on signs in the supermarket, as "ABCs," so her comments about Jameson's book struck me as a distinct commentary on her part, as if she knew it was some esoteric and inaccessible stuff (I wanted to use another word). Hell, many folks have picked up Jameson's book and a host of others like it and felt compelled to voice the same thoughts, but therein lies the challenge of this project. Though I have never claimed to be a postmodern critic, I have been struck by the few occasions when fellow African-American scholars have referred to me as such. I was ambushed at the national meeting of a black studies organization a few years ago by a group of decidedly Afrocentric scholars who wanted me to explain my affinity for postmodernism after I presented a very early version of chapter 4 of this book. Shortly thereafter, as I began to shop my first manuscript, *What the Music Said*, to various publishing houses, at least two responded that it seemed "postmodern." Since then I have come to accept my fate, which can be reduced to the crass logic, "If it quacks like a duck, then it's a duck." It is my desire with this project to use postmodern insights to illuminate the presentation of black life and culture, particularly within the realms of popular and mass culture; but to do so in a language (fat chance) that is accessible and readable to the publics that I am politically committed to, while employing examples that are recognizable within those same and other publics. Using the prism of what I call a "post-soul aesthetic," I hope to achieve this.

It is this desire for accessibility that perhaps led me to use R. Kelly as the focal point for my illumination of the post-soul aesthetic in chapter 1. Though Kelly is a fine singer and even finer songwriter and producer, he has also been a lightning rod for criticisms of how "vulgar" contemporary black popular music has become, as witnessed in ditties like "Sex Me" and "Bump and Grind." While some may excuse certain antics among so-

called gangsta rappers because they are "thugs," Kelly is more disconcerting to some, because it is so clear that this boy "loves his mama" and that
he "came up in the 'Chuch.'" But my interest in Kelly is based on those
very contradictions; the same artist who has penned his generation's first
standard, "I Believe I Can Fly," he is so clearly a student of the "soul man"
tradition that he regularly channels the likes of Charlie Wilson, Lenny
Williams, and Jeffrey Osborne. His latter talent is notable because
Wilson, Williams, and Osborne are not household names, in comparison
to the regular rent-an-R&B-vocalists who think they are the next Marvin
Gaye. For years I have been bouncing my opinions about R. Kelly's significance to my best friend Frank Paul Jr., himself a music critic for a
international news service, only to have him regularly question the state
of my sanity. I mentioned, for example, how useful I found one of Kelly's
most recent singles, "I Wish," where he brings his artistry full circle to
Sam Cooke, creating an aural space where one could imagine the late
father of male soul singers riffing, "Come on and braid my hair." In classic style, Frank responded that Sam Cooke would have never appeared in
the video for the song shoving his mug into the camera while "sipping on
Kristal." Of course Frank is right, but it is the very broaches of acceptable
public behavior in the work of Kelly or in Eddie Murphy's *The PJs* that I
want to recover in this project and translate into meaningful and useful
critiques of contemporary black life.

In chapter 2 I attempt to "recover" the very popular films done in the
mid-1970s by Sidney Poitier and Bill Cosby. Though the films were a clear
attempt by Poitier to sanitize the presentation of black life in film, which
had come to be dominated by the blaxploitation genre, the films themselves relied heavily on some of the very staples of those films, albeit less
violently, with their consistent focus on black gangsters. I argue that the
gangsters in the film trilogy serve the purpose of articulating the appre-
hensions and ambitions associated with the emergence of the "new" black
middle class in the 1970s, if not a commentary on both Poitier's and
Cosby's struggles in that regard, as black entertainment icons. Chapter 3
delves heavily into the gender politics of the post-soul era where I juxtapose the general desire to rehabilitate and "save" the black man to the
demonization of black women in popular culture. Referencing the theoretical insights of Hortense Spillers and Sharon Patricia Holland, I look
closely at the figure of John Amos, arguably the quintessential black television father; Dave Holister's "Baby Mama Drama" and the film *Soul Food*.

But this project is also a product of my own desires to place my intellectual project and those of my generation into some kind of historical context—a reflection on the impact of a post-soul generation of artists and critics or, dare I say, even intellectuals. On the mornings when I lose the battle with my daughter over radio privileges, I am forced to listen to my daughter's musical choices, most often the soundtrack from the film *Elmo in Grouchland*. Elmo is of course the three-year old "monster" who is easily the most popular of the current crop of *Sesame Street* puppets and whose dolls have been very popular sellers over the last few years. It will be some time before I can share with my daughter that I was literally in the first generation of children exposed to the ambitions of the Children's Television Workshop, which introduced *Sesame Street* on the Public Broadcasting System (PBS) in 1969—its theme song based on a riff from the song "Hi-heel Sneakers"—hoping to impact nappy-headed ghetto three-year-olds like myself, who were also in the first generation of Head Start graduates. That a program that initially aimed to "educate" the ghetto masses has become synonymous with public broadcasting and a mainstream children's program, as well as a franchise in its own right with the various *Muppet* movies and products—the most recent, *Muppets in Outer Space*, heavily indebted to funk music—speaks volumes about just how American the 'hood has become. The theme song to the Elmo movie, "Welcome to Grouchland," in fact includes a break that riffs off the Broadway musical *Bring in Da Noise, Bring in Da Funk* ("bringing the noise, bringing the *junk*"), which starred a definitive post-soul artist in dancer Savion Glover. What does it mean that contemporary popular icons in the 1980s and '90s, such as Michael Jackson, Bill Cosby, and even actor Morgan Freeman, who featured in the original cast of another Children's Television Workshop project, *The Electric Company*, were thoroughly consumed by the post-soul generation via the Saturday-morning cartoons *The Jackson Five* and *Fat Albert and the Cosby Kids*? What does it mean when that same generation comes to public voice during the Reagan era as critics and producers of hip-hop music and culture? How does this generation of voices, be they Joan Morgan, Aaron McGruder, Kevin Powell, Paul Beatty, Jill Scott, or myself, for that matter, differ from the critical voices of those prior to the post-soul era? Chapter 4 is a fairly explicit manifesto that aims to locate the formation of this post-soul intelligentsia, while chapter 5 attempts to identify those voices in the collective work of the aforementioned critics.

Acknowledgments

Though I'd like to steal a riff from Toni, Tone, Tony ("Toni, Tone, Tony has done it again!"), I'll simply thank Bill Germano at Routledge for his support and encouragement of this project. Support at the State University of New York at Albany has also been crucial to the realization of this project. I'd like to thank provost Carlos Santiago, my former colleagues in the Department of Africana Studies, and "new" colleagues in the Department of English, most notably Bret Benjamin, Mike Hill, Randall Craig, Donald Byrd, and Tom Cohen, all who seriously represented a "bruh" in the trenches. I'd like to thank also some of my most recent students, including Mohavi Wright, who also keeps a "bruh" centered, the brilliant Faith Corbett and no less brilliant Karima Fitzgerald, Jason Smith (thanks for the poem), Candace Douglas, John Roberts, Habiba Ibrahim, and David Hupp. I got special luv for my crew of grad students Wil "ABD like a MFer" Turner, David Curry, Laterrian (Teri) McBrewer, and Nicole "the critical one" Johnson. As drama went down all around us, the five of us bunkered ourselves into a collective I'll simply call "CIN" (Critical Interdisciplinary Niggas), fine minds all that I expect great things from. I must especially thank Teri and Nicole for the great care and commitment they showed to my undergraduate students as assistants, but also as fertile, vibrant, provocative intellectuals. It goes without saying that this project does not get done without their support.

SOUL BABIES

Peace to my homies in the western New York hinterlands of Fredonia, especially Jon and Wilma Kraus, Karen Mills-Courts and Pat Courts, Jean and Tom Malinowski, Bruce Simon, the Slaton and Torrain clan, Linda Phillips, Robert Jordan, Kathleen Bonds and family, and the rest of the EDP staff, particularly Barbara Yochyum. Much thanks to our family lawyer, Brendon O'Shea, and the staff at the Sleep Center at St. Claire's hospital, who helped a "bruh" finally get some rest. Got to thank the staff at the Wolf Road Starbucks in Colonie (Albany) for good coffee, great music, and the kind of customer service that keeps people coming back, particularly given the fact one of those eggnog lattes can a run a "bruh" close to $4.00.

Many thanks for folks who have supported my work these last couple of years, especially Sarah Zupko and Cindy Fuchs, editors of PopMatters, which allowed me to think out loud in print. Thanks to my man Jabari Asim, "the hardest working black man I know," who peeped my work in the most obscure of places and been showing me luv ever since. Gotta show my luv for Bob Davis and the rest of the "fam" on the Soul Patrol list. Thanks to Kevin Powell, Jeff Melnick, and Rachel Rubin for allowing my work a presence in their projects. Thanks to S. Craig Watkins, Craig Werner, Thomas Glave, and Winston Napier for the regular e-mail exchanges. In that regard I am even more thankful for my Toronto homie Richard "the R" Iton, who shares my love of good soul music and provocative criticism and has always been willing to allow me to vent and bounce ideas off him. Much thanks to Max Rodriguez, editor of the *Quarterly Black Review,* for giving me a regular forum at the Harlem Book Fair. To my man Robin "Where's the Monk book?" Kelley, who has shown me luv from the beginning. Got to represent for Mike and Marcia Dyson, who ALWAYS show a "bruh" some luv. Thanks to my sista/mentor, the Masani Alexis DeVeaux, for still lending her ear. Much luv, as always, to the only real homegirl I have, Jeanette McVicker (and Bill Spanos), whose teaching and intellect still hold me in awe. Lastly I have to thank Sharon Patricia Holland (and Jen Devere Brody). Though we were only colleagues for a short year, I am thankful for our far too brief conversations and your friendship. Your influence on me runs deep through this project. A quick "holla" to Todd Boyd, Tricia Rose, and Dipa Basu for the "sick" time we had at the "Hip Hop and Rap: Redefining the Black Public Sphere conference in Claremont, California, last spring.

Though I don't have that many real friends, I'd like to thank Denise Davidson, especially for the way she represented for me when we promoted *What the Music Said.* I have no doubt that there is a little of your

ACKNOWLEDGMENTS

spirit in these pages. Many thanks to Ana Robertson for your friendship to the family and being Misha's loving godparent. I don't have any brothers, but if I had one, he would be like my brother-in-law, Wesley Taylor. Thanks to Wesley and his bride, Jacqueline, for their love and support. And then there's the crew. Much luv to Charles Banks Jr. and Gary White (and wife Phoebe), and I got real special luv to my tightest niggas. Whether trying to be bourgie at B. Smith's, eating chicken wings and dirty rice at the crib, exchanging regular e-mail, or talking on the phone about being committed fathers and husbands, I can't do what I do without the constant support and affirmation from Gopal Burgher, esq., Sebastian Tate (with Jiann and them big boys Jason and Jamar), Dr. Julius Adams (with Carmon and baby Lisa), and Frank Paul (with Sonja and my goddaughter Imani). As R. Kelly would say, "My niggas, we out the 'hood now." To my father-in-law Willie ("don't know what my son-in-law does for a living, but he sure can cook") Taylor and my gracious and gentle mother-in-law, Odessa, thank you for *all* that you do.

Perhaps no people have shown me more love than my parents, who have taken great pride in me from the beginning, but even more so now that they can show folks my name in print or blush the few times I'm on TV. It has been the joy that they seem to derive from my successes that is perhaps most touching to me, because in my mind their work has been done for a long time and it is that work, of raising me, that remains most important to me. I know that I live the life of the mind twenty hours a day as I do because my father got up every day at 5:00 A.M. to travel two hours sometimes from the Bronx to work twelve-hour days in Brooklyn. I know that I chose to be an "intellectual" because my mother made that choice for herself when I was a boy. More than two years ago my wife and I were blessed with an addition to our lives. We often wonder aloud to each other what exactly we did with our time before Misha Gabrielle Neal came to dominate our lives. Whether calling her the "baby-girl diva," "Ya, Ya" (my favorite), or "Soul Sista" (after the Bilal tune), she has absolutely changed our lives. This project is a tribute to both my wife Gloria and my daughter Misha for their regular faith in me as a husband and father above everything else.

M. A. N.
Schenectady, New York
June 2001

i was searching for some abstract beats the other day
when who do i see down there on avenue a?
my man albert—head down, in the worst mental state
he used to live fat, but now that's only in weight
i played like mary j. and asked for the 411
he said, "if you knew what i knew, you wouldn't even ask, son.
HEY HEY HEY . . . my crew's in disarray
i think i saw weird harold comin' down on the subway train
asking people for change, almost out of breath
always was thin, but now he damn near looks like death.
russell dropped out of school, hangin' with the wrong cliques
bucky started hustlin' so that he could get his teeth fixed.
bill got out the ghetto, now's he got four kids and a wife
but, he ain't thinkin' 'bout us/too busy livin' the life
and mushmouth's servin' time in the penny
somebody talked about his speech impediment one time too many
so, all over the neighborhood it's known:
eff around with mushmouth, yes ya get blown.
dumb donald's locked up with the mentally retarded
and rudy's been pimpin' even before the show started.
i wish mudfoot was here; maybe then i could maintain
and forget about what's weighin' down my brain.
it was cool between '72 and '84,
but the m'hood ain't that good no more.
gonna have a good time, right?
gonna have a good time, true?
gonna have a good time, right?
gonna have a good time, true?

—**Jason Randall Smith, "A Lesson in Deterioration"**

"You Remind Me of Something"
Toward a Post-Soul Aesthetic

We need a voice like our music—one that samples and layers many voices, injects its sensibilities into the old and flips into something new, provocative, and powerful. And one whose occasional hypocrisy, contradictions and triteness guarantee us at least a few trips to the terror-dome, forcing us to finally confront what we'd all rather hide from.

—Joan Morgan-Murray

Many have described the contemporary American experience, including the experiences of the black diaspora within it, as an example of postmodernity, a term that is at best foreign within the African-American community and contentious among more traditional black intellectual circles. While there is really no catchall definition of postmodernism, many theorists suggest that fractures within society and culture have necessitated new modes of thinking, which in many ways render more traditional ideals, in this case modern ideals, obsolete.[1] Much of the criticism directed at the use of postmodern theory by black intellectuals has sprung from discomfort with the import of decidedly European-based theories to explore African-American life. As bell hooks relates, postmodern thinking is "dominated primarily by the voices of white male intellectuals and/or academic elites who speak to and about one another in coded familiarity."[2] Fears that "theory" could decontextualize the reali-

1

ties of black life are not without warrant. My own rejection of the work of Theodor Adorno in my first book, *What the Music Said*, was a product of such thinking—my own sense that a European theorist could do little, if anything, to help me better illuminate the significance of Aretha Franklin's voice on a Sunday morning.[3]

Nevertheless, as filmmaker Madison Davis Lacy suggests in his film on the life of Richard Wright, the latter's years as an African-American expatriate in France exposed him to a broader range of intellectual discourses, particularly the work of French existentialists Albert Camus and Jean-Paul Sartre, allowing Wright to take more intellectual risks in his telling of the black experience globally, including the burgeoning decolonization movement on the African continent. While I am not suggesting that Wright's earlier work did not entail profound risk on his part, I do think that Wright's myopic view of black life in America—no different than that of most African-American thinkers at the time—was a product of the segregated world that produced him, denying him and others the physical and metaphoric freedom to explore more aspects of the African-American experience. I am aware that the world that framed Wright's latter commentary and the one where African-American graduate students are regularly exposed to French poststructuralists are radically different. The current access that black thinkers have to European theorists is unprecedented, but using Davis's logic here, I am suggesting that postmodern theories, particularly when carefully considered within the context of even the simple nuances of black life, facilitate valuable intellectual insights that can and should be refracted into interrogations of the African-American and diasporic conditions. In fact, I am suggesting that such theories offer a wider range of vantage points to fully problematize the African-American experience, particularly in concert with more traditional modes of inquiry.

In this regard, I am struggling to find language that references tropes that are/were valued, recognizable, and even rejected within African-American vernacular and popular culture, to better critique the postmodern realities that confront the African-American "community." I believe the concept of the "post-soul aesthetic" will be the framework in which I will achieve this goal. In the post-soul aesthetic I am surmising that there is an aesthetic center within contemporary black popular culture that at various moments considers issues like deindustrialization, desegregation, the corporate annexation of black popular expression, cybernization in the workforce, the globalization of finance and communication, the general commodification of black life and culture, and the proliferation of black "meta-identities," while continuously collapsing on modern concepts of blackness and reanimating "premodern" (African?) concepts of blackness. I am also suggesting that this aesthetic ultimately renders many "traditional" tropes of blackness dated and even meaningless; in its borrowing from black modern traditions, it is so consumed with its contemporary existential concerns that such traditions are not just called into question but obliterated.

I use the term *post-soul* to describe the political, social, and cultural experiences of the African-American community since the end of the civil rights and Black Power movements. To my knowledge, Nelson George first used the term in a general description of black popular culture after the blaxploitation era. More specifically I locate the beginnings of the post-soul era in the *Regents of the University of California v. Bakke* challenge to affirmative action in 1978. I'm most concerned about those folks, artists and critical thinkers, who live in the fissures of two radically different social paradigms; folks born between the 1963 March on Washington and the *Bakke* case, children of soul, if you will, who came to maturity in the age of Reaganomics and experienced the change from urban industrialism to deindustrialism, from segregation to desegregation, from essential notions of blackness to metanarratives on blackness, without any nostalgic allegiance to the past (back in the days of Harlem, or the thirteenth-century motherland, for that matter), but firmly in grasp of the existential concerns of this brave new world. At the core of this indulgence is a radical reimagining of the contemporary African-American experience, attempting to liberate contemporary interpretations of that experience from sensibilities that were formalized and institutionalized during earlier social paradigms. In this regard I agree with S. Craig Watkins's notion that in "periods of great disorder and transition . . . new ideas, social movements, and ideological strategies are mobilized to make sense of societal flux and instability. In the process, the ideas, belief systems, and symbolic terrain of a given period become more fragile and vulnerable to competing ideological worldviews."[4]

Almost two generations ago, the concept of soul emerged as the most vivid and popular expression of an African-American modernity. Jurgen Habermas's notion that "modernity lives on the experience of rebelling against all that is normative" is useful here, though not necessarily so for the black bodies that had long been ascribed a status of inferiority.[5] As

3

Scott Malcomson explains, "modernity is often considered hostile to inherited social status, given that modern societies tended to undermine genealogical aristocratic privilege,"[6] but modernity also "created and fixed a global notion of inherited slave status and 'savage' status, and of an inherited racial identity for whites, blacks, and Indians."[7] This "inherited slave status" was a product of what Malcomson calls the "combining of black skin and pagan faith" into the bodies of Africans in Portuguese possession in the fifteenth century and the beginning of what might be referred to as "modern blackness."[8] However "blackness" has been inscribed socially and cultural on black bodies, blacks have often used "blackness," and their own bodies, for that matter, as sites to challenge prevalent notions of blackness.[9] In a more detailed analysis of black expressive culture during the 1960s, Kimberly Bentson argues that blackness emerged "as a term of multiple, often conflicting, implications which, taken together, signal black America's effort to articulate its own conditions of possibility."[10] African-American modernity—what else could it be labeled, given that twentieth-century African-American identity was initially constricted within the context of American modernity?—could thus be regarded as a "counter" or at least "alternative" modernity.[11] Consequently, as a "modern" aesthetic, soul challenged the prevailing logic of white supremacy and segregation in ways that were discomforting and even grotesque to some, regardless of race or ethnicity. Premised on the construction of "positive" black images that could be juxtaposed against the overextended influence of Western caricatures of black life, the soul aesthetic dramatically altered the projects of Harlem Renaissance artists and critics by sanctioning both vernacular and popular expression largely valued within the black community without concern for the reactions of mainstream critics or institutions. As William Van Deburg writes, "Soul was the folk equivalent of the black aesthetic . . . a type of primal spiritual energy and passionate joy available only to members of the exclusive racial confraternity." Thus important political and social claims, particularly in regard to identity and cultural self-determination, could be made—and were made—on the frenzy of Aretha Franklin's voice or the syncopated choreography present in any James Brown performance. The same claims could be made on the purported militancy of wearing dashikis and Afro wigs, claims that were at least tacitly useful in the creation of the generation of black elected officials that appeared in the post–civil rights era.

In his work *A Nation within a Nation: Amiri Baraka and Black Power Politics*, Komozi Woodard asserts that black nationalist sensibilities were products of the hypersegregation within American society that "laid the foundations for a distinct black national political community."[12] Though clearly not the first aesthetic that mirrored the segregated realities of black life, the soul aesthetic was the cultural component to the most visible black nationalist ideas of the twentieth century. Subsumed within these efforts to build and support a "nation within a nation" was a litany of ideological and identity constructs that were often perceived as undermining black efforts at inclusion.[13] The paranoia within the Black Power and civil rights movements about "alternative" black lifestyles and ideologies was legitimated by the widespread infiltration and intense surveillance of the movements by the FBI and local law enforcement agencies. During earlier eras, when the threat of state-sanctioned violence against them was more prominent and overt, blacks rigorously closed ranks around common notions of black identity, even if such homogeneity was a fictive gesture. By coalescing around the myth of shared heterosexual identities, themselves socially constructed in relation to mainstream American perception of the function of blacks in American society, African-Americans often protected themselves from the most heinous forms of violence. In other words, identity constructs that further marked blacks as different were thought to invite more violence upon the black community—and legitimately so; a case in point is the experience of musical icon Little Richard, who once admitted that he "went through a lot as a boy. They called me sissy, punk, freak and faggot. . . . Sometimes white men would pick me up in their car and take me to the woods and try to get me to suck them. A whole lot of black people have had to do that."[14]

The strict code of discipline directed toward black children is just one example of the violence directed within the community to protect it from the violence directed toward the community from beyond. But such inward violence—and *violence* is not too strong a term—was also associated with patriarchal and heterosexist tendencies that denied full agency to women, queers, and others within the black community. In an essay advocating stronger alliances between black political organizations and progressive gay and women's liberation organizations, even Black Panther Party cofounder Huey P. Newton was forced to admit that "sometimes our first instinct is to want to hit the homosexual in the mouth, and a woman to be quiet. We want to hit a homosexual in the mouth because we are afraid we might be homosexual, and we want to hit the woman or shut her up because we are afraid that she might castrate us, or take the nuts that we might not have to start with."[15] Newton's comments suggest that for some African-American men it has been difficult to separate their race pride from their anxieties about their masculinity. The fact that some of these men censured the efforts of black queers and women to publicly consider the implications of their racial, gendered, and sexual identities speaks to the level in which black masculinity was often synonymous with black identity. I am cautious not to suggest that the black community has been any more homophobic than mainstream white society—however that can be defined, beyond essential notions of white people—and I am very sensitive to basic desires within the black community to protect its "weakest" members. Despite the examples of Black Panther Party members Huey Newton and Bobby Seale, who at various points in their career addressed the issues of homophobia and "male chauvinism,"[16] during the 1960s this violence, rhetorical or otherwise, at best trivialized various expressions that were not in sync with nationalist desires to unify black identity and culture under a common rubric that would ideally best survive the bombardment of white supremacist discourses and practices.[17]

Like Habermas's notion that modernity is not a complete project, hooks contends that "certainly many of the ways black folks addressed issues of identity conformed to a modernist universalizing agenda. There was little critique of patriarchy as a master narrative."[18] While not clearly identified in relation to the hypermilitancy of the Black Power era, black "modernist" ideals of identity, in collusion with the infamous Moynihan report, still hold profound sway within black communities. These ideals effectively hold the black community in stasis because they are not in sync with the fractures and fissures—think suburban migration and class stratification as just two simple examples of these gaps—that frame the contemporary black experience. There is also no critique of the overdetermined influence of race in constructions of black identity. In a related critique of scholarship within the fields of African-American and black studies, Dwight McBride adds that "for far too long the field . . . has thought about race as the primary category of analysis for the work that proceeds from the field. The problem with such work has always been, and continues to be, that African Americans and the African American experience are far more complicated than this."[19] These points are not in any way a rejection of the common heritage or experiences that clearly have been framed by race, but an attempt to seriously consider the full meanings of black identity.

Now I am cognizant of the many nuances of black nationalist thought and the powerful ways it has been politically and culturally useful in articulating narratives of resistance, community, and empowerment. Even as the cultural nationalism espoused by early Amiri Baraka and other critics like Larry Neal has contributed to the problematic essentializing of black culture in this era, it forced black artists and the black masses to some extent to come to terms—in positive ways, I think—with their own organic cultural productions and the influences of what Joseph E. Holloway refers to as "Africanisms."[20] Accordingly this project emboldened various constituencies within the black community to appropriate its energy, creating the context in which black, queer, and poor youth, for example, located valuable social space, often via the marketplace, to articulate a broader definition of black community, which embraced difference as a strength and not a weakness.[21] These efforts challenged the traditional logic of the black community, which has suggested that such identity politics are partially to blame for erosion of black community in the post–civil rights era. Hortense Spillers adds that "if community is embedded in each, so to speak, then its restitution will commence with . . . the capacity to perceive community as a layering of negotiable differences. Doing so would allow us to understand how change, or altered positioning, is itself an elaboration of community, rather than its foundering."[22] A good example of these "negotiations" is the way some queer black men, given the homophobia present in most black Christian institutions, use social spaces like queer nightclubs not only to socialize but also to create a context to embrace their own spirituality and blackness.[23]

Soul has also been an aesthetic interconnected with the marketplace and the consumerist desires of black and white audiences alike. Despite the drive toward self-determination that the soul aesthetic encapsulated, it remained a project that essentialized black identity and culture for one consumer public demanding inclusion into the mainstream on its own terms (clearly a self-defined black identity was more likely to be achieved than secession from the United States), and another looking for nonthreatening markers of difference, which could be consumed as a measurement of the mainstream's positive response to the former's demands for inclusion. Robert Weems suggests that "when we consider the impact of black consumerism on white business, we see that any changes in busi-

7

ness practices among white-owned companies resulted from pragmatic white conservatism, rather than from altruistic white liberalism . . . they were able to maximize their profits and appear 'socially responsible' at the same time."[24] Even as the narratives of black nationalism stridently argued for distinct black institutions, the intense commodification of soul already suggested the coming realities of black expressive culture in the postmodern era. This is most powerfully represented in the complicity that an organically "black" genre like hip-hop has with the engines of global capitalism. The hypervisibility of hip-hop culture has been significantly enhanced, if not fully realized, by these engines. Thus even as the phrase "black-owned" rolls from the tongues of boutique-style record label owners like Shawn "Jay-Z" Carter, Percy "Master P" Miller, and Sean "P. Diddy" Combs, they are little more than middle managers within transnational corporations.[25]

I mention the above to highlight that even as African-American culture embraced modernity, it was already impacted by postmodern influences. Referencing W. E. B. Du Bois's trope of "twoness," Kali Tal writes, "The struggle of African Americans is precisely the struggle to integrate identity and multiplicity, a perfect model of the 'postmodern' condition—except it predates postmodernism by hundreds of years."[26] Of course, Du Bois's trope was already problematic; his concept of the "warring" African-American soul was premised on struggles over the body of the "black patriarch," effectively dismissing the gendered, queer, and uncultured (in Du Bois's view) bodies that littered the "battlefield." Again, I am aware that Du Bois was a product of the world he was born into, and thus is not altogether to blame for whom he didn't acknowledge in his most famous treatise, but the omission does again suggest that struggles over definitions of black identity have had a continued presence in twentieth-century African-American thought.

I also do not mean to single out black nationalist thought in this debate; more mainstream concepts of blackness have clearly also been complicit in denying a full range of black identities. For instance, the NAACP Image Awards for years have privileged the artistic performances of those who best "uplifted" the race. Given the logic of the segregated black societies that I address above, such a focal point is not surprising. What is surprising is that well into the beginning of the twenty-first century, these efforts to sanitize black life and culture still hold value—often unchallenged—in the black community. Ironically, such efforts were visible in the aftermath of Tupac Shakur's nomination for an NAACP Image Award in 1994 for his acting prowess. As one critic of the nomination expressed at the time, "Are these the sort of actions we want to elevate as examples of the best in the black community?"[27] Efforts to create the most "positive" historical read of the black experience and its various icons have often denied a full exploration of the humanity of black folks. Commenting on the legacy of Martin Luther King Jr.'s "I Have a Dream" speech, Michael Eric Dyson observes that the speech "has become an enemy to his moral complexity. It alienates the social vision King expressed in his last four years. The overvaluing and misreading of 'I Have a Dream' has skillfully silenced a huge dimension of King's prophetic ministry."[28] Likewise, the full complexity of African-American life and culture has also been censored by those within the black cultural and political mainstream, who are understandably apprehensive about the wide distribution of black images that could be construed as negative. The point here is that such efforts often deny the efforts of black artists and others to tease out radical political and social sensibilities in existing and often problematic (stereotypical) caricatures of black identity. The embrace of the "nigga" by many black youth is but one example of these projects.

I am well aware that many of my critical insights may counter more traditional readings of African-American culture, and worse still, they undermine the well-respected ethic of common sense that pervades traditional African-American culture. In his work on black culture, David Lionel Smith suggests that "common sense is not critically self-conscious, and its function is to facilitate conformity and adaptation to familiar circumstances. It thrives on familiarity and fears change, and therefore common sense is profoundly conservative. Thus, paradoxically, those who wish to change the status quo must combat common sense and thereby risk acquiring the semblance of fools."[29] Historically, the description of the black intellectual class as "educated fools" is one of the more prevalent folkisms within the black community. At the risk of sounding like one of those "educated fools," through the course of this chapter I am going to eschew many well-regarded African-American folk sensibilities and suggest that the future of the African-American community lies within the recognition and empowerment of those most ostensibly marginalized within it, and within the larger American society. In his work on postmodern culture and minorities, Philip Brian Harper posits that "what

'minority' subjects often experience as their primary source of disorientation—the social effects of their difference in contexts where it is construed
as negative—will complicate their experience of what has heretofore been
conceived as the 'general' disorientation characteristic of the post-modern
condition."[30] In this regard, I am accepting, as Larry Grossberg does, that
"the margins are not inherently marginal,"[31] or in other words, those folks
whom some blacks posit as on the margins of acceptable or even relevant
black life—the niggas, the bitches, the queers, the baby-mama, to name a
few—are as integral to that experience as those who try to keep them at
arm's distance, rhetorically, spatially, or otherwise.

In an explanation of just why postmodernity is so disconcerting to
some, Grossberg also states, "The commonplace has, after all, become
dangerous. . . . Whatever the historical facticity, everyday life feels threat-
ening, and we are all worried that Freddy or Jason is, in fact, our next door
neighbor."[32] The fact is that for black folk, that nigga, queer, crackhead, or
baby-mama is the "sista" or "brotha" who lives next door, drives the church
van, is a day-care helper or the homeless body picking up the cans on their
front lawns. I am not explicitly commenting on whatever perceived dangers these figures embody, but on how these figures are products of various postmodern configurations that remain explicitly tied to black
"community," if only because of efforts by black elites and others either to
distance themselves from these figures or to allocate their largely rhetorical and ideological energies to name these figures and thus administer
the exchange of them in the open market of political, cultural, commercial, and intellectual capital. Acknowledging my own complicity in this
process, I am going to examine those figures most ostensibly marginalized
within black life to examine the "post-Soul" condition, figures who themselves thrive on "folk" sensibilities uniquely suited to questioning the realities of the post-soul experience.

I am also interested in exploring the popular narratives and images
produced by these figures or ostensibly produced in representation of
these figures, much of which are widely distributed and available to a
range of consuming publics. While these are clearly a product of marginal experiences, at least in the context of my own admittedly problematic
notions of normal behavior, the current intense commodification of black
expressive culture suggests otherwise. Examining the role of avant-garde
art in contemporary society, Stanley Aronowitz writes that it has "become
a kind of 'futures' investment in the hope that today's margin is tomor-

row's center."[33] The case of hip-hop is endemic to this travel, to quote bell hooks, from "margins to center." While hip-hop publicly came out in the mid-1970s plugged into inner-city lampposts and youth culture and was later embraced for its postmodern sensibilities by "avant-garde" critics, by the end of the century it was the best-selling genre of popular music, in large part because of its relevance to the lived experience, both real and imagined, of white and Asian youth. While two decades ago critics already predicted that hip-hop was going to be the "surf music" of the 1980s, it is virtually impossible to imagine the contemporary world without its presence, in no small part due to the control and distribution of hip-hop music and culture by transnational conglomerates. Given hip-hop's global influence—as if best-selling groups the Backstreet Boys or N'Sync would exist without Bobby Brown's self-constructed bad-boy image within his bubblegum pop group New Edition—even among those who vehemently deplore its presence, it implores us to take seriously, not just the supposed negativity the genre engenders, but the realities it attempts to portray.[34] We cannot simply reject these narratives on a moral basis that is itself a product of a profoundly different world; we must at least critically engage them with the same energy and passion that many of these artists themselves inject into their creative efforts.

"You Remind Me of Something": A (Brief) Post-Soul Consideration of R. Kelly

By way of an admittedly brief introduction to the post-soul aesthetic, I want to examine the work of post-soul musical artist R. Kelly, writer and performer of perhaps his generation's first standard, "I Believe I Can Fly."[35] Kelly is part of a increasing cadre of R&B singers who have embraced "sensitivity" as part of their musical identities, convening around a stylistic tendency that Luther Vandross first embodied twenty years ago. What separates Kelly from other black male artists who, like Bill Clinton, aim to "feel your pain," is his desire to bring into conversation the raunchier aspects of black male sexuality and the frenetic power of the black church, elements largely absent in the music of Vandross and others like Maxwell and Kenny "Babyface" Edmonds. Kelly's referencing of the black church tradition and the attendant contradictions associated with spirituality and sexuality explored consistently in the work of Sam Cooke, Marvin Gaye, Al Green, and most recently Prince suggest that Kelly may be a quintessential (post) soul man. Kelly has been most renowned for the explicit sexuality in songs like "Sex Me" and "Bump and Grind," suggesting the same kind of "vulgar" imaginings commonly associated with contemporary forms of black popular music, most explicitly hip-hop. I reference Kelly's song "You Remind Me of Something" in the title of this chapter, in part, to suggest that the song represents a post-soul colloquialism that serves as a moment of social criticism. Kelly's penchant for sexually charged song lyrics and seemingly simplistic and even absurd song titles and lyrics—the chorus to "You Remind Me of Something" begins with the line "You remind me of my Jeep"—does not detract from my belief that his music provides meaningful critiques of contemporary black life.

Implicit to my argument that Kelly's music represents a mode of social criticism is a belief that he is conscious of the contradictions that his music generates. As Kelly reflected in an interview, "What I do now is what I know people want to hear. Sex sells."[36] Thus a song like "Sex Me" is part of a strategy, a successful one I might add, employed by Kelly to do what he is in the business of, namely, to sell records. His role as a social critic is buoyed by his willingness to code complex social experiences in a language that is accessible to his primary listening audiences. From my vantage point, the chorus to "You Remind Me of Something," in which Kelly states, "You remind me of my Jeep/I wanna ride it/Something like my sound/I wanna pump it/Girl, you look just like my car/I wanna wax it/Something like my bank account/ I wanna spend it,"[37] on the surface conflates black male sexual desire with the type of consumerist, material, and leisure desires that have driven the drug economy in many black communities. The description of cars in female-gendered language is embedded in the vernaculars of masculine cultures in the United States. Terms like *ride* and *pump* are commonly used metaphors for sexual activity. Specifically, the word *wax*, within black male urban vernaculars, is used to describe both athletic and sexual conquest, hence a phrase like "I waxed that ass." In the process black women are reduced not only to sexual objects, but to sexual objects to be bought and exchanged like four-wheel-drive vehicles, $5,000 sound systems, and money orders. It is not my contention that Kelly's objectification of female sexuality, at least within these lyrics, is not unproblematic; on the contrary I think such representations are intensely troubling. But my reading of Kelly here and of other popular culture artifacts throughout this project is based on a strong belief that radical and progressive possibilities can and should be teased out of images that common logic suggest are problematic.

Kelly's lyrics open up a space to critique the surveillance, exchange, and control of female sexuality, particularly black female sexuality, among various artists, corporate entities, and men in general. Whether or not Kelly sees himself as a social critic is not really of importance to me here, though to Kelly's credit, he has been responsible for some of the "pro-feminist" stances in the work of former protégées Aaliyah, Changing Faces, and Sparkle. His duet with Sparkle, "Be Careful," and his own "When a Woman's Fed Up" both offer a unique male perspective on domestic issues usually addressed by women. Kelly has often deflected charges that his work has objectified black female sexuality by suggesting, "Sometimes you can love a person so much it can go beyond love. Ain't no love like a religious love and when you love somebody religiously then that's the way God loves you. I love women and I love them religiously."[38] Kelly's response is largely a product of the inspiration that his late mother has provided in his life. In this regard, Kelly has also been critical of black male infidelity. On Kelly's track "Down Low, Double Life," which describes the travails of a man engaged in polygamy, the narrator of the song suggests that his mother's distaste for his activities was because of "what my old man did to her." Kelly subsequently defines those who engage in such activities as "niggas," referencing one of the most powerful tropes within African-American life, in this case, to highlight his own derisive scorn. While I am not going to explore the ramifications of Kelly's use of the word *nigga* in the context of his work, I am interested in providing some context to examine Kelly's commitment to engage in socially meaningful rhetoric as a songwriter and artist.

In 1997 Kelly recorded "Gotham City" for the soundtrack to the film *Batman and Robin*, the third sequel to the financially successful *Batman* film, which starred George Clooney in the title role. The sound track for the first film was wholly produced and performed by Prince, and "A Kiss from a Rose," the most recognizable single from the soundtrack of the third film, *Batman Returns*, was recorded by Seal. The inclusion of Kelly on the fourth sound track was logical, given the success of other black artists on previous soundtracks, though the decision to include Kelly in the project may have also been based on the success of Kelly's "I Believe I Can Fly," which was initially featured on the sound track of the film *Space Jam*, featuring basketball star Michael Jordan and characters from the Loony Tunes series, most notably Bugs Bunny. *Space Jam* allowed Kelly to reach a larger audience than his music generally allowed. Kelly also recorded a remixed version of "Gotham City," which he referred to in the song's lyrics as "Gotham city for the ghetto," that was included on the single release of the song. The alternative version of the song allowed Kelly to dramatically alter the urban landscape, as presented in the *Batman* film series. All of the films in the series present an urban world defined by surreal and sinister characters—queered by unnatural acts of human nature—who prey on the good-natured citizens of "Gotham." These characters and the darkened skies that define the *Batman* sets become powerful symbols of the malaise that has engulfed urban life. Time and space do not allow for a more detailed analysis of the symbolism present in the film series, but for my purposes, Kelly's remix allows him to address issues of race and poverty that are largely absent in the film but are integral to life for some urban communities.

Most striking about the remix recording—the equally interesting video featured Kelly driving through the 'hood in the Batmobile—was Kelly's spoken introduction, drawn from Gladys Knight's version of the Marvin Hamlisch composition "The Way We Were." Barbra Streisand, who starred in the film of the same name, first recorded the track in 1973. Knight's rendition of the song appeared in 1974. What distinguished the two versions, besides the obvious, was Knight's spoken intro, where she states, "Hey, you know, everybody's talking about the good ole days, right? Everybody, the good ole days, the good ole days, well, let's talk about the good ole days. Come to think of it, as bad as they are, these will become the good ole days for our children." Knight's commentary is prescient. More than two decades after her intro, "back in the day" narratives are widespread within contemporary black popular culture. Coming-of-age films like *The Wood* and *Love and Basketball* are rooted in the early 1980s, a time when Ronald Reagan, then in his first term, began to construct the political bureaucracy that would erode the civil rights gains of the previous two decades. Songs such as Notorious B.I.G.'s "Things Done Changed" and the Beanie Sigel and Eve collaboration "Remember Them Days" sentimentally long for an era when black-on-black crime, the crack cocaine epidemic, AIDS, and other social maladies began to hold the very cities that these songs invoke—Brooklyn and Philadelphia, respectively—under siege.

In his "for the ghetto" version of "Gotham City," Kelly repeats Knight's initial words regarding the "good ole days" verbatim. Where Knight waxed sentimental about how her children would view those "good ole days," Kelly instead reflects, "I remember me and my brothers. We used to sit up on the porch in the summertime and just talk about just making it. You know what I'm sayin'. Being successful, following after our dream. I believe that's every kid's dream . . . to rise and be somebody, but damn, sometimes we just get caught up."[39] Kelly's refusal to invest in the sentimentality that informs Knight's intro and the lyrics of "The Way We Were" is significant; as a thirty-something adult who grew up on the soul music of Gladys Knight and others, Kelly was probably of the same generation of "children" that Knight invokes. Kelly's remix thus serves the dual purposes not only of constructing his own racial subjectivity within the "Gotham City" narratives of the *Batman* film series but also of speaking for himself, as a way to counter Gladys Knight, and in reality many others of her generation who attempt to speak for him and his generation. Kelly's ability to write (sing) his own subjectivity into "back in the day" narratives, at least in this case, is predicated on referencing an existing performance done in a period that is, in and of itself, lodged in the black communal memory as a moment of stability and possibility. In my case, listening to the opening lines of Kelly's "Gotham City" places me in a state of familiarity, where his music "reminds me of something," in this case Knight's fabulous performance. Via my conversation about Kelly, I am suggesting that this sense of familiarity is a key component of the post-soul aesthetic, a familiarity that is exploited by post-soul artists to convey their own sensibilities in a way that heightens the sense of fracture and difference, generationally at least, experienced within the black community, simply because something that was so familiar is rendered "vulgar" and unintelligible.

Given the patriarchal focus of black struggle in the twentieth century, it's not surprising that the "Soul Man" publicly articulated the trauma and tragedy of the black experience in ways that black women were often not allowed. This sense of distress experienced by the black community conveyed via black male soul singing was often made more real by the tragic circumstances surrounding some of the genre's most significant figures. What made the "Soul Man" uniquely suited for this work at the "crossroads" was the Pentecostal tradition that many of them were reared in as children. In this regard, their invariably tragicomic circumstances can be read as "punishment" for their willingness to use their "sacred" gifts in the service of the secular desires. In his autobiography, *Take Me to the River*, Al Green writes, "Anybody can tell you that all the great soul singers learned their best licks in the choir loft, that the church is the mother of R&B and the grandmother of rock & roll. But no one can tell you the pain of having the choice between lifting up your voice for God or taking a bow for your third encore. That's something that you have to experience for yourself. Like Sam Cooke. Like Marvin Gaye. Like Al Green."[40] Kelly, who also has roots in the Pentecostal tradition, has been no stranger to the "tragic" circumstances that have defined the experiences of some "Soul Men." Gaye's struggles with cocaine and an abusive father and Al Green's spiritual conversion after potentially meeting his maker via a pot of hot grits are the most cited examples of these tragedies; for Kelly's part he was embroiled in a controversy over his purported sexual relations and apparent marriage to then-fifteen-year-old artist Aaliyah Houghton.

Kelly's connection to the legacy of black male soul singers is also witnessed in his penchant for generously borrowing the vocal styles of black male artists. On his five recordings to date, Kelly has mimicked the styles of Charlie Wilson, Jeffrey Osborne, Sam Cooke, Lenny Williams, Aaron Hall, and most significantly Ronald Isley, who has been reintroduced to "Generation Hip-Hop" as Mr. Big in a few video collaborations with Kelly. Kelly's vocals on his first release, *Born into the 90s*, were barely distinguishable from those of Hall, at the time the lead vocalist for pioneering "New Jack Swing" group Guy. Kelly's follow-up release, *12 Play*, documents the maturation of Kelly's awareness of the vocal strategies he could employ. Like jazz instrumentalists, who very often borrow liberally from existing musical voices in order to develop their own voice, Kelly's borrowing has offered a valuable acknowledgment of the talents that preceded him. The first track where Kelly actively acknowledges this exchange is the old-school remix of his "Bump n' Grind." In an effort to highlight the continuity of his music to earlier forms, Kelly samples lyrical riffs from "Forever Mine" and "Ooh Child," first recorded by the O'Jays and the Five Stairsteps, respectively, and he clearly invokes the sound of Ronald Isley in the song's chorus. In the spirit of Jason King's brilliant read of Luther Vandross, I would also suggest that Kelly, like Vandross, is an archivist of black male singing styles.[41] In this regard Kelly's "voice" is really a conflation of a generation of male rhythm and blues vocalists.

Kelly's referencing of the old-school sound augments his contention in the original version of the song that the hypersexual content of "Bump 'n' Grind" was not a rejection but an embrace of romantic narratives like those of previous generations of soul singers. Kelly's collapse of the sexual and the romantic—really a collapse of the public and the private dimensions of African-American sexual relations—naturally suggests that many of these narratives and artists simply represented a pool of resources that Kelly could appropriate to articulate his own existential concerns, while also acknowledging the constraints placed on previous generations of artists in terms of how they coded sexual innuendo in a language that could be widely distributed.[42] Kelly's vocal sampling embodies one of the basic impulses of the post-soul aesthetic, which is to borrow profusely from black modern projects in an effort to derive new meanings more in tune with contemporary experiences. In this regard, Ronald Isley had to be destroyed, or at least figuratively displaced, in order for "Mr. Big" to serve Kelly's own aesthetic desires, as evidenced in Kelly's "Down Low" video, which I examine later. Ironically, it was a symbolic death that benefited Isley commercially, since his collaborations with Kelly renewed interests in his then moribund career, much like the endless sampling of the Isley Brothers' music on tracks such as Ice Cube's "It Was a Good Day" ("Footprints in the Dark") and the Notorious B. I. G.'s "Big Poppa" ("Between the Sheets"). Like the commercial phoenix in which Isley was reborn, Kelly's old-school sentiments represented a savvy commercial sense. As Paul Gilroy has discussed, the ability of artists to remix their recordings for various publics allows them to engage in a mode of specificity that may not be conveyed to the broader audiences that those artists hope to reach commercially. Kelly, for instance, has often remixed his singles in a "Chicago" style to speak directly to those audiences in his hometown of Chicago and other parts of the Midwest.[43] Likewise, Kelly's old-school remix spoke to the sensibilities of a generation of musical audiences who might have come of age, for example, to the music of the Isley Brothers, the Stylistics, or the O'Jays. Pre-dating the retro-soul music of D'Angelo, Angie Stone, Erykah Badu, and Maxwell by a few years, Kelly's strategy also considered the generational shifts and fractures in urban radio programming, which allowed Kelly a significant presence in both "classic soul" and contemporary urban (read young, black, and brown) formats.

Kelly is seemingly very conscious of the ways his music and its focus on sex and sexuality have impacted the soul music tradition, as witnessed in the very bizarre and provocative video that he conceived for "Down

Low." At the video's opening, Kelly is invited to his boss Frank Biggs's house. Mr. Biggs (Ronald Isley) requests that Kelly take care of his "woman," Lila (Garcelle Beauvais), specifically telling him, "Here's a pound of money, keys to the Bentley . . . take her out, show her a good time." But Mr. Biggs's request comes with a specific warning: "Kelly, I don't have to tell you, you know Lila means everything to me. Now I want you to take her out, give her everything she wants, but you are never, never to touch her."[44] It is my contention that the video can be read as a very public exchange between Kelly and Isley regarding the contemporary nature of rhythm and blues and soul music, where Lila is the personification of those genres. My vulgar appropriation of Andreas Huyssen's concept of "Mass Culture as Woman"[45] notwithstanding, I am suggesting that when Mr. Biggs exhorts Kelly to "never touch her," he is in fact warning R. Kelly about diminishing the soul music tradition with sexually explicit lyrics, like those that Kelly has been synonymous with. My interpretation of Lila as the embodiment of classic soul is buoyed by the various scenes in the video in which she is stylishly dressed, harking back to the kind of feminine look that the late Jackie Kennedy Onassis made prominent during the 1960s. Lila's look also recalls that of the Supremes, during the height of their popularity in the 1960s. Though the Motown corporation contained many acts that were crucial to its success, most notably Marvin Gaye and the Temptations, it seems clear that Berry Gordy viewed the Supremes and later Diana Ross as the flagship product of his record label. Mr. Biggs's later castigation and punishment of Kelly in the video for defiling Lila is ironic, given that Isley's recordings during the 1970s and early 1980s as well as Marvin Gaye's recording output after *What's Going On* are primary influences on contemporary black male R&B singers. The closing scene of the video finds Kelly sitting in a wheelchair at the bed of the dying Lila, who apparently has also been beaten by Mr. Biggs and his bodyguards. The video suggests that the very tradition that Isley attempts to maintain is in fact killed off by his own hand, as witnessed in the failure of his generation of soul singers to make earlier traditions of the music relevant to contemporary audiences. It is with the "death" of that tradition, and presumably of "Ronald Isley," that Mr. Biggs is born, as witnessed by recurring roles in "Ronald Isley" videos and the video for the R. Kelly remixed version of Kelly Price's "Friend of Mine."[46] In the latter video Isley's Mr. Biggs appears as the uncle of Price, whose husband, portrayed by Kelly, is involved in an extramarital affair with her best friend.

Kelly's use of Isley/Mr. Biggs as a way to connect across generations is not just a simple commercial gesture. On the aforementioned "Down Low, Double Life," where the main character is physically attacked by the two women he is involved with, Kelly specifically references the Persuaders' "Thin Line between Love and Hate," which is the lyrical basis of the Kelly song and in fact states that he was attacked with "a pot of hot grits," which of course is a reference to Al Green. The incident where Green was attacked by "hot grits" was a catalyst in his spiritual conversion, in which he largely gave up singing the secular music that made him an icon to begin a successful career as a gospel singer. Green's conversion was predicated on his own belief that he needed to pay spiritual restitution for his former lifestyle, particularly his often predatory relationships with women. Green later admitted, "It took me awhile to figure this out, but God's not displeased with his servant Al Green for singing 'Tired of Being Alone' . . . or 'I'm Still in Love with You.' He wants his people to feel good, to laugh and carry on and remember what it was like when they were young."[47] Nevertheless Kelly's reference to the incident was an acknowledgment of his own attempts at conversion, in the aftermath of his controversial relationship with former protégée Aaliyah, in which it was suggested that Kelly had illegally married the then-fifteen-year-old artist. "Down Low, Double Life" appeared on Kelly's *R*, which was released late in 1998. His previous project, simply titled *R. Kelly*, was recorded and released during the height of the controversy surrounding his relationship with Aaliyah. Both project titles suggest that the recordings represent some aspect of the real R. Kelly, that they are autobiographical portals into the life and experiences of the artist. Regarding the adulation exhibited by his fans, Kelly states, "I think they love me because I'm real, you know. I think they're into me, R. Kelly, because they feel something real even though they don't know me personally. I don't try to be nothing else except myself."[48]

The *R. Kelly* project, not surprisingly, opens with one of those moments of realness, as Kelly openly responds, without specifically mentioning Aaliyah, to the charges made against him. His response, which is titled "The Sermon," is notable because Kelly consciously chose to acknowledge his "sins" within the familiar aural confines of the black church and more specifically in a mode of address known within that tradition as "testifyin'." Kelly's choice of address is significant because of his acknowledgment that he was most concerned with the opinions and reactions of the black community and that the black church remains the moral center of that community. His response was thus coded in familiarity with those who shared his cultural sensibility. Referencing one of the most popular blues lyrics in the African-American experience, Kelly asserts, "Just like the song says, ain't nobody's business what I do," which was a reflection of how intensely previous generations of black folk guarded their privacy as a response to how distinctions between private and public were eroded by the logic of chattel slavery and Jim Crow segregation.[49] Ironically, Kelly's own fame, which he suggests is recognized on a national scale, was largely predicated on his own willingness to air "dirty (sexual) laundry" in public, as he admits in "The Sermon" that "even the Statue of Liberty wants to 'Bump and Grind.' Can I get a witness?" A common theme in Kelly's work, as witnessed in his "Gotham City" remake, is his acknowledgment of the struggles he faced to be successful. As Kelly states in one portion of the address, "I remember when I was tryin' to be somebody. But I just didn't know nobody. . . . Ever since God has blessed me it seems like, everything is going a little bit different. It's funny how things have changed." In this regard, Kelly is not so much seeking forgiveness as he is seeking affirmation for his means to an end. In this regard, Kelly taps into a communal psyche, particularly among contemporary black youth audiences, that has craved representations of financial success.

Kelly's own "Only the Loot Can Make Me Happy," which samples "Happy" by Surface, and Puff Daddy's "All about the Benjamins" are but two examples of the fixation with material wealth among contemporary artists, though in many ways these desires are no different than those of previous generations of black folk who saw such desires as emblematic of success and protection from various forms of economic oppression. What marks the difference in desires generationally has been a willingness on the part of post-soul artists to appropriate and reproduce "vulgar" representations of blackness to achieve this material success, which is in its own right deeply indebted to African-American notions of "making a way out of no way" in order to survive and in this case thrive. This is not to suggest that I am radically opposed to depictions of "post-soul" art as problematic. I too am alarmed by the rampant sexism, misogyny, homophobia, and crass materialism that is regularly presented on, say, BET (Black Entertainment Television or Black Entertainment Tragedy, take your pick) or within mainstream popular culture in general. My point is to suggest that Kelly and many of his contemporaries are a product of and a response to the world that they live in and that their complicity in rendering those things "familiar" in forms that seemingly undermine the sensibilities and struggles of previous generations of black folk is a legitimate engagement with a world that itself more powerfully undermines those strategies and struggles.

A classic example of this was the controversy surrounding the Outkast song "Rosa Parks." Named after the civil rights icon whose principled stand against segregation of public transportation in Montgomery, Alabama, was the catalyst for the modern civil rights movement, the song, which appeared on the full-length recording *Aquemini* (1998), was largely a reference to the group's prowess as lyricists and performers, as the song's chorus—"Ah ha, hush that fuss/everybody move to the back of the bus/Do you wanna bump and slump with us/We the type of people make the club get crunk"[50]—suggests. Many viewed the song, which does not mention Rosa Parks explicitly, as a simple bid to take advantage of her fame, and Ms. Parks in fact sued the group and the group's label and distributors for the unauthorized use of her name in a song that was "vulgar" and "profane."[51] Setting aside the implications that one's name can exist in and of itself as a type of intellectual property, at the root of the Parks lawsuit was the fact that her name was "dragged into the gutter," if you will, by a rap group that presumably was both ignorant and disrespectful of the legacy of Rosa Parks. In this regard the lawsuit, which was eventually thrown out by a Michigan judge, was emblematic of a general feeling within the traditional civil rights leadership that the post-soul generation was unappreciative of that leadership's sacrifices. My own experiences with students in the classroom has often borne out that many black students do take those struggles for granted, but I would like to suggest a brief alternative reading of the "Rosa Parks" song, one more representative of the ways in which the post-soul generation(s) negotiate history, memory, and identity.

Given the general erosion of black communal networks during the post–civil rights era and the equally profound impact of popular media and popular culture in framing contemporary sensibilities relating to history and identity, the very specific struggles of the civil rights movement have often been reduced to thirty-second bites during the King holiday or when one of the icons of that movement has died. In this regard many of the events and people who were instrumental in creating the post–civil rights world have been reduced to singular events and people that serve as metaphors for the movement and its participants. In the absence of sustained study and immersion in the ideas that framed the movement, this is often the only way that any semblance of the movement has been recovered by this generation, save showings of *Eyes on the Prize* during Black History Month. For many within the post-soul generation, the Montgomery bus boycott is representative of a small number of communal memories, such as the March on Washington in 1963 and the assassination of Martin Luther King Jr., that propel their own perceptions and understanding of that moment. The mute character of Smiley (Roger Guenveur Smith) in Spike Lee's *Do the Right Thing*, who simply carries postcards of King and Malcolm X (El-Hajj Malik El-Shabazz) in his pocket, reflects this dimension. While the postcards themselves—or Smiley, for that matter—cannot articulate the nuances of the two men's ideologies in relation to themselves or each other, the postcards become broad metaphors for differences in leadership style between the two men. Thus a group like Outkast can find obvious value in appropriating the name of Rosa Parks because she metaphorically represents their own struggles as marginalized black men within the recording industry and the larger society. Specifically, the "bus" becomes the vehicle for their own personal empowerment. Also given the realities of surface transit in many urban municipalities, the invocation of the "back of the bus" is also an invocation of the temporary "imagined communities," to use Benedict Anderson's term, constructed by black youth and others during their daily travels to work and school. More than a simple appropriation of Ms. Parks's name, the recording likely had the impact of stimulating interest in the civil rights icon among those communities of youth who were otherwise oblivious to her. In this regard the song can be seen as a tribute to her and the movement that her actions helped incubate. I see the use of Rosa Parks in this context as one of the components of post-soul strategies that willingly "bastardize" black history and culture to create alternative meanings, a process that was largely introduced to the post-soul generation via the blaxploitation films of the 1970s.

2

Sweetback's Revenge
Gangsters, Blaxploitation, and Black Middle-Class Identity

Yet my concern is not whether Cosby was properly black; I am interested in using Cosby as a metaphor for a past era . . . the bottom line
for me has to do with media access, cultural representation, and the
death of a popular form. Cosby assumed a great deal of importance
throughout the 1980s, almost to the point of denying any other form of
popular African American imagery. As far as mainstream culture is
concerned, it is as though the representation of African American culture operates monolithically, and that only one form of popular representation may be available at any given time.

—Todd Boyd

I think that smiling in public is against the law
'Cause Love don't get you through life no more
It's who you know and "how you, son?"
And how you getting' in, and who the man holding
Hey yo, and how was the scam and how high
you what's up, huh? I heard you caught a body
Seems like every man and woman shared a life with John Gotti

—Posdonus (De La Soul), "Stakes Is High"

23

At the conclusion of Melvin Van Peebles's groundbreaking film *Sweet Sweetback's Baadasssss Song* (1971), the phrase "A BAADASSSSS NIGGER IS COMING TO COLLECT SOME DUES" appears scrawled across the screen. Sweetback did in fact return shortly in the forms of John Shaft, Youngblood Priest, and a host of other blaxploitation staples that *Sweet Sweetback's Baadasssss Song* provided the cinematic formula to reproduce. Given the historical moment, particularly in relation to the sensibilities of Hollywood and the political climate of the moment, Sweetback was in fact a revolutionary character, paving the way for portrayals of black masculinity previously absent in mainstream film. Though these portrayals are rife with many problematic elements, including unchallenged expressions of patriarchy, queer bashing, misogyny, and crude political ideas, *Sweetback* did help usher in a cultural moment in which African-American male identity was presented in broadened ways. The closing frame suggests that Sweetback, on the run from various law enforcement agencies, will return to the black community and take his rightful place as the revolutionary patriarch that the film's modern runaway-slave narrative prepares him for. Sweetback's "crossing of the sands," or in this case the Los Angeles Canal, is triggered by the supposed awakening of his dormant revolutionary consciousness, leading him to attack two police officers in an effort to protect Moo Moo (Mau Mau?), a local militant, from being a victim of police brutality. The attack is followed by a very telling scene where Sweetback responds to Moo Moo's query about where the two of them should find refuge with an acerbic, "What is this we shit?"

The runaway slave's run to freedom, or at least the self-actualization of freedom, has rarely provided the kind of social capital that could empower the masses of black folks, except as an inspirational symbol of the ability of some to overcome various oppressions. In this regard the film's core theme could have been written, and to some extent was, by Fredrick Douglass in his first autobiography. In the case of Douglass, it made him the prototypical African-American "public" intellectual, which in some ways makes his work the equivalent of the various self-help books of self-defined black spiritualists, athletes, and talk-show hosts. I don't mean to discount the power of symbolic inspiration, but in the worst-case scenario, the runaway-slave narrative can be read into a situation like the O. J. Simpson Bronco Chase (Simpson having been enslaved, apparently, by his own penchant for wife battering), which has not only not empowered African Americans but negatively influenced the judicial system's view of potential black jurors. In other words, the "freedom" of the run-away slave rarely means any significant freedom for the community of folks the runaway leaves behind, and often is the stimulus for retribution against them. In theory, it is this retribution against those left behind that potentially provides the basis for a community-based resistance that rarely gets portrayed in African-American film, Hallie Gerima's *Sankofa* notwithstanding. In this regard, *Sweetback* represented the status quo—a less politically sophisticated version of the various Nat Turners and David Walkers that litter the pantheon of black male martyrs throughout history.

In his book *Redefining Black Film*, Mark Reid posits that "resistance connotes any independent form that empowers black culture and the blacks who make the film."[1] While *Sweet Sweetback's Baadasssss Song* was not necessarily an independent film by Reid's standards, the notion that the film "empowered" black culture is useful for my purposes. On the surface, such "resistance" can be read in Van Peebles's willingness to have Sweetback engage in gratuitous sex throughout the film, but what is more significant is the workmanlike quality of Sweetback's sexual escapades. Reid observes that Sweetback's "ability to perform skillfully requires the discipline of a soldier intent upon killing the enemy; such a performance cannot be interpreted as primitive lust nor a reflection of emotional desire."[2] Reid's point here was that Sweetback represents a revision of historic portrayals of black male sexuality as animalistic and predatory in nature. While Reid's comments are legitimate, they do not take into account how such "warlike" sexuality informs sexual violence against black women and others by black men. On two occasions in the film, women, one black and one white, are constructed as gatekeepers or obstructions to Sweetback's desires for freedom, and in both cases his proficiency at providing sexual pleasure for the two consenting women provides the realization of that freedom. Though the subsequent "satisfaction" of the black woman challenges the legitimacy of historic claims that black women are insatiable, the sequences do not adequately problematize the use of sex as a tool of control.[3] In this regard, more alarming, as Ed Guerrero asserts, were the "implications of Sweetback raping a woman at knifepoint out of 'revolutionary' expediency."[4] Toward the film's conclusion, Sweetback forces himself upon another black women in a field to camouflage himself from the law enforcement officers who are in pursuit. The willingness of the officers to disregard the "couple," presumably because there is nothing unusual about black folks engaging in public sex, reinforces the notions of primitive sexuality that Reid suggests the film works against.

But Reid's description of Sweetback's sexuality is useful in another way. The dispassionate, workmanlike nature of Sweetback's sexual activity is largely predicated on his role as a sex worker. Sweetback makes his living and earned his initial notoriety performing in "sex-plays" at a local whorehouse. Rescued by a community of prostitutes as a youngster, Sweetback apparently honed his skills as a sex worker with expert tutelage by the woman in the brothel he is raised in. This connection is made very early in the film when a young Sweetback, played by Van Peebles's pubescent son Mario, is subjected to a form of rape, which is portrayed in the film as a rite of passage. This scene led Black Panther Party founder Huey Newton to suggest that the woman "baptizes him [Sweetback] into his true manhood."[5] Like the sexual violence that Sweetback performs later in the film, Newton's logic speaks volumes about the subjugation of the weaker bodies of the black community, in this case children, to further the "revolutionary" agenda of the ruling patriarchs. Newton's comments also intimate that rape should somehow be regarded as a natural initiation into black manhood, and presumably an initiation for black women into the black institutions in which they have been historically subjugated by black men. Nevertheless, to see Sweetback as a dispassionate, disaffected, and disenfranchised laborer in some ways captures the continued discontent of the black working class with the pace of the "revolution." The imagery of a black man confronting "the Man" notwithstanding, the film's connection to some of the black audiences that supported it was Sweetback's image as an everyday man who woke up and went to work every day, just as working folks in the black community have done for centuries. *Sweetback* was at a marked distance from the cinematic jet-setting, fast-talking, black "super spades" that he spawned.

Ironically, Van Peebles does not offer the prostitutes that open the film, who are also laborers, to the audience for the same kind of connection. Where Sweetback did not enjoy his work, the prostitutes derived pleasure in their labor, again as witnessed in the disturbing opening sequence with Mario Van Peebles. This perception of pleasure, like historical perceptions of the singing "darkies" in early Hollywood cinema, suggests a complicity on the part of those who find pleasure in such labor with the structures that are ostensibly oppressing them. The director's choice here is not only emblematic of the general erasure of women's narratives in the film but, given the black community's own discomfort with heightened black female sexuality, explicitly reinscribes black women's sexual pleasure as deviant, particularly when not used in the service of the "revolution." Such a notion has been powerfully reflected in ongoing debates within black communities about the nature of sexual relations between enslaved black women and various plantation owners and overseers during the antebellum and Jim Crow periods. It has often been easier for black men to suggest that black women derived some privilege from these relationships than to admit that black women have been victims of sexual violence, ironically also at the hands of black men. While the prostitutes featured in the beginning of the film may consent to the sexual relationships they engage in, Van Peebles offers no critique of the socioeconomic conditions that often force women, particularly poor women, into such a "profession."

Van Peebles, who experienced some mainstream success directing *The Watermelon Man*, was cognizant that a highly political film would not empower him as a movie director and instead opted for a more conventional action-film style, like that found in the highly profitable sequence of *Dirty Harry* and *Death Wish* films. As Van Peebles was quoted at the time, "If Brer [the black community] is bored, he's bored. One of the problems we must face squarely is that to attract the mass we have to produce work that not only instructs but entertains."[6] Almost twenty years after the release of *Sweetback*, KRS-One released his definitive recording, *Edutainment*, a blatant attempt to weld politically relevant commentary to the "party and bullshit" ethos that informed the early hip-hop aesthetic. Notably the recording featured the track "30 Cops" ("When they arrests a black man, they need thirty cops or more"), which samples dialogue from *Sweetback*, including the final chase scene in which Sweetback realizes his freedom across the Mexican border. KRS-One's borrowing of Sweetback to articulate his own generation's concerns with police brutality speaks to the value of blaxploitation narratives, despite how problematic they were. Sonic references to *Sweetback* were also made on Main Source's recording *Breaking Atoms*, most notably on the track "Just a Friendly Game of Baseball," which used the sport as a metaphor for police brutality. In many regards, the blaxploitation era is the textbook example of the stereotyping of African-American life and culture, and as such I am not really interested as much in reexamining this terrain as in

teasing out the more radical questions of black identity that some blaxploitation films provide space for. Particularly I want to examine the construction of black male middle-class identity, as represented in the Bill
Cosby and Sidney Poitier trilogy *Uptown Saturday Night*, *Let's Do It
Again*, and *A Piece of the Action*. Though the three films were not really
blaxploitation fare in the sense that we think of black cinema from that
era, they are implicitly linked to the blaxploitation moment because of the
efforts of the writers and director of those films to counter the negative
imagery of the genre, while still employing some of its elements.

Uptown Saturday Night and Other Black Middle-Class Fantasies: The Cosby/Poitier Trilogy

Buoyed in part by his own status as a legitimate Hollywood icon and his
own desires to counter the worst aspects of the blaxploitation industry,
Sidney Poitier made the conscious effort to direct and produce "black"
films that presented acceptable black images to a mass audience. In
response to criticisms of the sanitized nature of some of his previous portrayals, Poitier began to accept roles that better articulated the political
sensibilities of most African Americans in the late 1960s. His roles in *For
the Love of Ivy*, which costarred jazz singer and activist Abbey Lincoln; *In
the Heat of the Night*; and *The Lost Man* were examples of the "new"
Poitier, as was *Buck and the Preacher*, the first feature that Poitier produced, which costarred fellow Hollywood icon Harry Belafonte. In 1974
Poitier directed and produced *Uptown Saturday Night*, the first of a three-
film cycle that featured Poitier and comedian Bill Cosby in the lead roles.
Though distributed by Warner Brothers, all three films were produced by
First Artist, a collective of major actors and actresses that Poitier helped
found in 1969 with Robert Redford and Barbra Streisand, among others.
While Poitier may have desired to broaden perceptions of the black community, he also realized the need to reach the broadest audience possible,
which may explain the comedic and often slapstick nature of the first two
films, *Uptown Saturday Night* and *Let's Do It Again*, incidentally both
written by Richard Wesley. As noted film critic Vincent Canby wrote at
the time of the film's release, *Uptown Saturday Night* "is an exuberant
black joke that utilizes many of the stereotypical attitudes that only black
writers, directors and actors can decently get away with. You've never seen
so much eye-popping fear and unwarranted braggadocio used in the serv-

ice of laughs. Yet the result is not a put-down comedy but a cheerful gape that has the effect of liberating all of us from our hangups." [7] But Poitier's efforts also suggested a desire to "sanitize" the black experience in ways that would make black life, both cinematic and real, more palatable to white audiences. The controversy that preceded the film's wide release on July 26, 1974, is an example.

In support of the film's release, Bill Cosby did a trio of radio advertisements that were sent to major radio stations in New York City, including the black-owned WBLS[8] and WABC, which then dominated and defined the concept of Top 40 pop radio formats. In one of the commercial spots, which aired between July 3 and 6, 1974, Cosby states, "Remember the good old days when you used to go uptown to Harlem and have a good time—before it became very, very dangerous. Well you can still go uptown without gettin' your head beat in by going downtown to see 'Uptown Saturday Night.' This way the people are all on the screen and won't jump off and clean you head out."[9] Understandably, many Harlemites found the spot offensive. One of the spot's most vocal critics, Walter Brecher, then operator of the famed Apollo Theater as well as the Sixty-eighth Street Playhouse in New York City, called the spot "a vile characterization of a community."[10] Brecher believed that the spot conveyed the desire of the film's distributor, Warner Brothers, to reach the broadest (white) audience possible, figuring that a Harlem opening would inscribe the film as a "black" film.

Brecher's contentions disregard the fact, however, that the film's three major stars, Poitier, Cosby, and Belafonte, had long transcended a status that would limit them to only making "black" films. This does not mean that Brecher's claim that motion picture companies were attempting to siphon audiences away from Harlem movie houses was unjustified. Ed Guerrero has suggested that the blaxploitation moment began to peak in 1973, the year before *Uptown Saturday Night*'s release.[11] Recognizing that black audiences were apt to also support mainstream fare like *The Godfather* films or *The Exorcist*, the film industry began to pull back on its commitment to producing black-themed films and focus on "crossover" films. According to Guererro, "crossover power was accomplished on a narrative level by constructing black stories to accommodate white sensibilities and values. . . . Crossover films also recouped commercial cinema's star making system by relying on a few, isolated, big name stars for their box-office draw, rather than filling productions with casts of dozens of black actors looking for a break."[12] It is this crossover logic that led to the mega-star film careers of comedians Richard Pryor and Eddie Murphy in the late 1970s and 1980s. In films such as *48 Hours, Some Kind of Hero, Stir Crazy,* and *Beverly Hills Cop,* the antics of Pryor and Murphy were juxtaposed against decidedly white mainstream context. *Uptown Saturday Night* and *Let's Do It Again,* which took advantage of the popularity, if not acting talents, of Jimmy Walker of the television sitcom *Good Times,* were products of the beginning stages of the crossover phase of Hollywood filmmaking, a phase that has now survived to accord some semblance of star power to former television comics Martin Lawrence and Jamie Foxx. Given the desire to produce crossover features, there was a diminishing need for "black" films to run in predominately black neighborhoods, a trend that would reach its apex with the creation of the multiplex and mega-multiplex exhibition models in the early 1980s.[13] Also considering that suburban black middle-class audiences often returned to urban centers to view films that were not likely shown at suburban movie houses, the Cosby spot was as much about drawing whites to the film as it was about drawing black audiences to the film, as witnessed by the diverse audiences of the radio stations on which the ad was placed.

The aforementioned Cosby commercial spot undergirds the relationship that white audiences in New York City had with the Harlem community. Dating back to the Harlem Renaissance or "New Negro" period of the 1920s, white audiences flocked to Harlem nightclubs, theaters, and dance halls to consume various forms of entertainment.[14] In many ways Harlem was New York City's uptown funhouse. With the stock market crisis of 1929 and the subsequent economic depression, the quality of Harlem life for its residents and its institutions began steadily to erode. At the time of *Uptown Saturday Night*'s release, Harlem was still deep in the throes of an economic collapse. It is important to also remember that New York City was also deeply entrenched in a fiscal crisis at this time; we might recall the *New York Daily News*'s now-infamous cover page, which quoted then-president Gerald Ford as telling New York City to "drop dead." Civic life in Harlem was one of the casualties of this crisis—the famed Apollo, forced to close its doors for a significant time, became a vivid symbol of the community's demise. Cosby's commercial spot spoke to this dramatic transition in the quality of Harlem life, as the struggle for diminishing resources and the influx of recreational and debilitating drugs such as heroin and later "angel dust" helped create a crime-ridden environment. But Cosby's spot also spoke to the ways in which the black community or black folks were equally demonized by the highly visible demise of Harlem, which to this day remains a measurement of African-American success. The presence of Poitier, Cosby, and Belafonte was a calculated attempt to distinguish some forms of black film from the blaxploitation fare that had come to dominate the genre. Perhaps a larger question is whether filmmakers had an obligation to support black-owned venues, even though they actively sought white audiences. It is my contention that Cosby and Poitier, with the assistance of writers Timothy March and Richard Wesley, address issues of racial obligation and community responsibility, particularly as they pertain to black middle-class aspirations, throughout the trilogy of films.

Mark Reid has suggested that such films were examples of hybrid minstrelsy, in which the presence of black actors, actresses, writers, and directors, "like the black minstrel performer in blackface, enabled the naturalization, validation, and repetition of minstrelsy in a postmodern age."[15] Reid's point is validated by one reviewer's claim that Harry Belafonte's character, Geechie Dan Beauford, was "Marlon Brando's Godfather in burnt cork."[16] While Reid correctly absolves black screen actors and actresses in the 1930s and '40s for their willing complicity in the production of stereotypical images by an industry that granted them little if any control over those images, he seems less willing to grant the same exemptions for the work of Cosby, Poitier, or Ossie Davis (*Cotton Comes to Harlem*). Reid's criticisms are understandable, if only because Cosby, Poitier, and Davis were the standardbearers of positive black imagery at the time. According to Reid, films such as *Cotton Comes to Harlem*, which is based on a Chester Himes novel, and *Uptown Saturday Night* eschew any significant analysis of the socioeconomic and sociopolitical aspects of black life; "hybrid minstrel humor necessarily lacks any significant dramatization of African-American life." Reid recovers the idea of a comedic oppositional black cinema in the notion of a "satiric hybrid minstrelsy." While I share Reid's position on satire, it is my contention that even the "hybrid minstrel" form, in this case the Poitier and Cosby films, are invested with representations that are significantly relevant to the black community. Reid insists that a "focus on financial success and mainstream approval misses the underlying value of black humor and black film production. The traditional purpose of black humor has been to resist and subvert humor that ridicules members of the black community."[17] While Reid may find ridicule problematic in these films, for my purposes such ridicule often contains powerful critiques of the objects disparaged. My claim here is premised on the idea that given the constraints of the film industry and popular culture, most notably in regards to fuller explorations of race, gender, and ethnicity, popular culture workers often find ways to undermine these constraints in ways that can't be viewed simply as forms of satire.

The Cosby/Poitier trilogy is an example of such efforts. The duo portray the roles of Wardell Franklin (Cosby) and Steve Jackson (Poitier), two working-class men who presumably live in a midwestern industrial city. Over the film's opening theme, sung by Dobie Gray, who had success in the mid-1960s with the single "The In Crowd," the film provides audiences with glimpses of Jackson, a smelter by trade, at work and then on the bus ride home. The opening sequence, which also features a panoptic view of the town's landscape, including the factory smokestacks that rise in the distance, serves to frame Poitier's character with the traditional working-class identity that even a diverse black audience could relate to. The plot of the film is centered on a trip Steve and Wardell take to an upscale black after-hours club called Madame Zenobia's. The club is an example of the various covert social spaces that members of the black middle class often support, which provided them with a sense of entitlement and privilege that they cannot seek outside the black community. To buoy their chances at entry into the exclusive club, Wardell forges a letter of introduction on stationery from the law offices where his wife works. Wardell's efforts speak in some small ways to the desires among some working-class blacks to enjoy some semblance of this ultimately flaccid privilege, if only for a night. Steve in fact uses a significant portion of his vacation pay simply to gain a space for Wardell at the craps table, which requires a minimum bet of $100. During the course of the night, Zenobia's is held up by a group of disguised men, who we later find out are led by Silky Slim (Calvin Lockhart), a local gangster. It is only after reading the newspaper the next day that Steve realizes that his wallet, which was stolen during the robbery, included a winning lottery ticket worth $50,000. Steve and Wardell then collaborate with "Geechie Dan" Beauford, Belafonte's brilliant caricature of *Godfather* patriarch Don Corleone, and his rival "Silky Slim" to retrieve the stolen wallet under the pretense that a document—the same letter of introduction—

that was included among the stolen goods contains information about the whereabouts of over $300,000 in diamonds. Ultimately the two outwit Geechie Dan and Silky Slim and retrieve the wallet and the lottery ticket.

The first scene after the film's opening montage finds Dave at home with his wife Sarah, who is portrayed by the late Roslind Cash, a veteran of the Negro Ensemble Company, founded by Douglas Turner Ward in the 1960s. Cash was part of a generation of black actors and actresses like Richard Roundtree, Roxie Roker, Roscoe Lee Brown, Frances Foster, Esther Rolle, Cleavon Little, and Denise Nichols who all worked with the ensemble, which was created within the context of the black arts movement. Many of these actors and actresses became the first generation of black actors and actresses to take advantage of the greater opportunities post–civil rights cinema offered, and incidentally Foster, Brown, and Nichols all appeared in at least one of the Cosby and Poitier films. In this regard these films brought together black actors like Cosby and Poitier, who had achieved some degree of success within mainstream Hollywood, with those who had struggled on, for lack of a better term, the "chitlin' circuit." In the opening sequence with Sarah, Steve queries her about the possibility about moving back down south to the country. The scene in which the two reminisce about the "good ole days" and life in the country is ironic, given the general history of black folk who lived in the South prior to and during the civil rights movement. While the scene romanticizes the lived realities of black folk in the South, it does speak to the way black migrants in the North continue to relate the South as a place where they were able to build and maintain a sense of family and community. Steve's query also speaks to the emergence of the "new" South, reflected in real terms by the mayoral elections of Maynard Jackson in Atlanta, Ernest Morial in New Orleans, and Richard Arrington in Birmingham shortly before and after the film was released. Not surprisingly, the second film in the Cosby/Poitier trilogy, *Let's Do It Again*, was set in both Atlanta and New Orleans, further suggesting the renewed vibrancy of southern cities for blacks.

This same generation of black officials is also an object of contempt, as when the duo attempts to enlist the assistance of local congressman Lincoln, played by Roscoe Lee Brown. Steve and Wardell's attempts to meet with Lincoln underscore the depth to which Black Power politics and the early manifestations of Afrocentric thought were already used as perfunctory symbols by black elected officials to convey a sense of belonging with the black masses they were ostensibly elected to represent. This is perhaps best reflected in the Afrocentric "transformation" of former Washington, D.C., mayor Marion Berry in the aftermath of his crack cocaine/prostitute scandal. His political and cultural metamorphosis was a vulgar attempt to garner black voter support in his successful attempt to be reelected as mayor of the city. In preparation for receiving Steve and Wardell, Lincoln literally labors to transform his identity—he replaces a picture of Richard Nixon with one of Malcolm X and dons a dashiki—to one he sees as more in line with his core constituency, whom he describes as being the "real salt of the earth." The class difference between Lincoln and his constituents is made even more apparent by Roscoe Lee Brown, whose general demeanor throughout his acting career suggests that he would exude regal presence in a pigsty. When Steve and Wardell explain that they were victims of black-on-black crime, Lincoln responds pretentiously, "My people, my people. How long? How long?" highlighting the very pretentiousness that Duke Ellington identified in his song "My People." As Lincoln begins to contact the local police chief to help the duo pursue "justice," he becomes reticent when he is informed that the robbery took place in Madame Zenobia's, which he describes as an "illegal after-hours den of iniquity."

Lincoln's class aspirations and desire to distance himself from those who might most threaten his aspirations are articulated via his exchanges with his wife, Mrs. Lincoln (Paula Kelly), who was introduced earlier in the film sharing the same craps table with Wardell as "Leggy Peggy." As Leggy Peggy and Steve and Wardell exchange colloquial pleasantries and memories of the robbery at Zenobia's, Lincoln says to his wife, "Must you always speak in dialect? It's so condescending. We must rid ourselves of these linguistic shackles." Lincoln's response here suggests that many black politicians of his ilk often related the crisis of blacks urban life to a self-inflicted pathology that itself could be equated with the tragedy of chattel slavery. "Pathological" blacks were often easy targets for black municipal leaders, who couldn't translate the power that their positions suggested into real policy changes that could meaningfully address the crises of the very people who became the object of their scorn.

Leggy Peggy discloses that a possible source of Lincoln's reluctance to have the police investigate the robbery at Zenobia's is his own connection to the club as a charter member. Leggy Peggy's disclosure then compromises Lincoln's desire to distance himself from that world via the "respectable" world of politics and the higher sense of privilege that Zenobia's world conveys to him as the only real space where he can exude any privilege. In response to her disclosure, Lincoln queries, "How can one work for the good of one's people, if one's wife continually airs in public one's dirty laundry?" Lincoln's comment speaks powerfully to the continued protection that most black male leaders, continued to benefit from in the era. Thus the community was expected to close ranks not only around truncated identities but also around its leadership, even in the face of impropriety on the part of that leadership. The desires to rehabilitate the images of former Washington, D.C., mayor Marion Berry, boxer Mike Tyson, and the Reverend Henry Lyons, the former head of the National Baptist Convention, are but a few contemporary examples of this dynamic. The verbal lashing that Lincoln gives his wife after her disclosure is analogous, albeit superficially, to the heavy criticism that Desiree Washington faced after she accused of Tyson of sexually attacking her.

In the aftermath of Congressman Lincoln's inability to address their issues, it is not so ironic that the duo turns to respected members of the criminal underground, whose names, incidentally, were provided to them by Mrs. Lincoln. Leggy Peggy's apparent comfort with the various elements of the community, which can be legitimately assumed to be a byproduct of her possible experiences with grassroots organizing during the civil rights movement, is dwarfed by the more prominent focus on her physical features. As Joy James observes about the generation of Panther women who emerged in the 1960s and early 1970s, "Unlike their black female predecessors and elders in the southern civil rights movement . . . Panther women leaders were romanticized as icons, noted for a particular form of physical appearance tied to 'fashion,' skin color, and youth that led to their commodification."[18] Angela Davis's popularity as the most prominent of the "revolutionary sweethearts"[19] was as much about her proclivity for wearing a full Afro and miniskirts as it was about her radical politics. As such Leggy Peggy's potential status as an effective political leader is obscured by "segments of the culture that tended to idolize . . . rather than critically engage with radical heroes and heroines."[20] Ironically, Wardell's comic misrepresentation of her name as "Peggy Leggy" can be read as an attempt to challenge the reduction of Mrs. Lincoln's identity to her physicality.

Steve and Wardell initially confront Little Seymour, played by the legendary tap dancer Harold Nichols, and his associate Big Percy. In a humorous sequence Steve, at Wardell's urging, attempts to call out Little Seymour by playing the dozens. When Little Seymour and Big Percy appear and subsequently show that they are not pushovers but in fact formidable opponents, Wardell intervenes with an unconvincing tale, attempting to build some common ground with Little Seymour with the statement, "I know you can identify with picking cotton." This latter statement incenses Little Seymour and only intensifies his rage at Steve and Wardell's efforts to "call him out of name" and "make a fool out of him." Little Seymour's response to Wardell's attempt to build a common link with him via a suspected shared experience with the Jim Crow South is notable because it is just that, only a suspected shared experience. This moment in the film speaks significantly, at least in Wardell's view, to the limits of essentializing African-American identity based on the notion of a common oppression. Wardell's comments deny the legacy both of African Americans whose lives were not explicitly defined by Jim Crow oppression and the progeny of free blacks who built enclaves within free black societies in the North during the antebellum period. Little Seymour's response may also bespeak his own middle-class sensibilities, in which any reference inferring a connection to the economic poverty and disempowerment experienced by black sharecroppers would naturally be offensive. Such a response could be related to the responses of some middle-class black college students, who are regularly asked to explain what the ghetto is like in classes predominated by white students. My point here is that this is an example of the film's attempt to broaden the definition of black identity, which would be totally in line with Poitier's own desires to make a film that could legitimately be distinguished from the general fare to be found within the blaxploitation genre.

Steve and Wardell's attempt to gather information about the robbery from Little Seymour, and later Geechie Dan Beauford, also speaks to the relative amount of respect and social status assigned to "traditional" gangsters within black communities. This respect has been conveyed contemporarily with the lionization of the "OG" or "original gangsta" by the hip-hop generation.[21] With activities primarily consigned to the underground economy of numbers running, protection, prostitution, and to a lesser extent drug dealing, these gangsters were often an integral part of black urban life, providing jobs (particularly if we accept that prostitution, among other things, is also a form of labor) and some semblance of authority to the criminal element within the black community. One of the reasons that Steve and Wardell were encouraged to seek out Little Seymour and Geechie Dan was because of the sense that nothing happened within the black criminal underground without the knowledge and sanction of black gangsters. At the time that *Uptown Saturday Night* was filmed, black communities were in the midst of the dramatic post–civil rights shifts that changed the demographic and economic profile of black communities, many of which still remained segregated spaces. In the context of black middle-class flight and the contraction of economic opportunities in formerly stable working-class communities, a new generation of gangsters appeared, such as Silky Slim, who broadened the activities of that class with no compunction, at least by comparison with the relative morality and decency exhibited by previous generations of gangsters. This is reflected in the meeting between Geechie Dan and Silky Slim in which they agree to a truce. Upon meeting Silky Slim face-to-face for the first time, Geechie Dan insists to his younger competitor, "You got no class . . . drug dealing, prostitution and bungled stickups like Madame Zenobia's."

Black gangsters and con men are featured prominently in all three of the Cosby/Poitier films, and in the last, *A Piece of the Action*, that class is cast as legitimate members of the then new black middle class, in part because of their graduation from the underground economy of black communities into the extralegal and illicit economies of "mainstream" America. Given the centrality of the black gangster element in the three films, I contend that these narratives serve as the space where writers Wesley and Timothy March and director Poitier examine the dynamics and intricacies of black communities in flux during the post–civil rights era. Whereas the primary themes of the first two films center on the middle-class aspirations of the two main characters, the often contentious relationships between various gangsters within the subplot encapsulate the generational tensions between blacks who came of age during legal segregation and those among the emerging black middle class of the 1970s. This is particularly evident in the film *Let's Do It Again*, where Lockhart is typecast as the youngish, stylish Biggie Smalls opposite John Amos's portrayal of "veteran" gangster Kansas City Mack.

In the second film, Cosby and Poitier return as working-class denizens who, as leaders within a religious/Mason's organization named the "Sons and Daughters of Shaka," are responsible for helping the "church" acquire a loan to begin construction on a new building. The new building is needed because the city of Atlanta, where the film is set, was not willing to renew the lease on their current building. The situation that the church faces is analogous to the impact of "urban renewal" in many black urban communities. In her examination of the cultural politics of post–World War II Detroit, Suzanne Smith examines the Detroit Plan, one of the first urban renewal programs in the country: "The plan . . . argued that the city should purchase and then demolish slum property in order to sell the real estate to private developers at prices well below cost. The first stages of the Detroit Plan began in 1947 and 1948. . . . By 1953 Mayor Cobo had overseen the demolition of 700 buildings in Black Bottom, a process that displaced over 2,000 black families."[22] The deterioration of black housing conditions is obviously one of the most significant aspects of urban renewal, but as the film suggests, it was also a challenge to black institutions, particularly those that provided cultural and social stability for black urban communities. In the film, the church was an obvious reference to the Nation of Islam and the mythology that surrounds the sect's development. The reference is furthered correlated with the appearance of Ossie Davis as the church's leader. Davis, of course, eulogized the slain martyr El-Hajj Malik El-Shabazz (Malcolm X) at the latter's funeral service in February 1965. Davis's character's constant references to the "great, great Grand Warrior of the Kingdom of Shaka" who "stamped his feet on the ground . . . in Africa and the earth shook" are thinly veiled allusions to Nation of Islam founder Elijah Muhammad, who incidentally died the year that the film was released. The precarious status of the church represents a critique of the limits of black nationalist economics; the church is incapable of sustaining itself, and its congregation is unwilling to support it in any way that might be detrimental to their own precarious economic status. But the church also presents another context for black nationalist economics in its desires to provide community-based organizations like day-care facilities and senior citizen housing.

The church is saved by the guile and savvy of the two working-class protagonists, who place a bet on a championship boxing match in New Orleans using their own personal money and the church's savings. The bet is placed on the heavily underdogged challenger Bootney Farnsworth, portrayed by physical comedian J. J. Walker, whom Clyde then hypnotizes into believing that he can beat the champion, "Fortieth Street" Black.

Farnsworth's upset victory provides Clyde and Dave, who have placed $10,000 bets with both Kansas City Mack and Biggie Smalls, the money to build both a new church and a community day-care center in the basement of the church. When Kansas City Mack and his crew figure out that they have been duped by the duo, they track down Clyde and Billy and force them to return to New Orleans for the rematch between Farnsworth and Black, under the premise that Clyde will hypnotize Farnsworth in the days prior to the fight to help generate bets on the new champion and then rehypnotize him back to his former self the day before the fight, to allow Mack and his cohorts to win back the money they lost in the initial fight. Unable to hypnotize Farnsworth to his normal self the day before the fight, Clyde instead hypnotizes Fortieth Street Black, which leads to a draw, as both fighters simultaneously knock each other unconscious. Clyde and Billy ultimately outwit both Mack and Smalls, whom they also place a heavy bet with, by betting that the two fighters will fight to a draw. Billy and Clyde then lure Kansas City Mack and Biggie Smalls into a police station entrance camouflaged as a bathhouse. Thinking that the duo has set them up, Mack and Smalls are shocked when informed that a donation has been made in each of their names to support the police youth league and the Daughters of Shaka day-care facility. Billy deflects attention from their abrupt entrance by suggesting that Mack and Smalls were so moved by the needs of the youth league that they came in "running." Clyde and Billy protect themselves by presenting the station chief with a sealed envelope that could incriminate the gangsters in the event that Clyde and Billy meet with bodily harm or death. Their proxy efforts on behalf of Mack and Smalls have effectively "sanitized" the gangsters. For their part Billy and Clyde become the faces of decency and morality as they return their remaining winnings to the gangsters. This is part of a recurring theme in the trilogy; gangsters are not only presented as integral to the social fabric of black urban life but are also "rehabilitated" and mainstreamed, largely because of more intimate connections with the working-class and working poor folks that they more often than not exploit.

The audience is initially introduced to Kansas City Mack as he castigates his associates for not making enough money from their primary activities, "gambling, joy houses, and the liquor business." In acknowledging the threat that Biggie Smalls posed to his underground empire, Mack states that his adversary "got them educated faggots doing his thinking for him." Mack's commentary here is both on the general disregard for higher education among some black populations and also on how the younger generation, who are positioned to empower themselves via their cerebral talents as opposed to their physical skills, are essentially viewed as inauthentic representations of the type of masculine sensibilities that has apparently informed previous constructions of black masculinity. Smalls, on the other hand, first appears via an address to some of his new associates, where he states his intention to take over the territory currently run by Mack. Smalls asserts, "We believe in change and we're prepared for it, with new techniques and new approaches. And for our part, we feel that you are the best pieces of manpower available in this whole region. We hope to be able to move into this area peacefully . . . no violence." Smalls's language is closely related to some of the black middle-class rhetoric of the era, which eschewed the more militant language used by Black Power activists in the 1960s. In this regard Smalls's comments reflect a belief among some that the real political and social change would occur when blacks gained an economic foothold, change that would occurs nonviolently. Given my belief that Smalls's monologue articulated the philosophical ideals of the screenwriter and director, it is not surprising that Kansas City Mack, as representative of the old guard of political leadership, would be an object of scorn.

When Mack and Smalls confront each other at a sparring match days before the second match, Smalls greets his adversary by stating, "Well, if it ain't shuffle along Mack and his old-time donkeys." When Mack responds with a query about Smalls's mom working in "$10.00" sex houses—the narrative equivalent to simply responding, "Your mama!"—Smalls retorts, "You're colorful, Mack. . . . Dumb, old-fashioned, out of style, but colorful." Biggie Smalls's comment serves as a critique of the often emotional and animated sensibilities of some race leaders whose performances of "black rage" often obscure the substantive issues that they were ostensibly expected to represent. Mack's "Your mama" response is emblematic of the empty rhetoric of those same race leaders, as his comments, while entertaining and witty, do nothing to dramatically address the challenge that Smalls's presence poses. Thus Mack's comments are parallel to the rhetoric of black political leaders who, while providing analysis of the issues that face blacks and instilling some sense of solidarity among blacks, do little if anything to posit solutions to the problems identified. Biggie Smalls and his cohorts, on the other hand, are positioned, via the constant references of their college degrees, to provide those kind of solutions. The confrontation between Mack and Smalls also illuminates the changing nature of the entertainment industry in segregated black urban spaces during the 1970s. Toward the end of the sequence Smalls states, "You know how things are nowadays with gambling and the sporting in the black belt. There's no need for two of us." With the civil rights movement helping to accord blacks greater choice in how and where they spend their money, the type of social spaces that were so integral to black life have become increasingly obsolete as businesses that formerly served a largely white clientele now court black customers.[23]

Furthermore, many of those Black Belt institutions often serviced the needs of those whites who were more willing to inhabit those spaces, often under the premise that the Black Belt contained a more "authentic" and thus more satisfying experience. This concept correlated with the perceptions of some whites that blacks were somehow the perfect balance between (sub)humanity and the primitive. While the community of Harlem, particularly during the 1920s, was the most prominent example of these spaces, southern cities like New Orleans and the Gulfport region of Mississippi were also popular spots for hedonistic pleasures associated with prostitution and gambling. In this regard Biggie Smalls's comments are prescient, as the era witnessed the state annexation of gaming activities that had been largely controlled by the criminal underground. The state-sanctioned lotteries that have appeared during the past thirty years are an example of this. While the legalization of some forms of gambling rightly addresses issues of corruption that may have been present in these formerly "illegal" activities, it was also a recognition of the powerful underground economy that was often integral to the survival of the urban poor. In the face of the challenges posed by the legalization of gaming under various state and municipal jurisdictions, the black gangster class was forced to develop new strategies to compete with state-run programs that had access to many more resources, including advertising budgets.

Ironically, one model that appeared in the late 1980s was the tribally controlled casino, like Foxwoods or Mohegan Sun, run by the Mashantucket Pequot and the Mohegan tribes, respectively. Despite the sharp decline of tribal landholdings over the last century, largely due to the federal government's insidious "Indian Policies," the Indian Gaming Regulatory Act of 1988 allowed some tribes to transform their reservation status into productive gaming industries. Despite the real physical

SOUL BABIES

connections between Black Belts and the black bodies that inhabited them, blacks did not have ownership or real autonomy in those spaces. This might explain the historical focus by blacks on the failure of the federal government to deliver on their promise of "forty acres and a mule" during the Reconstruction era and the current fixation on reparations in popular African-American thought.[24] Rather than tribal homelands, some blacks exist in what could legitimately be called neocolonial states. As black "gangsters" were forced to diversify the "services" that they provided for an admittedly desiring public, it is thus not really surprising that the crack epidemic that continues to afflict some poor communities occurred under the auspices of the next generation of "OGs." The examples of former drug dealers and gang members turned legitimate record industry executives and "chitlin' circuit" stage producers are representative of this dynamic.[25] Further emblematic of the new "vision" that Biggie Smalls advocates is a gesture toward a more diversified organizational structure, which in the film includes whites and at least one black women, the latter not explicitly linked to Smalls romantically. The film ends with the police chief effective banishing Biggie Smalls and Kansas City Mack from the city of New Orleans.

Though Bill Cosby and Sidney Poitier were constants, *Let's Do It Again* and *A Piece of the Action* were not sequels to *Uptown Saturday Night*. The only other constant in the films was the significant presence of black gangsters. Thematically there is a sense of continuity between the latter two films, which were both written by Timothy March. March's story line, unlike the one written by Wesley for *Uptown Saturday Night*, treats black gangsters or con men as they are portrayed within *A Piece of the Action* as a metaphor for some of the tensions associated with black life, specifically black middle-class mobility. As Kansas City Mack represented the demise of one generation of black gangsters, and Biggie Smalls a tentative step into new possibilities for that class, *A Piece of the Action* more fully articulates a vision of the black criminal class that is interconnected with the aspirations and challenges faced by the black middle class. The significance of the narrative is buttressed by Cosby and Poitier taking on the characters of con men—albeit new and improved versions, when you consider Richard Pryor's star turn as a shady detective in the first film—positioned opposite their working-class identities in the previous films. Their characters are legitimated by their challenges to white-collar corporate structures like the banking industry and more traditional

42

criminal elements like the Mafia. In the context of *A Piece of the Action,* Manny Durrell (Sidney Poitier) and Dave Anderson (Bill Cosby) are both "legitimate" businessmen—at one point during the film Anderson suggests that he "manages" money by moving it from one place to another, wherever the interests rates are highest—and members of the black middle class. Their elevation to this status is not unlike the "road to respectability" traveled by fictional mafioso don Michael Corleone in the *Godfather* chronicles. Poitier first explored this theme in the film *For the Love of Ivy*, in which he is cast as the owner of a trucking company who uses his trucks after business hours as traveling gambling casinos that can transcend local gaming restrictions. In the film, Poitier is portrayed as a successful black businessman who becomes romantically linked to the maid, brilliantly portrayed by jazz artist and political activist Abbey Lincoln (Aminata Moseka), of one of his major clients.

The film opens with Anderson, a safecracker by trade, successfully burglarizing the offices of the "Consumer Credit Corporation." The name of the corporation is notable because of the ways in which various corporations have extended credit to working-class and working poor communities, often at exorbitant interest rates. These "credit" corporations, in this regard, help stimulate consumption among those who otherwise would have not have been likely to spend beyond their means. Most credit companies allow debtors to pay only a minimal portion of their overall debt balances, hence the popularity of the cards among poor populations, though this also means that some debtors are likely to purchase goods and services well above the market price. By identifying the Consumer Credit Corporation as a target of his criminal activities, Anderson implies a concern for the equally, if not more, criminal activities of financial institutions that prey on the material desires of poor people, particularly those who are black or Latino/a. Not surprisingly, Anderson orchestrates a second heist, this time attacking a banking officer delivering a briefcase full of cash to an unnamed destination. Unspoken in this narrative is a subtle critique of the ways redlining policies by the banking industry have impeded black economic development.

Unlike Anderson, Durrell works with an ensemble that includes a group of Puerto Rican men from New York City and an older African-American woman. Durrell coordinates a heist of $475,000 from a local Mafia boss named Bruno, whose illicit activities include "numbers, girls, cigarettes . . . secured loans." In one telling sequence, Bruno asks one of his associates about the pharmacy business, to which the associate replies "higher and higher . . . South Chicago . . . Terrific." The "pharmacy" business is a reference to the illegal drug business, which in this context is focused on the largely black communities on Chicago's South Side. This sequence in the film also references the memorable scene in *The Godfather* in which Don Corleone reluctantly agrees to become involved in the illegal drug industry, on the provision that his associates will only deal to the "moulies."[26] Durrell and his associates are able to pull off their heist by masquerading as federal agents, supposedly readying themselves for a bust of Bruno's residence. Hastily attempting to destroy evidence of their activities before the bust, Bruno asks his maid, Mrs. Lucy Foster (Frances Foster), to deliver the briefcase containing the $475,000 to his cousin. To show his gratitude, Bruno even gives Mrs. Foster $20 for her efforts. Unbeknownst to Bruno, Foster, whose real name is Bea Quitman, was planted in his house as a domestic by Durrell and his associates and is in fact the most pivotal catalyst to their scheme. Though space does not permit a fuller exploration here, Foster's role in this dynamic speaks to the ways in which black domestics use cunning and guile to take advantage of employers, who often assume that their domestics are blindly loyal to them and incapable of arranging complex schemes like Foster's.[27] All of the heists follow a Robin Hood theme—steal from the rich and give to the poor—that is seemingly at the basis of the criminal activities of both Anderson and Durrell. On the contrary, both Anderson and Durrell engage in what Durrell later describes as "hustling," more or less done in the interests of their own material desires as opposed to the legitimate and sometimes competing interests of black communities.

Ultimately it is the efforts of Joshua Burke (James Earl Jones), a retired police detective, that force Anderson and Durrell to be more socially responsible to their communities, particularly the generation of black youth, who in large part don't have the resources or the opportunities to "hustle" at Anderson and Durrell's high and relatively safe level. Burke, whose work as a detective allows him to recognize the signature criminal styles of Anderson and Durrell, chooses to blackmail the two rather than turn them over to the authorities. Burke's decision here suggests an empathy for their activities, though he has the more personal motive of forcing the two to "volunteer" at the Benjamin Banneker Community Improvement Center. The center, which provides child care and senior services, an arts program, and family counseling, was the passion of Burke's late wife, Martha Burke. (Martha Burke's death, at the relatively young age of forty-three, was in part the product of her overextending herself in meeting the challenges posed by the center.) Existing as only a voice on a telephone (ironic, given James Earl Jones's later role as a spokesperson for the Bell Atlantic/Verizon communications company), Burke "encourages" Anderson and Durrell to accept his terms of becoming traditional "9 to 5" laborers for the periods of "5 years" and "4 years and 6 months," respectively. The specific time periods coincide with the time that would be served in the state penitentiary system if the duo were turned over to the authorities. The center's director, Lila French (Denise Nichols), who was mentored by the late Martha Burke and who is initially unaware of Burke's plan, proposes that Anderson and Durrell specifically focus on the job-preparedness program, which attempts to find employment for black youth assigned to the program by juvenile court. It is this relationship between the "volunteers" and the assignees that frames the film's overall critique of black middle-class identity and responsibility.

Upon meeting Anderson and Durrell for the first time, one of the youths at the center describes them as "male roles models . . . bourgies . . . they work with the CIA I betcha." The young man's comment speaks volumes about black youth's perceptions of the black middle class at the time. The idea that the black middle class, particularly those with certain "bourgeois" sensibilities, is reserved a special role model status was a crucial aspect of W. E. B. Du Bois's original "talented-tenth" thesis and continues to be present in the thought of prominent contemporary black intellectuals, most notably William Julius Wilson.[28] But the young man's comments also suggest a complicity on the part of the black middle class in the maintenance of the youth's own misery. This is particularly apparent in a confrontation between center assignee Barbara (Sheryl Lee Ralph) and the job-preparedness instructor Sarah Thomas (Hope Clarke). Ms. Thomas accuses Barbara—who ignores her lecture, choosing instead to read a copy of *Iceburg Slim*—of having a short attention span, to which Barbara explosively responds, "Time dammit . . . Time out . . . bad mouthing me about my attention span. I've been paying attention, that's what's wrong. I paid enough attention to peep your game Ms. Thomas, so don't give me all that bull shit." In an animated display, Barbara goes on say, "I ain't never gonna get no damn job . . . not with people like you around. I said if we all get jobs it'll blow your game. Yeah, game. All you middle-class bourgie ass niggas. . . . All of y'all got the jobs, and you making your money off of us. Administering to your lesser brethren and sisters . . . all of us poor ghetto deprived chillen." After commenting on how well-paid Ms. Thomas and others are, Barbara goes on to charge, "Well, if it wasn't for niggas like us, y'all wouldn't make shit. . . . I recognize a poverty pimp when I see one. . . . What's happening is bourgeois bullshit."

Ms. Thomas, who has been largely silent during Barbara's outburst, finally responds by asserting her own experiences of going to college and the fact that she works hard, to which Barbara responds, "So now you work hard on your game of underprivileged nigga." Barbara's comments powerfully present some of the anger and derisiveness that some poor black youth reserve toward the black middle class and the relative privilege extended to that class. While Barbara's tirade may have been the product her own need to "read" Ms. Thomas publicly in response to the latter's "calling her out of name," many of her claims are legitimate critiques of those black elites who may benefit from some blacks remaining in destitute conditions because it legitimates their positions as spokespeople and brokers for that segment of the black community. Implicit in Barbara's comments is also the idea that being black in America is to some extent "all a hustle," but that the "hustling" of the black middle class is validated by their college degrees and their finely tuned social sensibilities. In a later conversation with Durrell, who also witnessed the "attack," even Ms. Thomas is forced to admit, "I do make my living from their misery," though she is also careful to criticize the bankrupt conditions of public schooling in black and poor communities.

The exchange between Barbara and Ms. Thomas articulates the distance between generations of blacks in the 1970s, but also a presumed distance between the black middle class and the black community, which is characterized throughout the film series as primarily working class and poor. *A Piece of the Action* is the first of the trio of films in which Cosby and Poitier were not previously linked. In the previous films, their relationships between themselves, their wives, and community institutions like the black church enhanced the sense of community that was part of the appeal to black audiences. While the film doesn't consistently speak to the reality of black middle-class flight during the period—Barbara's tirade is the one scene in which it is explicitly addressed—the unfamiliarity between the Poitier and Cosby characters at the film's opening depicts the sense of distance and dislocation that the black middle class began to experience in relation to the black community. This is articulated during the duo's first meeting, where they share a deep mistrust of each other. This is not to say that the black middle class abandoned black urban communities en masse, but even those who remained vital and productive members of black communities forged decades earlier because of legal segregation were often still marked as "different" because of their economic and social class. Durrell lives in an expansive apartment that has a white doorman, one marker of black middle-class status. This was explored throughout the run of the popular sitcom *The Jeffersons*, in which the main character often articulated his disdain for the poverty and racism he experienced as a child through the abusive way he treated the building's white doorman, Ralph. While the film does not focus on Anderson's home life, he is witnessed on several occasions coming back to the 'hood to frequent a local disco. Overall, the characters' personal lives suggest a distance from black community.

When the black church, arguably the most important black social institution of the twentieth century, is referenced, it is done so in a way that suggests that it is more intrusive to the personal lives of the black middle class than helpful. Specifically this occurs when the parents of Durrell's live-in partner, Nikki, come for a visit. As the daughter of a minister and a mother who seems well attuned to communal perceptions of their daughter "living in sin," Nikki is castigated by her mother for not setting a proper example for her younger sisters. In previous eras, as Kevin Gaines attests in his work, black middle-class identity was often conflated with religious identity and a morality code connected to the black community's need to present the most positive aspects of their identity and culture.[29] Perhaps unspoken in this sequence of the film is the fact that Nikki has also failed to set a proper example because she chose a dark-skinned black man for a mate. Though my specific interest in the film does not permit a more detailed account of the color caste politics of the black community, I do want to suggest that the efforts of the black middle class to reproduce themselves socially and morally often entailed an intraracial discrimination against the darker end of the black skin color spectrum. The fact that Nikki and Durrell were able to maintain their relationship and even convince her family of the value of it highlights one of the ways that the influence of the black church had begun to erode in the 1970s. This is perhaps most profoundly articulated in the apparently absolute absence of the black church in the lives of the black youth portrayed in the film.

In an effort to get information on the male voice responsible for blackmailing them, Durrell and Anderson decide to "hit" the center's safe, hoping that the safe will contain information on the various supporters and benefactors of the center. As they escape the center via a back alley, they are confronted by a quartet of black men, likely petty burglars, who refer to Anderson and Durrell as "Errol Flynn" and ask for their "cut" of the take, figuring that the duo is cutting in on their territory. The "Errol Flynn" comment helps to again reinforce the Robin Hood "take from the rich and give to the poor" theme of the film, but it also marks the difference between the petty criminals present in black communities and the style of "high" crime that Durrell and Anderson engage in as con men. After a physical confrontation with the quartet, the duo races back to Anderson's car, only to find out that the tires have been stolen and the car is sitting on a quartet of concrete blocks. The scene is reminiscent of a recording from the era by the O'Jays, "Don't Call Me Brother," in which the song's narrator, Eddie Levert, details the everyday occurrences that challenge attempts to maintain community in the 1970s. Ironically, it is this experience that begins the process in which Anderson and Durrell begin to connect more significantly to the black community as it is presented in the film. This process is also represented in the increasingly closeness between Anderson and the center's coordinator, Lila French.

When the duo finally identify Joshua Burke as the likely source of their problems, simultaneously Bruno also identifies Durrell as the mastermind behind the heist at his home. Bruno was able to do this by first tracking down his former maid, Bea Quitman, who had fled to Copenhagen, since she was the only one that Bruno could visually identify. Bruno lures Quitman, who had a lengthy career as a con woman in her own right, back to the United States under the threat that he will harm her grandson, who still lives with his parents in Chicago. Earlier in the film Quitman had voiced some apprehension about leaving her grandson after Durrell suggested that it was in her best interests to flee to Europe, beyond the reach of Bruno. Ultimately it is the pull of family that leads Quitman back to the States—the same pull of family that has been the stimulus for those within the black middle class who no longer reside in black communities to remain engaged with the neighborhoods in which many of them were born and raised. Quitman is then used as bait to kidnap Nikki, so Bruno can offer an even exchange of her for Durrell and the money he stole. The role that Nikki plays at this junction highlights one of the more troubling aspects of the film, in that women are largely used as vehicles to further the plot or the specific agendas of male characters. The most blatant example of this is Anderson's initial interest in Lila French. Anderson specifically seeks a relationship with her, figuring that such intimacy will accord greater access to the inner workings of the center and those who support it. While the film eschews some of the more blatant distortions of black female sexuality prevalent during the period and presents black women in the film as reasonably independent thinkers, it also recalls the historic economic and social value assigned to black women with light skin.

Given the increased value that black female quadroons and octoroons garnered in the open exchange of black bodies during the slave trade, the value of Nikki and her light skin, which in the film is two-thirds of the original $475,000, or a little more than $316,000, can be considered as part of the contemporary skin trade that continues to assign increased value, for example, to light-skinned black women within the film and music video industry, in particular. I understand that my reading here in some ways distorts the intentions of the film, but it is a consideration buoyed by Durrell's frequent assertion that he wants *his* woman back. Nikki is thus something to be owned, likely to be bought and sold, as theoretically she is in the film. This notion also speaks to the historic values assigned to light-skinned black women and white women as the trophy pieces of "elite" black men, as those women presumably convey a higher social status than dark-skinned black women. As the romantic opposites of Cosby and Poitier, Denise Nichols (Lila French) and Tracy Reed (Nikki) played central roles in the film's plot. That they are both light-skinned black women may have been incidental to the casting process, though the heightened promotion of light-skinned black women in the film industry, Lena Horne and the late Dorothy Dandridge being the most potent examples, has been an industry fact.[30]

More telling is that the darker-skinned Ms. Thomas is a source of scorn and ridicule for Barbara, perceived as cold, unfeeling, and calculating, qualities attributed in part to the lack of a sex life or male sexual counterpart. At one point during their exchange, Barbara suggests that Ms. Thomas should return to her middle-class neighborhood to use her "vibrator," or whatever, as she states to Ms. Thomas, "turns you on." In this particular sequence, Ms. Thomas is "queered" because of the absence of a male, black or otherwise, in her sexual life and because she is presumed by Barbara to instead satisfy her self "unnaturally" via a mechanical apparatus or a female sexual partner. All of these attributes are firmly assigned to the body of a dark-skinned black woman. As a dark-skinned woman, even Barbara, played brilliantly by a young Sheryl Lee Ralph, is subject to these color dynamics, representative as she is of the aggressive, bitchy, emasculating black woman who dominated black popular culture in the twentieth century. Barbara's dark skin and character within the film also reflect a connection between skin color and social class. More broadly, Ms. Thomas can be seen as the black woman who is forced (tragically) to serve her people as a teacher/nurturer; presumably she is too unattractive to find a black heterosexual mate because her dark skin is deemed unattractive to such suitors, particularly among the black middle classes. In this context, such women would presumably accept a state of intraracial peonage within the black community rather than pursue "alternative" relationships, in which her own "blackness" and devotion to the "race" may be questioned. Even as her relationship with Barbara softens toward the end of the film, Ms. Thomas's blackness is still questioned. To celebrate the end of the six-week training program, the program's participants give gifts to the center's director and Ms. Thomas. The class's peace offering to Ms. Thomas, presented to her by Barbara, is the collected works of black musical genius Stevie Wonder. The gift suggests that Ms. Thomas, given her middle-class status, would in some way be unfamiliar with Wonder's work and thus could begin to reconnect with her "blackness" by immersing herself in it. The most visible album cover within the bundled collection of albums that Ms. Thomas receives is the recording *Music of My Mind*, which contains one of Wonder's most popular recordings from the era, "Superwoman." An alternative reading of this exchange suggests that the gift instead represents a recognition on the part of Barbara of the struggles and sacrifices that Ms. Thomas endured as she strove to succeed in a racist and sexist society and in spite of the color-caste politics of the black community. This reading is bolstered by the fact that as a "bright" dark-skinned woman, Barbara is likely to endure the same kind of struggles that Ms. Thomas has.

It is after Durrell finally exchanges his own freedom for Nikki's that he is able to fully articulate his own reconnections with blackness, albeit in the role of spokesperson and power broker for the working class and poor on Chicago's South Side. In their initial confrontation, Bruno says to Durrell that he interferes with the "normal flow of things, boy. You shouldn't deal with other people's money." Durrell's first response to Bruno's claim is to assert that he is a "man," countering Bruno's depiction of him as a boy. This aspect of the exchange is an old narrative in which black men both real and imagined have attempted to assert their masculinity or manliness in the face of a culture that has at times deemed them childlike. But Bruno's comments also represent a broad commentary on the travels that the black middle class had begun to make in the era by "integrating" spaces that had formerly been defined by white male privilege. While Durrell and Anderson are metaphors for black middle-class mobility, it is useful to note that it is a mobility largely defined by *black male* privilege. Despite whatever privilege Nikki and Lila French may derive from their light skin, both remain in the position of nurturer; Nikki nurtures Durrell and French provides that support for the center and those who benefit from it. Thus a general theme throughout the film is not just the rehabilitation of Durrell and Anderson from their status as con men and criminals but their reclamation as privileged black men willing to represent the race. Durrell begins to accept this role as he retorts to Bruno, "You should take your own advice Bruno, that [the money Durrell has stolen] was other people's money, money you took from poor people." Durrell's desire now to represent the interests of poor people is ironic, given that he had to be blackmailed to help train the students at the community center. Though Lila French is likely the character in the film who could best articulate the interests of the "people," the film presumes that black male middle-class privilege also conveys that status, even to the exclusion of a character like French.

Bruno defends his practices by stating, "I don't steal that money. People give it to me. I provide a service," to which Durrell responds, "Dope is a service? Gamblers, whores, twelve-year-old junkies are informed consumers?" Bruno's defense is not unlike those used by black drug dealers contemporarily, though Durrell's comments speak to the role that he sees for himself and by extension the black middle classes in administering to the less fortunate and the dysfunctional, even though he has generally had little if any contact with that particular community. Durrell attempts to place his conning of Bruno on a more principled plane by admitting, "So I touched ya and I touched ya good. Alright I owe you. You owe people. You owe a lot of people in *my* [emphasis mine] neighborhood. So in a matter of touching other people's money, we're even." Durrell's "claiming" of his neighborhood is one way for him to acknowledge his race pride, which had been largely absent throughout the film, and this pride, in concert with his middle-class status, conveys a right to represent his community, even in absentia. Throughout the film Durrell had not shown any inkling of being concerned for his community, though it becomes a way for him to buttress problematic activities, suggesting that he does it all for the "folks." When Durrell and Anderson are presented with the opportunity to actually continue to serve the interests of the youth at the center, they jokingly decline, though in the film's closing scene the youth at the center join most of the film's major characters, including Ms. Thomas, Detective Joshua Burke, Lila French, Durrell, and Anderson, in a dance cipher reminiscent of the Soul Train line so popular in the television show of the same name. The scene, which features the music of vocalist Mavis Staples, conveys a sense of community, despite the ill-will originally felt between many of the folks in the scene. This "happy" ending suggests that when all is said and done, the pull of race and community will help blacks transcend intraracial differences. Noticeably absent in this scene is Nikki, whose general absence at the center throughout the film suggests her domestication by Manny. This perception is buttressed by the fact that quadroons and octoroons were also "domesticated" as the sexual "pets" of elite white men in the South during the antebellum era.

The popularity of the Cosby and Poitier films has been confirmed in the ways elements of them have cropped up in contemporary black popular culture. The best example is the Notorious B.I.G.'s original moniker, Biggie Smalls. In another example Rachid Lynn, whose musical persona is Common, named his recording imprint Madam Zenobia. *A Piece of the Action* was the last film that Poitier acted in for almost a decade, though he would also go on to direct other films, including *Stir Crazy*, which starred Richard Pryor and Gene Wilder. In some way the film marked the definitive end of the blaxploitation cycle and the beginning of the entrenchment of the crossover film. Only with the much-ballyhooed release of *She's Gotta Have It* in 1986 and the ascension of Spike Lee as the most visible icon of "independent" black cinema did the film industry begin, tentatively I might add, to invest in projects by black directors and screenwriters. Whereas all three films in the trilogy were in many ways validated by the presence of Poitier, who played straight man to the Cosby comedic forays, it was Cosby who emerged in the aftermath of *A Piece of the Action* as a hypercommercial black entity. With the debut of the highly rated *Cosby Show*, which premiered in the fall of 1984, Bill Cosby solidified his status as the ultimate black crossover icon, rivaled only in the 1980s by Michael Jackson and Magic Johnson and perhaps Eddie Murphy. Opposite Raquel Welch and Harvey Keitel in *Mother, Jugs, and Speed*, the film version of Neil Simon's *California Suite* (ironically with Richard Pryor, who like Eddie Murphy would come to be recognized as the anti-Cosby), Cosby attempted to craft a crossover film career, perhaps to transcend his success as a stand-up comic and television star. Films like *Uptown Saturday Night* and *Let's Do It Again*, which was one of the highest-grossing black films of the 1970s, dramatically increased Cosby's potential in this regard. It is important to note even the changes in Cosby's characters in the trilogy of films he did with Poitier. Wardell Franklin and in particular Billy Foster, could have legitimately been drawn from the ever-present Jim Crow caricatures that existed in the late nineteeth and early twentieth centuries. In contrast to these characters, Dave Anderson was cleanly shaven and his Afro was neatly intact. While this may have just been the necessary style for a character who for all intents and purposes was upper middle class, it was also a return to Cosby's clean-shaven and cultured role on the television series *I Spy*.

Cosby had had several short-lived television shows, among them *The Bill Cosby Show*, in which he portrayed high-school gym teacher Chet Kincaid, and an attempt at a variety show, *The Cos*, which debuted in the mid-1970s. Besides *I Spy*, Cosby's major success in a television series prior to *The Cosby Show* was the very popular Saturday-morning cartoon *Fat Albert and the Cosby Kids*, which presented an animated and often surreal view of Cosby's childhood in Philadelphia. For the generation of black youth and children who came to adulthood in the 1980s and 1990s, shows like *Fat Albert and the Cosby Kids* and *The Jackson Five Cartoon* were part of our introduction to the multicultural and multiethnic world that the television industry tried to craft for America in the post–civil rights era. While such shows may not have dramatically altered the realities of a racialized society, clearly some aspects of them enhanced the hyperpopularity of Cosby and Michael Jackson in the 1980s.[31] In some regards *Fat Albert and the Cosby Kids* allowed Cosby the opportunity to publicly meditate on his own ascension from a working-class black community in Philadelphia to successful black crossover star. The show, which was filled with anecdotal material and tales of moral and social responsibility, helped articulate Cosby's notion of the possibilities of the American Dream, which he legitimately was afforded the opportunity to realize. As Michael Eric Dyson has suggested, Cosby "has risen to such phenomenal stature precisely because he embodies so much of the power of the ideology of Americanism: an individual who, despite a poor beginning, overcame problems of race and class in order to become a great stand-up comedian, actor, and spokesperson for several companies."[32] Although Manny Durrell and Dave Anderson were con men, they epitomized American notions of hard work and "pull yourself up by your own bootstraps" dictates. Is there a more American story than that of those Italian and Jewish ethnics who transcended poor working-class existences, often in the illicit economies of large urban centers, and whose children later become quintessential members of the American middle class? In many ways, *A Piece of the Action* presents that story in blackface, though with strong doses of social responsibility to the race.

It is this strong sense of social responsibility that perhaps foregrounds the success of *The Cosby Show*. While Cosby eschewed any real engagement with the political realities of race in America during the show's run (1984–92), his responsibility may have been just the presentation of a black middle-class alternative to the negative stereotypical images of black life that littered television programming. Dyson has argued that the show "created cultural space for the legitimate existence of upper-middle class blacks on television," though he also admits that the show also has a "responsibility to address more pointedly" issues of race, sex, and class.[33] This disconnect was perhaps most visible during the show's final broadcast, which celebrated the graduation of Theo Huxtable (Malcolm Jamal-Warner) from New York University as the Los Angeles "revolt" of 1992 dominated news broadcasts.[34] But Cosby's points had been made: black middle-class families do exist, black men do graduate from college despite debilitating conditions like "dyslexia," a work ethic and college education are still viable means to the middle class, and black men can and do sustain productive and respectful relationships. The absence of narratives on the experiences of the black poor and underclass in Cosby's show was itself a critique of those who suffer under dire economic conditions, in many ways no different than Manny Durrell's very pointed comments to the youth at the Benjamin Banneker Community Improvement Center. It is perhaps too much to have expected Cosby to devote significant time to the issues that affected a broader segment of the black community within the confines of a situation comedy that was largely devoted to the ebb and flow of middle-class family life. But ironically, television, film, and music continue to play a significant role in how various constituencies within the black community articulate their positions within that community. The next chapter will be devoted to examining those tensions within gender relationships in the post-soul era.

3

Baby Mama (Drama) and Baby Daddy (Trauma)
Post-Soul Gender Politics

Got the baby-mama drama, make me want to scream and holla. Tryin' to get for my dollars, ain't nothing but the baby-mama drama.

—Dave Hollister

Let's face it. I am a marked woman, but not everybody knows my name. "Peaches" and "Brown Sugar," "Sapphire" and "Earth Mother," "Aunty," "Granny," God's "Holy Fool," a "Miss Ebony First," or "Black Woman at the Podium": I describe a locus of confounded identities, a meeting ground of investments and privations in the national treasury of rhetorical wealth. My country needs me, and if I were not here, I would have to be invented.

—Hortense Spillers

In 1966 Bill Cosby debuted in the television program *I Spy*, which costarred Robert Culp. Cosby and Culp portrayed intelligence agents Alexander "Scotty" Scott and Kelly Robinson. It was one of the first major television roles for an African American in a regularly scheduled action-drama series. Given the political climate of the time, the show and Cosby's role within it—his character was a Rhodes scholar, among other things—were widely celebrated. Two years later Diahann Carroll appeared as the lead actress in the television show *Julia*, which was also widely recognized as emblematic of the changing political terrain of the time, though some black audiences felt that it was an inauthentic portrayal of black life. Film historian Donald Bogle has suggested that for some black audiences during the 1960s, "Diahann Carroll represented one more dehydrated and lifeless accruement of a decadent capitalist society."[1] Black audiences were also leery of the fact that Carroll's character was single black mother, albeit a widow whose husband was killed serving in Vietnam. Given the mainstream appeal of Cosby and Carroll, they were logical choices for television programmers hoping to win over white audiences that were at best uncomfortable with the increased visibility of blacks on television. The good-natured personality of both characters provided another vantage point to view blacks, contrasting with that generally presented in news stories surrounding black demands for political equality during the 1960s. Carroll had already attained some crossover success on Broadway and in film, notably opposite Sidney Poitier in the film *Paris Blues*, which also starred Joanne Woodward and husband Paul Newman.

Despite the symbolic value of *I Spy* and *Julia*, both programs were marked by a noticeable absence of sustained heterosexual romantic relationships in the lives of the black leads. Both absences likely centered on the inability of the shows' writers and producers to adequately represent the nuances of black identities, but also a real fear of how black masculinity should be constructed in these programs. In the case of Cosby his character was presented as nonsexual, as opposed to asexual—a savvy decision on the part of the show's producers and writers, given the anxieties and sometimes outright terror that colored mainstream perceptions of black male sexuality. While *Julia* featured potential romantic suitors for Carroll's character, including Paul Winfield and former NFL star Fred Williamson, there was little if any significant attention paid to that aspect of her life. Given that the program was a star vehicle for Carroll, who had been comfortable in crossover roles throughout her career—Bogle describes Julia as "Doris-Day-in-blackface"[2]—the presence of a "strong" black male character may have complicated efforts to craft the show in a way that reached the widest audiences. Presumably this absence was also affected by the "Poitierization" of black male roles in film and television; these roles were tight binary constructions, where black actors were cast based on how closely they hewed to Poitier's acting sensibilities. During the 1960s Hollywood's version of the good-negro-vs.-bad-nigger dichotomy was itself historically based on the inability of many whites and more than a few blacks to recognize the complexity of black identities. Bill Cosby probably benefited from his proximity to Poitier's style as well as his success as a crossover stand-up comic, while former football star Jim Brown became the "anti-Poitier," both on screen and in real life.[3] *Julia* demanded more nuanced representations of black masculinity, and femininity for that matter, which the time and theme constraints of the sitcom format does not often allow. Cosby's *I Spy* character was afforded a subtler reading in an hour-long drama, as well.

The sitcom *Sanford and Son* premiered in January 1972, featuring comedian Redd Foxx and Demond Wilson as the lead characters. Foxx and Wilson played father and son Fred and Lamont Sanford, junk dealers in the Watts section of Los Angeles. Wilson's "straight man" character provided a welcome balance to the often absurd antics of the show's patriarch Fred Sanford (Foxx), but the show also highlighted a trend in black-themed television shows, where stable family structures were largely absent. This is not to suggest that the familial relations in *Sanford and Son*, or *Julia* for that matter, were unstable or that they would necessarily be made more stable by the presence of heterosexual parents, but the family structures within these programs were "abnormal" given the television industry's consistent use of the nuclear family to center situation comedies.[4] Fred Sanford's late wife Elizabeth was generally referred to only when Fred attempted to gain some degree of sympathy, usually from his son Lamont (Wilson), for one of his failings. The image of Fred Sanford clutching his chest as if having a heart attack and uttering the line, "Elizabeth, I'm coming," was the show's signature comedic moment, one in which an absent black female character is used to buttress the joke. Another key comedic element was the contentious and acerbic exchanges between Fred Sanford and the show's only major female figure, Aunt Esther, who was played by Lawanda Page. Though Aunt Esther serves as a stand-in matriarchal figure for Lamont, her personality is clearly dramatically different from that of Elizabeth, who was likely more accommodating to Fred's cantankerous personality—particularly in death. Given the nature of Fred and Aunt Esther's exchanges, which are marked by different perceptions of fixed gender roles, I wonder whether Fred simply mourns Elizabeth's absence or her absence as a potent symbol of his patriarchal privilege. Whereas Elizabeth is constructed as a sentimental figure, Aunt Esther is the object of some of Fred Sanford's most mean-spirited jokes. The exchanges between Fred and Aunt Esther were some of the most memorable moments of the show's run, so much so that Page has been unable to separate herself from the character. A testament to the character's influence can be seen in the drag performances of Jamie Foxx and Martin Lawrence, whose characters "Wanda" and "Mama Payne" from the shows *In Living Color* and *The Martin Lawrence Show* seem directly drawn from Aunt Esther. Page even did an Aunt Esther–like reprisal in a spate of commercials for the Church's Chicken fast-food chain during the 1990s.

My larger point here is that Page's Aunt Esther role (with a subtle nod to Moms Mabley) in some ways embodied the emasculating and independent black women that were mythified in the late 1960s. Aunt Esther, for instance, owned an apartment complex next to the Sanford junkyard and held significant sway over the life of her husband. Such characters, particularly in comedy films and television sitcoms, have become staples, as witnessed by the role of Pamela James (portrayed by Tichina Arnold) on *The Martin Lawrence Show*, Maxine Shaw (Erika Alexander) on the sitcom *Living Single*, and, most classically, Florence (Marla Gibbs) on the highly rated sitcom *The Jeffersons* (1975–85). In their exchanges with Martin Payne (Martin Lawrence), Kyle Barker (T. C. Carson), and George Jefferson (Sherman Helmsley), respectively, all three woman are presented as emasculating "bitchlike" women, marked by the absence of men in their lives. Skin color also played a part in these particular constructions, particularly in the case of Arnold, whose character was often portrayed as the opposite to the light-skinned (or what some black folks would refer to as high-yellow) actress Tisha Campbell (who plays Gina Waters).[5] The aforementioned female characters comprise sets of comic tropes within black popular culture that became the basis for black popular culture's presentation and critique of gender relations during the post-soul era. Some of the anxiety and animosity present in discussions of contemporary black gender politics have something to do with battles over the role of patriarchy within contemporary black life and the perceived absence, both real and imagined, of black men in "traditional" family settings.

BABY MAMA (DRAMA) AND BABY DADDY (TRAUMA)

The origin of much contemporary discourse on black gender relations was the publication of the now infamous report *The Negro Family: The Case for National Action*. The report, coauthored by Daniel Patrick Moynihan and two staff members in the Department of Labor's Office of Policy Planning and Research, essentially suggested that the absence of fathers in black families, in concert with the more stable positions of black women in the labor force and within their families and communities, place the black family in crisis in a society that "presumes" that men provide leadership in both the public and private sphere. More tellingly, the report suggested that the apparent prominence black women hold within black institutions, including the black family, "undermines" the position of black fathers within those same institutions. Donna Franklin points out that Moynihan's thesis was not new; social scientists including Elliot Liebow, Thomas Pettigrew, and noted black sociologist E. Franklin Frazier had argued as much prior to Moynihan.[6] Moynihan's report was given more visibility, however, because it was released shortly before the Watts insurrections of 1965. As many pundits grappled for explanations for the explosion of violence in the Watts district of Los Angeles, *The Negro Family: The Case for National Action* helped fill in the blanks and has continued to do so for nearly four decades.[7] In this regard, Jimmie Reeves suggests that the Moynihan report and subsequent studies of its ilk—a discourse that he has labeled "cultural Moynihanism"—provided the New Right in the Reagan era and beyond with "seemingly 'objective' research that justifies eliminating affirmative action programs, cutting welfare funding, and prosecuting a brutal war on black youth under the guise of the war on drugs."[8] Ironically, perhaps, the report also gained credibility among black nationalist thinkers who found Moynihan's thesis on the recovery of black patriarchy useful to their ideological concerns. The embrace of black patriarchy within these circles was so powerful that it led the late filmmaker Marlon Riggs to suggest that the civil rights and Black Power movements had been reduced to an "erected" black phallus.[9]

Many authors have taken Moynihan to task, so I feel no need to critique his report in such a way here.[10] In my mind, the crisis that black men face in American society in terms of unemployment, health care, violence, and so on is very real, but the focus on these "male" issues should not come at the expense and eclipse of black women and their own critical conditions. The conditions that black women face in American society are perhaps even more critical—if we accept even the logic of the

Moynihan report—because they are also responsible for the care of "fatherless" children. It is within this context that the current feminization of poverty is witnessed within the black community.[11] In this chapter, I will examine how these "conversations" about black fatherlessness and black matriarchy play out within black popular culture, particularly within music videos. I am particularly interested in the ways in which the absences of black men and women are often mourned, though for radically different reasons, and how some black women are scorned because of their failure to resemble their kind of black matriarchs deserving of mourning, and the roles these women have in the "removal" of black men.

"Damn, Damn, Damn . . . James!": Mourning James Evans Sr.

In the fall of 1998 the Atlanta based hip-hop act Outkast released their third full-length recording, *Aquemini*. Included on that recording was the track "SpottieOttieDopalicious," which chronicles some of the everyday experiences of what rapper Andre refers to as "Niggerville, USA." One of the recurring features of the song was the phrase "damn, damn, damn, James," which was repeated throughout the song by background vocalist Patrick Brown and group members Andre and Big Boi. The phrase was a direct quote from the second part of a two-part episode entitled "The Move" from the popular sitcom *Good Times*. The first of the two episodes originally aired on CBS in September 1976 as the premiere episode of the 1976–77 television season. *Good Times* was a spin-off of the popular sitcom *Maude*, which starred actress Bea Arthur in the title role and was itself a spinoff of the groundbreaking and controversial *All in the Family*, which tackled social controversies like racism, abortion, and the Vietnam War head on. All three shows were either created or developed by Norman Lear for his Tandem Productions, which also oversaw the creation of *The Jeffersons*, another spinoff of *All in the Family*. *Good Times* matriarch Florida Evans, portrayed by Negro Ensemble veteran Esther Rolle, originally appeared in *Maude* as a maid. In 1973 Michael Evans, who had a recurring role as Lionel Jefferson on *All in the Family*, and writer Eric Monte, who later wrote the screenplay for the nostalgic film *Cooley High*, pitched the idea of a sitcom that focused on a black inner-city family to Norman Lear. The end result was the series *Good Times*, which first appeared on CBS's primetime schedule in February 1974 and introduced the Evans family to television audiences.

BABY MAMA (DRAMA) AND BABY DADDY (TRAUMA)

"The Move" begins with the announcement that family patriarch James Evans Sr. (John Amos), who often struggled to maintain the kind of regular employment that could help him better sustain his family economically, had been offered gainful employment in Mississippi. His new job necessitated that the Evanses move from their apartment in the notorious Cabrini-Greene housing projects and relocate, or rather remigrate, back to the South. "The Move" was a not-so-subtle hint that for many blacks, whose families migrated to cities like Chicago and Detroit after World War II in pursuit of better job opportunities, the promised land was just that, only a promise. As witnessed by the dire living conditions that the Evans family faced, black migrants were often forced into economic conditions arguably worse than those in the South. The series' appeal to black and nonblack audiences alike revolved around the concept, presented on a consistent basis, that nuclear and extended families were potent buffers against the often absurd and challenging features of urban living. But the episode's early theme also suggests that the great social experiment that was the mass migration of blacks from the South after World War II was a failure for families like the Evanses whose lack of formal education, among other things, was a significant hindrance to their success in post–civil rights America. Thus the South became the "new" promised land for a man like James Evans Sr. precisely because he never made the transition from a "plantation" laborer to the more "cerebral" laborers that could be found in the emerging black middle class of the 1970s and that "thrived" in the urban and suburban economies of the postindustrial city. Throughout the series, which ran from 1974 to 1979, the Evans family was consistently juxtaposed to the emerging real-life class of black managers and professionals. That juxtaposition suggested that the Evans family was a product of an old "Negro" paradigm that was destined to die off as more blacks were afforded the educational opportunities that would better prepare them for what was being touted, at least within popular culture and liberal political rhetoric, as post-race America.

The sense that the Evans family was a product of the past was powerfully supported by the presence of James Evans Jr., portrayed by stand-up comedian Jimmy Walker. Walker's portrayal of the character's "coonish step 'n' fetchit" antics increasingly became the show's most popular feature. James Evans Jr., or JJ, as he was regularly referred to, became a potent symbol that even in liberal, post-race America, some blacks, even those born in the "promised land" like JJ, could not be saved. At the height of the program's popularity, Esther Rolle was quoted as saying of the character, "He's eighteen and he doesn't work. He can't read or write. He doesn't think. The show didn't start out to be that. . . . Little by little—with the help of the artist I suppose, because they couldn't do that to me—they have made him more stupid and enlarged the role."[12] Within this context daughter Thelma (Bernadette Stanis) was already being trained to be a dutiful domestic and wife like her mother, though her often contentious exchanges with her brother JJ suggest that she also was of the ilk of those emasculating black women that Moynihan claimed were increasingly a staple of black life. Only the character of Michael, the youngest of the Evans children, suggested a diversion from the old Negro paradigm that the family generally represented. Michael, who was portrayed by teenage stage actor Ralph Carter, was an emerging intellectual in his own right, whose commitment to social activism was a refreshing counter to the antics of JJ and implied in some ways the impact the civil rights and Black Power movements had on black youth in the post–civil rights era. But the character of Michael was also marked by a distinct militancy that some mainstream audiences may have found discomfiting. While I cannot at this time provide a more sustained reading of Michael Evans, I will suggest that for some audiences his character may have justified their fears about the militancy of the Black Power movement. Given the ways black political radicals were represented in mass media during the 1960s, what could be more disconcerting to some audiences than the idea of a ten-year-old black male who embraced black nationalist thought?[13]

What may have been of value in the show to many blacks was the idea that the presence of a strong patriarchal figure and the stable family structure that a strong patriarchal figure presumably generates was an absolute necessity if families like the Evanses were to have any chance to survive. That idea was thrown into significant crisis at the conclusion of Part 1 of "The Move," when audiences were made aware that James Evans Sr. had been killed in an automobile accident down south. James Sr.'s death became a symbolic reminder of the violence that remained a part of southern soil for blacks, but also an example of the presumed connection between patriarchal presence and the stability of black familial relationships. In this regard, James's death placed the Evans family in social stasis. One of the key story lines in Part 2 of "The Move" is the inability or unwillingness of Florida Evans to publicly mourn the death of her husband, a lack of mourning that is juxtaposed to the histrionic mourning of a neighbor. Throughout the episode Florida rebuffs the efforts of friends and family to get her to open up and publicly acknowledge her pain, as the Evanses' neighbor Wanda, in a memorable performance by the late character actress Helen Martin, feigns mourning at every turn, because it's the right thing for her to do. Florida's failure to mourn James Sr. is viewed as strange and distasteful, even disrespectful, given the reality that she had lost a "strong black man." Her children are particularly incensed when Florida laughs and jokes with some of James's old friends. It is only at the end of the episode that Florida finally breaks down. Alone in the living room, Florida, who is cleaning up after postfuneral festivities, drops the crystal punch bowl that she is carrying and cries out loud, "Damn, damn, damn, James!" Only at this moment does Florida really begin the mourning process.

I have been struck by that moment in the series because of the number of times it has been recovered by post-soul performers. Besides the aforementioned use by Outkast on the track "SpottieOttieDopalicious," Florida's line also appeared in episodes of the television series *Living Single* and *The Martin Lawrence Show*. Though it is used in the latter two cases simply as a comic reference, the recovery of Florida's moment of mourning in "The Move" suggests that it may be a moment lodged in the collective memory of the post-soul generation. Following this logic, I am suggesting that in the social imagination of the black community, the fictional death of James Evans Sr. has become a metaphor for the absence of black men in the black community, and that this absence represents a kind of trauma for the community. Furthermore, Florida's initial ambivalence toward the death of her husband informs perceptions that some black woman are indifferent to and sometimes complicit in the "removal" of black men from the community. My reading of the significance of James Evans Sr.'s death is supported by some of the initial commentary on his death and subsequent comments by members of the *Good Times* cast.

The stimulus for the removal of James Evans Sr. was the ongoing dispute between actor John Amos and the show's executive producer, Allan Manings, and developer, Norman Lear. Prior to the 1975–76 season, Amos was given a "hefty" raise in an effort to quell his demands that the writing staff address the increasingly prominent role that JJ garnered. Both Amos and Esther Rolle had been very vocal about the "coonish" antics of the JJ character.[14] Actor Jimmy Walker most likely also attracted acrimony from his fellow actors because he was the only "nonactor" in the cast, yet was its most popular member. Though there is some dispute as to whether Amos was fired in the role of James Evans Sr. or asked to be released from his contract, his character was written out of the series beginning with the 1976–77 season. In an interview Amos explained, "It was something other than dramatic and creative differences, it was an ongoing struggle to say no, I don't want to be a part of the perpetuation of this stereotype. . . . Despite the fact that I had a writing background, they didn't want to accept whatever ideas I had as a writer. . . . So when I would pose arguments about JJ's role being too stereotypical, I was regarded as a negative factor."[15] Amos began his professional career as writer for the Leslie Uggams variety show, which debuted in 1970, and as a stage actor. After a brief appearance in Melvin Van Peeble's *Sweet Sweetback's Baadasssss Song*, Amos had a small recurring role on *The Mary Tyler Moore Show* as Gordy the weatherman. His role as James Evans Sr. was his fist major role, and to all intents and purposes made him a star.

Series creator Eric Monte has suggested that the inclusion of a father figure in the series was an bone of contention, as Lear and others expressed fears that a strong black male character would not be "funny."[16] Along these lines, Esther Rolle asserted, "I introduced the black father to this country. There never had been one in the whole of the country. And I risked my job by saying I won't do it unless you give me a husband for my children."[17] While I am not interested in the validity of the late actress's boast, it provides an understanding of the criticism that Lear and the show's producers and writers faced after the announcement that James Evans Sr. would be written out of the series. One of the most vocal critics was Pluria Marshall, then chairman of the National Black Media Coalition. In Marshall's view the absence of James Evans Sr. would result in the loss of the "only positive black adult character in primetime television."[18] Citing a Howard University survey of eighty-four black children in Washington, D.C., Marshall urged Norman Lear and CBS to "restore the character so as not to give 'new roots' on television to the stereotype of the fatherless black family."[19] Marshall's comments are notable because of the implied erasure of Esther Rolle's character Florida as a "positive" adult character and his clear investment in the notion that a strong patriarch would naturally counter stereotypical perceptions of black life on television. *Good Times* executive producer Allan Manings responded to Marshall's criticism by saying, "There are other realities that deserve exploration—the fatherless family does exist in the ghetto."[20] In a recent interview, Ralph Carter admitted that "things were never the same" for him after the death and departure of James Evans Sr./John Amos. The responses to the "death" of James Evans Sr. revealed what Hortense Spillers has labeled "a cultural situation that is father-lacking."[21] In her own reading of this condition of "father-lacking," Sharon Patricia Holland has argued that it has become a "founding and necessary condition/experience of what it means to be black. . . . While the condition of the child is to be 'father-lacking' it is also therefore the condition of the community to reiterate this lack as loss in a process of mourning that requires no dead body, per se, but merely the idea of one looming and therefore returning in the not so distant future."[22] Defending his position in the removal of John Amos, even Manings's response suggests that "father-lacking" is an "authentic" aspect of black family life.

During Amos's final season on the show, the concept of father-lacking was specifically addressed in a particularly emotional episode titled "The Family Tree," which was broadcast originally on December 23, 1975. In the episode the family is preparing for a surprise birthday party for James Sr. Thelma has been excused from some of the preparty preparation because she is immersed in a school project in which students are responsible for creating a family tree. Ironically, Florida makes reference to Alex Haley's book *Roots*. Thelma finally returns home, excitedly announcing, "Hey we got a grandfather. I found Daddy's father." The announcement was a shock to the rest of the Evans family, as James had often maintained that his father had died when he was a young boy. Unbeknownst to his family, James had claimed that his father had died to obscure the fact that his father had in fact abandoned James and his family when he was a young boy. The episode suggest that James's own concept of being an engaged and committed father was predicated on his desire not to be like his father. This is made more apparent later in the episode, when James is confronted with his "surprise" guest. Initially James refuses to meet with his father. It is only after a conversation with Florida, in which he acknowledges that his father's absence was so traumatic that he was unable to share the pain of it with her, that he finally agrees to meet with his father. Attempting to at least provide some explanation, if not a justification, for his absence, James's father, Henry (Richard Ward), explains that his abandoning of his family was the offspring of the dire economic realities associated with the system of share-

67

cropping ("I wasn't making enough money sharecropping to feed a tick"). Close to tears, James responds, "Man, how come you never tried to find me?" which is followed shortly thereafter by an emphatic, "Where you been, man?" Toward the end of their "reunion," father and son sit next to each other as Henry says, "Jimmy, I've missed over thirty-five years without a son," to which James adds, "and me without a father." It is within the context of the dual pain they individually experience at not being allowed to be a father and not having a father, respectively, that they can finally share a bond with each other and begin the healing process. Holland identifies such a bond in the seemingly disparate black masculinities of queer dance artist and choreographer Bill T. Jones and the late gangsta rapper Tupac Shakur. Citing Shakur's frequent laments at not having a father figure present and Jones's self-admonishment that his sexuality denies another black child the opportunity to have a father, Holland writes, "Their dual reflection upon fathers and fatherhood is precisely, I would argue, what makes them identifiably black and male. . . . Jones and Shakur mark their participation as black men in African-American culture by sharing the trauma associated with the absence of fathers."[23]

Such a bond was also apparent in an earlier episode of the series in which JJ is shot by a gang member. In a two-part episode titled "JJ and the Gang," which originally aired in November 1974, JJ is forced into a gang named the Satin Knights. As James attempts to intervene, JJ is shot during a scuffle between James and the gang's leader, Mad Dog (Oscar DeGruy). JJ only receives a flesh wound, and much of the "comedy" in the two-part episode relates to a pair of hot red pajamas that Florida gives to JJ to wear during his recovery. Eventually Mad Dog is charged with attempted manslaughter, though he is released on probation because both the juvenile detention center and the county prison are overcrowded. After his sentencing, Mad Dog, whose real name is Cleon, is confronted by his mother, who in her anger says, "There ain't nothing can be done for you, Cleon. . . . I never thought I could feel this way about my child, but I hate you. Sometimes I wish you was never born. . . . If only your father was here." Mad Dog emotionally responds, "What if he was? He'd be a wino in the gutter," to which his mother responds by slapping his face and hurriedly leaving the courthouse. As his mother departs, Mad Dog yells, "He ran out on you, didn't he?" James, in attendance at the hearing, witnesses the exchange between Mad Dog and his mother. When Mad Dog, who is near tears, asks James if he "wants a piece" of him also, James dissents, later wondering aloud to Florida, "What kind of father am I that I have sympathy for the boy that shot my son?" Unlike Mad Dog's mother, James chooses not to lash out at Mad Dog, because he intuitively understands the condition of father-lack that the episode suggests is at the root of Mad Dog's delinquency. Both episodes acknowledge not only the ways in which the character of James counters the condition of father-lack but also the wide range of emotions that John Amos is allowed to examine within the character, including a particular vulnerability and sensitivity to issues surrounding the lack of fathers in his life and the larger community. Part of the appeal of James Evans Sr. to black audiences remains that he was one of the fullest and most balanced representations of black fatherhood in commercial television history.

By comparison, Bill Cosby's Cliff Huxtable emerged in the mid-1980s as the quintessential television father, though not necessarily the ideal black father in the view of some black audiences. The firm upper-middle-class (and quite frankly, also working-class) values that the Huxtables exuded were often seen to be more derivative of fathers in Scarsdale, New York, or the Garden District in New Orleans than in the Compton and Bed-Stuy (Bedford-Stuyvesant) sections of Los Angeles and Brooklyn, respectively. Herman Gray has suggested that "positioning *The Cosby Show* in relation to the previous history of programs about blacks helps explain its upper-middle-class focus."[24] Thus Cliff Huxtable was a conscious attempt on Bill Cosby's part to counter a history of black televisual fatherhood that included a generally "unsophisticated" Fred Sanford and an often jobless James Evans Sr. Despite ongoing critiques of Cliff Huxtable's "authenticity" in relation to black life and culture,[25] he and his televisual peers Fred Sanford and James Evans Sr. were much less problematic than Reginald Vel Johnson's Carl Winslow, the patriarch of the family-oriented sitcom *Family Matters*. The series was popular in the early 1990s, largely because of the popularity of its young star Jaleel White, who portrayed Steve Urkel, a character that was initially inserted in the show as a fringe character. Though Urkel's character evoked memories of JJ from a decade earlier, in my opinion White may be the most gifted physical comic actor of his generation, recalling the early television careers of Larry Hagman (*I Dream of Jeannie*'s Major Nelson), Dick York (the original Darren Stevens on *Bewitched*), and most recently, the late Christopher Farley. In my mind Carl Winslow, who later simply existed on the series to set up White's comic moments, was the more troubling character. As he was the only black male adult regular throughout most of the series' run, Carl Winslow's buffoonery, particularly given that he was employed as a law enforcement officer, often undermined perceptions that he was capable of being a productive parent, or for that matter a productive adult. That the series was a comedy does not, in my view, make Carl Winslow's antics any less problematic; they presented a negative critique of black male professionalism and competence within black domestic spheres, particularly given the paucity of such representations in contemporary television. It is not my intention to engage in a sustained critique of the representations of black fatherhood throughout television history, however, but to present admittedly sketchy comparisons of James Evans Sr. with a small cadre of popular father characters in black television sitcoms.

At the time that Amos's departure from *Good Times* was announced, he was already negotiating to accept the lead role as the adult Kunte Kinte/Toby in the miniseries adaptation of Alex Haley's "fictional" family account *Roots*. The miniseries went on to become one of the most highly rated television events in history and helped garner Amos recognition, including an Emmy nomination, that he was unlikely to have earned had he remained in his role as James Evans Sr. on *Good Times*. As Amos admitted years later, "I'd rather say 'Toby be good nigger' in *Roots* than 'Toby be good nigger' on *Good Times*."[26] Amos's comments here are strikingly reminiscent of the oft-cited comment by actress Hattie McDaniel that she would rather play a maid in the movies than actually be one in reality. Whereas McDaniel was often criticized for taking on demeaning roles in her career, Amos felt that his treatment on the set of *Good Times* was more demeaning than any slave role he could take in miniseries like *Roots*. Amos's comments are also significant when considered within the context of *Roots*'s importance to the black communal imagination. If Amos's James Evans Sr. was viewed by many as the quintessential "strong 'black' father" on television, then his role as Kunte Kinte/Toby helped establish Amos as the "original" black patriarch, one who consistently engaged in blatant acts of resistance against efforts to acculturate him to the "new" world and the system of domination that blacks suffered under during the period of legalized chattel slavery. Within this context, James Evans Sr.'s death allowed for the birth of Kunte Kinte and the rebirth of possibilities for black fatherhood and patriarchy. In a particularly insightful reading of the miniseries, Herman Gray proposes that for the post–civil rights generation(s) of black youth, "*Roots* also opened—

enabled, really—a discursive space in mass media and popular culture within which contemporary discourses of blackness developed and circulated."[27] Gray adds that the popularity of *Roots* provided "some of the enabling conditions necessary for the rearticulation of the discourse of Afrocentric nationalism."[28] But even as the series and the figure of Kunte Kinte resurrected the possibilities of an "enabled" African heritage and a reconstructed black patriarchy, Kunte Kinte remained a source of mourning. Part of this sense of mourning can be received in the ambivalence associated with his name: the Kunte Kinte character was the focal point for questions of African-American identity and the presumed loss of "authentic" African culture. This is best represented in the character's principled stand against his renaming.

Some of the most dramatic and meaningful segments of the miniseries were those in which Kunte Kinte (who as a youth is portrayed by Levar Burton) resisted the imposition of the name Toby upon his body. As witnessed in the miniseries, the name Toby was violently inscribed upon the young Kunte Kinte's body via the lash. It is within the context of a very brutal whipping that Kunte Kinte forcibly accepts the moniker "Toby," which marks the breaking of his "African" spirit. It is of some significance, I think, that John Amos makes his first appearance as the adult "Toby" in the very next segment after the dramatic beating of the young Kunte Kinte. Kunte Kinte's acceptance of the name Toby became a popular metaphor in the African-American imagination for the loss of African influence on the lives and cultures of African Americans. Because this loss was inscribed upon the body of the original African-American father, it also can be read as the loss of the "father," the specific source of that which was "African," as represented in the narratives of the miniseries. Notions of fathers in absentia and the erosion of masculinity and patriarchy are consistent themes throughout the later stages of *Roots*. Kunte Kinte was responsible for making his daughter Kizzy (Leslie Uggams) a powerful receptacle for those things "African" that remained within him—Kizzy's attempts at literacy is one of the most important aspects of the series, in my mind—but was rendered incapable, even flaccid, in any attempt to protect the removal of his daughter from the plantation where they lived. It is in the context of Kizzy's removal that she herself is subjected to the sexual violence of her new "massa," Tom Harvey. While Kunte Kinte was marked by his inability to perform the patriarchal duty of "protecting" his family, Kizzy is marked by the absence of a protector or father. This become much clearer with the birth of Kizzy's son, George, who is nicknamed "Chicken George" because of his success at cockfighting. The nickname, which suggests that George had an apparent affinity with chicken, is a subtle marker of the violent miscegenation or "cross-breeding" that accompanied his inception. Chicken George's ability to "buy" his freedom via his winnings as a cockfighter also becomes the stimulus for his own absence in the lives of his family, as the slaves codes of the day forbade him residence where his family lived for more than thirty days, at the cost of his freeman status. I am again struck by the ways in which "Kunte Kinte" is simply referred to as "the old African" throughout *Roots* and *Roots: The Next Generation*. This speaks to the ways in which Kunte Kinte and absent black fathers, in general, remain nameless and the concept of black fathering amorphous, though still rooted in an "African" context.

As the specific moment of Florida Evans's mourning of her husband has been recovered, so has John Amos been recovered as a patriarchal figure. The best example of this was his role as Cleo McDowell in the Eddie Murphy comedy film *Coming to America*. For a brief moment, Amos even made peace with Norman Lear and portrayed the patriarch in the short-lived sitcom, *804 Hauser Street*, named for the address of the home that the Bunker family lived in Lear's flagship series *All in the Family*. Amos is here cast as a conservative African American, whose son lives in the house with his white wife. I have been most interested in the ways Amos has been cast in various vehicles for hip-hop artist O'Shea Jackson (Ice Cube), as in the disturbing video for the song "Natural Born Killers." Released in 1994 and marking the first collaboration between Jackson and Andre Young (Dr. Dre) since Jackson's very public and bitter departure from their seminal "gangsta" rap group NWA (Niggas with Attitude), the duo suggested that it was they, not O. J. Simpson, who were responsible for the killing of Nicole Simpson-Brown and Ron Goldman. Holed up in a warehouse and under siege from various law enforcement agents, it is John Amos who appears as the one in charge of "capturing" the suspects and stabilizing a critical situation. In this role, Amos returns to reinstill discipline and stability in the lives of the video's two primary characters, Ice Cube and Dr. Dre, and to suggest that part of the reason that the duo were "natural born killers" is the absence of a patriarchal figure like John Amos. Jackson has also cast Amos in several of his film projects, including most recently *The Players' Club*, in which Amos portrays a law enforcement officer.

BABY MAMA (DRAMA) AND BABY DADDY (TRAUMA)

Baby Mama and Baby Daddy: Post-Soul Gender Politics

The term baby daddy, a black southern colloquialism of "baby's daddy," was first introduced to the lexicon of black popular culture with the release of the "bass" recording "My Baby Daddy" by B Rock and the Bizz. In a society and culture historically obsessed with identifying lineage, particularly in relation to property rights, inheritance, and the ownership and control of family names and legacies, "baby daddy" helps to link the offspring of unwed and often casual sexual encounters. In this regard "baby daddy" and its gender opposite, "baby mama," have become markers of these "alternative" parenting relationships. On a basic level, the song is an example of the various kinship networks that single parents employ, as in theory the "baby daddy" remains a vital part of the child's life. The song's lyrics, in fact, suggest that a more substantive relationship exists between the unnamed female narrator and her baby daddy. Specifically the phrase "that's just my baby daddy" is employed by the baby mama as a response to her current boyfriend (T-Bird)'s queries as to the nature of her relationship with the baby daddy. The name and identity of the actual baby daddy remain elusive; he is referred to as "Lavell," "Jay," and "Ken" at various points of the song. The ambiguity of the baby daddy's real identity suggests that the baby mama has been with multiple partners, and thus the true identity of the father of the baby mama's child is also subject to this ambiguous state. Equally problematic is the amorphous identity of the baby mama herself. By the time the baby mama says, "T-Bird, I need some money for my baby," it seems clear the proverbial "welfare queen" has been recast as the "baby mama." The baby mama becomes the latest entry in a collection of widely circulated identities that Patricia Hill-Collins has labeled as "controlling images."

According to Hill-Collins, the "mammy," the "matriarch," the "jezebel," and the "welfare mother" comprise a set of "socially constructed controlling images of Black womanhood, each reflecting the dominant group's interest in maintaining Black woman's subordination."[29] Within this particular fictive narrative, the baby mama preys not only on the state for resources, but also on black men. With an increased dependence on the welfare state over the last forty years, Hill-Collins describes the "welfare mother" as "an updated version of the breeder woman image created during slavery."[30] Accordingly the welfare mother "provides an ideological justification for efforts to harness Black women's fertility to the needs of a changing political economy."[31] The welfare mother, who like Aunt Jemima has gone through both subtle and dramatic facelifts, including a stint as the "crack mom," has been employed as a nonracialized sign of black women's social deviance and obsolescence.[32] A derivative of the welfare mother has been the "welfare queen," which implies that some welfare mothers have exploited the welfare state to the point of living in fairly luxurious circumstances. The term *welfare queen* became widely circulated as one of President Ronald Reagan's favorite anecdotes to justify his own administration's dismantling of the welfare state as it existed in the early 1980s. Because the popular press often equated intense poverty with "blackness" and the quintessential welfare recipient with a black woman, the terms *welfare mother* or the more insidious *welfare queen* have functioned as nonracialized monikers of social deviance and dysfunction. This has been particularly useful for political pundits and politicians, who can then be hypercritical of the welfare state without, in theory, being perceived as racist. Donna Franklin points out that the conflation of "black" and "welfare queen" has been so complete that the "queen" portion of the moniker "expresses attitudes that are not simply antiwelfare, but racist, for it has been used against black professional woman as well."[33] Franklin cites the labeling of law professor Lani Guiner as a "quota queen" and former surgeon general Jocelyn Elders, who advocated the use of masturbation and educating American youth about condom use, as the "condom queen" as examples, to which I might add that Alexis Hermann, labor secretary in the second term of the Clinton administration, might have been interpreted as the "campaign finance queen" when criticized for her role in that administration's campaign finance controversy.[34] A crucial aspect in the marking of black women as "queens" is allusions to their educational, moral, and cultural impoverishment. In the case of Jocelyn Elders, for example, Karla F. C. Holloway makes the cogent argument that Elders was publicly demeaned not only because of the content of her comments but also because of their style. Holloway writes, "Elders' dialect retains some of the nonstandard features that identify her region and ethnicity . . . Elders' sentiments about sex education were powerful enough antagonists; but what encouraged her easy and disrespecting targeting were the dialect codes in her speech that separated her from the standarized mainstream.[35]

In the competing discourses of welfare reform, the welfare mom/queen has been presented as a failed parent whose predilection for reproduction continuously siphons off valuable public resources from the state. Whereas the welfare mom/queen has largely been the creation of media outlets and political elites, the baby mama has been a creation of black communities themselves. Generally speaking, the baby mama can seen as an attempt by various and sometimes competing black communities to mark those black female bodies that remain outside "mainstream" black culture. "Uneducated," "impoverished," "lazy," and "undisciplined," such bodies are seen by some in the black community as threats to nearly a century of attempts to sanitize the most negative perceptions of black life and culture. But the baby mama also serves as a particular sign within contemporary black male discourses that are connected to black male desires to be seen be as competent and meaningful players within social and political spheres perceived as the white male domains of capital and material accumulation. The ability of some young black men to "handle their bizness" takes place in realms of accumulation as diverse as the illicit drug economy; the burgeoning urban popular culture industries, including the record and dot-com industries; and traditional corporate settings. Within this context the baby mama and her cousin the "chickenhead" are seen as threats to this provinces of black male ambition and autonomy, in that they are solely interested in generating status and finances from their "partnerships" with black men.[36] For example, when relating the impact of an infamous *Sports Illustrated* feature on out-of-wedlock fathers in the National Basketball Association, Julianne Malveaux has suggested that these women are "depicted as predatory sperm collectors whose pregnancies are part of a 'plot' to collect child support from high earning hoopsters."[37] Whereas the "chickenhead" is largely seen as succeeding in this arena via the employment of her sexuality—rarely are black men critiqued for their own objectification of black female sexuality in this process—the baby mama succeeds, via her employment of sexuality and the reproductive process. The baby mama is perceived by some as the more dangerous of the two because she creates a permanent biological bond (the child) that cannot be easily broken.

The construction of baby mamas in relation to the production of child "commodities" can be traced to public perceptions of unwed black women in the post–World War II period. In her study of single mothers and race prior to *Roe v. Wade*, Rickie Solinger writes that many black single mothers were charged with having babies "in order to be eligible for

SOUL BABIES

larger welfare checks," an assumption that "these females were treating their reproductive capacities and their children as commodities, with assigned monetary values . . . black unmarried mothers were portrayed as 'economic women' making calculated decisions for personal financial gain."[38] Solinger further details that single black mothers were effectively criminalized by their actions, with various judicial and political figures suggesting that these women should be incarcerated or sterilized.[39] In the context of contemporary black life and culture the single mother or baby mama is seen as also engaging in these "calculated" decisions, except her interests no longer lie in attachment solely to the state, but also to black men of status, be they professional athletes, rap artists, drug dealers, or corporate lawyers. Ironically, black women are often denied access to abortions because of the Supreme Court's decision in *Webster v. Reproductive Health Services*, which denies women the right to attain abortions in publicly funded hospitals or clinics. As Dorothy Roberts recounts in her book *Killing the Black Body*, reproductive rights are not seen as an issue for black women, either within the black community or among organizations who struggle for reproductive rights for women; thus, without access to inexpensive abortions, poor black women in particular have little choice than to be inscribed within the black community as economic pariahs.[40]

My intention is not to corroborate or discount the validity of claims that black woman engage in such activities; it is clear that some single mothers, regardless of race, use the offspring of sexual and romantic encounters to generate some semblance of financial stability from men with the reasonable means to provide such stability. To simply accuse such women of being gold-diggers is intensely problematic, however, given the reality that the economic stability of some women in American society is largely tied to their capacity to remain in relationships with "money-earning" men, even if such relationships are exploitive and abusive. But "gold-diggers" and "chickenheads" do exist. Joan Morgan admits as much in her exploration of a "hip-hop feminism"; as she states, "Strippers out-earn women with college degrees and antiquated alimony and child-support laws guarantee some women higher standards of living than most 9-5's could ever. Chickenheads rely on punanny for the same reasons drug dealers don't struggle through four years of college: In a world of limited resources, trickin' is a viable means of elevating one's game."[41] Within this

76

context there are obviously women who legitimately employ the power of the state to garner resources in the aftermath of failed heterosexual relationships. In any case, my concern is primarily how black single mothers or baby mamas have been demonized in the discourse surrounding the issues of father-lacking and black male absence, particularly as represented within black popular culture.

It is my contention that the baby mama has become a singular trope employed to explain the absence of black fathers and the loss of a meaningful patriarchy/masculinity that also condones modes of violence, both physically and rhetorically, against black women for their roles in diminishing these entities within the black community. Holland has argued that "Black women's bodies serve as the point of articulation of this loss— rather than being responsible . . . for passing on a 'condition' to her children, she is even more culpable for being the visible representation of a community's fatherlack."[42] Using Holland's logic here, baby mamas have become a powerful "representation" of the state of father-lack within the black community, more dangerous since they are seen as angry, vindictive, and irresponsible, to the point of willingly assisting the state in the removal and incarceration of black men and fathers in an era in which the astronomical incarceration rate of black men (and women) represents a legitimate crisis. Ironically, many critiques of the baby mama obscure the more powerful role of the state in the removal of black men, laying a good portion of the blame on the baby mama. I would suggest that part of the function of these narratives within the popular realm is to obscure the more powerful players and institutions that impact the "traditional" black nuclear unit. Two separate recordings, which share the same title, are indicative of this thinking within popular culture.

In 1998 Daz Dillenger, formerly of the Dogg Pound, released his first solo recording, *Retaliation, Revenge and Get Back*. Accordingly, one of the objects of Dillinger's wrath was the baby mama, as expressed on the track "Baby Mama Drama," which features cameos by C-Style and Lil' C-Style. The track opens with Dillenger yelling, "What the fuck is this? Child support papers?" which is followed by the chorus, "You didn't have to file on me, you turned my child on me." There are several aspects of the song's lyrics that are of interest to me, the first being the apparent connections articulated between anti-baby-mama narratives, perceptions of productive fathering acts, and the consistent invocation of religious themes. The first verse of the song finds Dillinger praying to God so that he can "try to do right" as he expresses his commitment to "live the righteous life for the path of my babies." Here Dillinger's "prayer" is reminiscent of those bizarre moments during music-industry award shows in which those who perform distinctly vulgar and profane forms of music begin their acceptance speeches by thanking God ("First, I'd like to thank God, and then all the bitches, hos, and niggas who supported me"). Halfway through the first verse, the tone of the narrative changes as Dillenger directly addresses his baby mama, stating, "I've been taking care of you and your kid all of my life . . . mad at me 'cause I wouldn't make you my wife." Dillenger implies that the baby mama files child support on him simply because he rejected her as a romantic/sexual partner. Ironically, Dillinger is willing to invoke a higher religious power to find sympathy for his "crisis," while rejecting how that very power has been employed by religious fundamentalists and others to criticize out-of-wedlock pregnancies and to privilege the institution of marriage as the primary social relationship in which to raise and support children. More than a simple contradiction, Dillinger's invocation of religious themes suggests the ways in which he sees "religion" as protective and supportive of his patriarchal desires.

This perception of religion is clearer during the song's second verse. The invocation of God is repeated as Lil' C-Style states, "I walk by faith, and not by sight/living day by day, praying night by night." Admitting to his weaknesses of the flesh ("lust, lust, lust, and every pretty girl I see, I wanna touch, touch, touch"), Lil' C-Style reveals that the object of his primary sexual affections is the preacher's daughter. Within Lil' C-Style's narrative, it is he that is "righteous," as opposed to the preacher's daughter, who is seen as beyond the spiritual/religious realm of her minister father, as witnessed by her inability to hold her liquor and her sexual escapades with Lil' C-Style ("everytime she drinks she gets drunk and throws up . . . looking her best, from the back bent over"). As she is described here, the daughter's later efforts to "file" on Lil' C-Style seem like a natural progression. Despite his own admission to lustful emotions for other women, Lil' C-Style has created a spiritual and patriarchal bond within black religious expression that transcends these emotions because they are viewed as a natural aspect of black masculinity. Alternatively, the preacher's daughter's "lust" for alcohol and sex is not protected or excused within this same expression. Her sin is the failure to remain within the boundaries assigned to "good" girls, including her challenge to the autonomy of black patriarchy by "filing" on Lil' C-Style. It is significant that she is a "preacher's daughter," precisely because of the ways black patriarchal figures within some black religious institutions have created an autonomous space for their own problematic proclivities by invoking a special bond with the discourses of black religiosity. In his critique of Martin Luther King Jr.'s own philandering, Michael Eric Dyson writes, "As surely as King learned from the black church the use of brilliant rhetorical strategies that would change America . . . he learned in the same setting about the delights of the flesh that were formally forbidden but were in truth the sweet reward of spiritual servants."[43] Dyson's comments are as critical of the black church as they are of King himself. Presumably this reading of the black church can explain the affinity that Lil' C-Style can have with black religious expression, and by extension, the "preacher." Though the preacher can be read as a failed father, and Lil' C-Style a failed romantic partner, ultimately it is the power of the patriarchal-sexual-religious bond between the two that cast the daughter or baby mama as the one deserving of scorn.

As protégés of gangsta rap icon Snoop Doggy Dogg (Calvin Brodnous), Daz Dillenger and Kurupt recorded as the Dogg Pound. The popular appeal of gangsta rap artists was in their ability to collapse their recording personas into their public ones. The escapades of Dr. Dre (Andre Young) and the late Tupac Shakur were textbook examples of this. The thinking at the time was that gangsta rap recordings needed to be interpreted as an authentic distillation of gangsta culture for audiences to remain interested in the consumption of the genre. That authenticity was validated by real-life escapades that often transcended those detailed in the studio, creating what Todd Boyd refers to as the "hyperreal" in gangsta rap culture, adding that the hyperreal "creates a media image that directs attention away from the actual occurrences and thus puts us in the realm of pure spectacle."[44] Though the "OGs" and "Gs" that populate gangsta rap recordings can be seen as oppositional to mainstream constructions of masculinity, it is again their experiences with "chickenheads" and "baby mamas" that place their experiences within the domain of traditional masculine interests. This can be read in Lil' C-Style's incredulous query, "Do gangsters get filed on child support? Hell yeah, they do." In this regard the baby mama has even been able to undermine the alternative and privileged spheres that gangstas themselves create in opposition to the challenges they face within mainstream culture. In the end these women are also presented as uninterested and selfish mothers, as Big C-Style laments: "It's not like it's for my baby, it's more like for you and your nigga." This line suggests that these women as so calculating that once they "trick" one man, they move on to the next, presumably to "trick" him also. In this regard, these women are seen as little more than professional "hos," who also have the power of the state on their side in their efforts to "trick."

The demonization of single black women within popular culture is even more explicit in the video for the Dave Hollister recording "Baby Mama Drama." Hollister came to prominence within R&B circles as the lead vocalist of the group Blackstreet. After financial and creative disputes with the group's impresario, Teddy Riley, Hollister embarked on a solo career. The track "Baby Mama Drama" appears on Hollister's first full-length solo recording, *Ghetto Hymns*. With heavy allusion to the artistry of the late Donny Hathaway—in publicity photos for the project Hollister is a dead ringer for Hathaway, particularly as the latter is presented on the covers of his *Everything Is Everything* and *Extension of a Man* recordings—*Ghetto Hymns* features Hollister's attempts to convey the gospel, if you will, of contemporary black urban life. Released on the Def Squad/Dreamworks imprint that was founded by hip-hop icon Erick Sermon (EPMD), Hollister's recording was emblematic of a generation of R&B recordings that were heavily influenced by hip-hop, particularly within the realms of production styles and the construction of masculine personas that countered the sweet, smooth love-man personas of definitive male R&B performers such as Luther Vandross, Keith Sweat, and Maxwell. In this regard, Hollister attempted to distance himself from the more palatable image of Blackstreet, as he admits in the song's lyrics: "Back on Blackstreet shit was sweet, but now I'm so low." The line is an acknowledgment both of his solo status as a performer and of his embrace of the "ghetto" underground. Hollister's debut solo recording is notable because, like R. Kelly and the aforementioned Daz Dillenger, he attempts to bring his spiritual upbringing, both musically and personally, in conversation to the ghettocentric spaces he inhabits, at least within the realm of his recording career. In an interview Hollister admitted, "Gospel and Hip Hop are all that I listen to and my album is what you get when you mix the two."[45] Given the historic position of the black church as one of the most influential institutions within the black public sphere and hip-hop's current role in the distillation of certain "authentic" aspects of contemporary black "ghetto" life, Hollister's music can potentially resonate in very powerful ways across various segments of the black community. In this regard his recovery of Hathaway is crucial to this project, particularly in light of Hathaway's own brilliance at crossing musical boundaries in his own music.

Hollister's musical sensibilities aside, I'd like to pay some attention to the "Baby Mama Drama" video, the visuals of which provide a more densely layered articulation of the threats that baby mamas are perceived to pose. The video, which was directed by Steve Carr, features actor Allen Payne in the role of the baby daddy. Payne, who would be considered on a B list of young African-American actors, got his start via a recurring role on the *Cosby Show* as Lance, the good-natured boyfriend of Charmaine (Karen Malina White), the best friend of the Huxtable niece Pam (Erika Alexander). Payne has routinely portrayed low-key, good-natured characters in his film and television career, playing opposite Angela Bassett in *Vampire in Brooklyn*, Nino Brown (Wesley Snipes)'s good-hearted lieutenant Gee Money in *New Jack City*, and as the romantic interest of Jada Pinkett in *Jason's Lyric*. Payne's previous roles are noteworthy because some audiences would likely feel more empathetic toward his travails as they occur within the video for "Baby Mama Drama." In other words, such empathy may not have been extended to a young actor such as Bokeem Woodbine (the "bad" brother opposite Payne's "good" brother in *Jason's Lyric*), who has regularly played ghetto villains with an alarming sophistication, such as his star turn as resident and rapist in the now defunct urban hospital drama *City of Angels*. Payne's "every good man" persona in his previous roles is critical to the director's attempts to portray the baby mama, not the baby daddy, as outside of the community.

The most compelling aspect of the video is in fact contained in the footage and dialogue that appears prior to the song's introduction. The video begins with the couple arguing as they emerge from the darkness of the baby mama's home into the sunlight. The scene is shot from the rear, giving the audience the impression that they are following the couple out into the front of the house. The dramatic juxtaposition of darkness and light in this sequence suggests that the couple, particularly Payne's character, are emerging from a domestic sphere that is dark and foreboding. It helps convey the sense that this domestic space, over which the baby mama presides, is unwelcoming to Payne's character. In contrast, the larger community outside the home is seen as more hospitable. The dialogue in this sequence confirms that this domestic space is inhospitable to the baby daddy, as he is heard to yell "I can't believe you taking me through this bullshit," to which the baby mama responds, "Why don't you stay away from my house?" The baby mama's emphatic statement that it is *her* house subtly reveals the way the baby daddy, or father figure, has been displaced from one of the realms of his patriarchal influence. Presumably the baby mama may have gained ownership of the house as part of a divorce settlement. Without the ability to own or control or rule his own domestic space, which is very different from being domesticated within that space, the baby daddy is effectively put out on the street. The baby daddy responds to this particular instance of being cast into the street by asking, "What's wrong with you, huh?" This question effectively "queers" or "others" the baby mama by suggesting that she was somehow different from what should be expected of black women and mothers.

Shortly thereafter it is revealed that the dispute is over child support payments, as the baby mama refuses to let the baby daddy spend time with his son unless he gave her some money. Pulling paper bills from his wallet, the baby daddy shouts, "Everything you do is about money." He then pelts her with those paper bills, punctuated with the phrase, "Here, take it, take it, take this shit." Again the director paints the baby mama in an unfavorable light: the possibility that the baby daddy may in fact be a deadbeat dad is not considered or explored. In his anger, Payne's character finally hollers, "You got me acting like this in front of my son. . . . I should smack the shit out of you." This acrimonious and disturbing exchange is pregnant with implications of how the baby mama should be perceived by audiences. First, the baby mama is censured because it is *her* actions, not the baby daddy's inability to control his own emotions, that are seen as the impetus for his outburst. In this regard, the baby mama is then seen as responsible, in this instance, for the inability of the father to be a positive influence on his son. Secondly, the baby mama is also culpable for instigating the baby daddy to the point of almost inflicting violence on her, an act that, given the patriarchal focus of the video's opening segments, may be justified in the minds of some audiences. As the song's introduction begins, the baby daddy is put into handcuffs by law enforcement agents, likely called to the house before the video's action began by the baby mama, who incidentally is seen laughing as the baby daddy is taken away. It is fairly clear that this particular baby mama, and apparently others like her, are seen as complicit with the state in the detention and incarceration of black men and fathers. Per the video's opening narrative the baby daddy's crime was that of simply wanting to see his son, as any good father would want to do under similar circumstances.

The video then shifts between Hollister's postmodern Donny Hathaway–as–griot/sage narration and flashbacks to the opening confrontation between the baby daddy and baby mama. The flashbacks provide a more detailed glimpse of that opening exchange, as the two are seen at various times pushing, shoving, and cursing at one another. In most cases the baby mama is the one presented as the aggressor. In one sequence, which revisits the baby daddy's arrest, the baby mama mouths, "Bye bitch," as he is cuffed by law enforcement officers. This moment helps frame the idea that the baby daddy is being both feminized and emasculated, heightening the demonizaton of the baby mama. The baby daddy's emasculation becomes clearer in a later exchange with the baby mama at a local bar. The baby daddy enters the bar, apparently after his release from police custody, to have a drink. The video of course fails to draw any connection between this particular scene and the baby daddy's possible alcoholism, except to suggest that if he is in fact an alcoholic, it's largely because of the pressures placed on him by the baby mama. While sitting at the bar, the baby daddy calls the baby mama, only to find out that she is not home. It is his son that conveys this information, though it is important to note that in an earlier version of the video, the baby daddy talks with the baby mama's mother. The absence of the child's grandmother in the second version of the video further emphasizes the baby mama's recklessness, as it suggests that she has left her son home alone. In fact the baby mama is at the same bar as the baby daddy, providing the context for their in-bar confrontation. In this particular scene the baby mama's sexuality is also "othered" or "queered," as she is seated at a bar with a man—another potential "chickenhead" victim—and another woman. The way that both women are presented, to all intents and purposes fondling their willing male counterpart, raises questions about the nature of their relationship and the willingness of the baby mama to engaged in what some audiences might perceive as "unnatural" or deviant sexual acts. When the baby daddy questions his estranged partner about her activities, she throws her wallet/pocket-book at him— a subtle suggestion perhaps that with a new and potentially more liquid benefactor present, the baby daddy's money, presumably the cash in her wallet, is no longer needed.

Enraged by the baby mama's actions and her suggestion that he "fuck off," the baby daddy throws a drink her. In my view the throwing of the drink can be read as a last desperate attempt by the baby daddy to assert some form of masculine power/privilege and is symbolic of an act of sexual violence. My reading of this act is influenced by narratives within black gang culture and gangsta rap that describe violent gun acts as "wetting."[46] In line with the video's suggestion that with the emasculation of the baby daddy, the baby mama is now invested with some semblance of phallic power, the baby mama also picks up a liquor glass and tosses a drink back at the baby daddy. In the video's closing sequence, the baby daddy is viewed the next day, sitting outside the house with his son as the baby mama returns from her evening. When the baby daddy immediately queries her about her activities of the previous night, she gives him the "hand," a gesture that has often been synonymous with sassy "bitchlike" black women. Hollister's vocals at this juncture of the video are important, evoking as they do communal empathy and sympathy for the travails of the baby daddy. As the video ends, Hollister simply asks, "Somebody out there know what I'm talking about?" which is followed quickly with the riff, "Can I get a witness?" Hollister's spoken lyrics are a subtle revision of a signature Hathaway riff in which the late singer would state in midsong, "Ya'll don't know what I'm talking about." Hathaway improvises such a riff in the song "Thank You Master for My Soul" to suggest with the context of the song's lyrics his very personal and spiritual relationship with the "Lawd." Hollister's revision of the phrase helps translate the baby daddy's experiences into a wider public of baby daddies, insinuating that his experiences have been shared by other black men. This notion is further articulated with the last riff, which, like R. Kelly's "The Sermon," aims to gain sympathy within the definitive space of black morality the black church. Hollister "testifies" on behalf of baby daddies, so that the full moral judgment of the black community can come to bear on the devious, deviant, and defiant baby mama who is not willing to acquiesce to patriarchal privilege within the black community. This represents another way in which black religious discourses have been complicit in the maintenance of black patriarchy.[47]

Given historical narratives that imply that black men have not been responsible fathers and patriarchs—the Million Man March in 1995 was organized so that black men could atone for past lapses and accept the mantle of responsibility—some aspects of songs and videos like "Baby Mama

Drama" resonate strongly within some traditional African-American settings. Many find value in these narratives because the patriarchal figures within them articulate desires to take the parenting process seriously. The crux of Hollister's song and video is that, despite all, the baby daddy is mainly concerned with being a good father. Narratives of this nature have been valuable within popular culture for offsetting the decades-old perceptions that black men are not "responsible" fathers, a perception strengthened by Bill Moyers's controversial award-winning program *The Vanishing Family: Crisis in Black America.* In the opinion of the jurors who awarded the 1986 CBS special the highest honor in the annual Alfred I. Du Pont–Columbia University Awards in Broadcast Journalism, the program gave "life to the statistics through intimate portraits of young black adults facing the difficulties of single parenthood."[48] Arguably the Moyers program and the Moynihan report have had singular impacts on public policy strategies designed to address black poverty, unemployment, and the reliance of some blacks on welfare relief. Perhaps there is no small irony in the fact that Moyers was the White House press secretary at the time that the report was initially leaked to the Johnson administration. The black communal imagination, particularly in the post-soul generation, has reserved a special warmth for those young black men who publicly affirm their desires to be non-absentee fathers. Laudable as these moments may be in popular culture, they remain problematic because often black mothers are constructed within these narratives as the primary obstacle to the realization of an engaged fatherhood. This is evident in the song and video "Why You Wanna Keep Me from My Kid."

"Why You Wanna Keep Me from My Kid" appeared on *Guy III,* the third full-length recording by the R&B trio Guy. The trio's groundbreaking debut in 1988 established the group and its founder and producer, Teddy Riley, as the definers of a new sound, at the time dubbed "new jack swing." Riley's productions for Bobby Brown, Keith Sweat, and a host of other artists, including the gospel group the Winans and Michael Jackson, were quintessential examples of new jack swing. The production style helped resuscitate interest in R&B among black youth who had been increasingly immersed in hip-hop music and culture. The formula behind Riley's success was a conscious effort to layer "traditional" gospel and soul vocal styles over rhythms closely associated with those found in some forms of hip-hop. After the release of their second recording, *The Future,* in 1990, the group decided to split, largely because of increasing demands on Riley as a producer. Both remaining members, the brothers Damien and

Aaron Hall, recorded solo projects. Aaron Hall's first recording featured the lovelorn track "I Miss You," the video for which featured Hall mourning the death of his wife during childbirth. While maintaining a fairly lucrative career as a producer, Riley went on to found a second vocal group, Blackstreet. As mentioned above, David Hollister was the group's first lead vocalist. *Guy III* was significant because it was the first release by the trio after a nearly ten-year hiatus. After a lukewarm response to the project's initial release, "Why You Wanna Keep Me from My Kid" was released as a single in early 2000.

Directed by Tim Story, the video opens with Hall sitting alone in an empty house. This opening scene places Hall within a domestic sphere that is crucial to the director's attempts to invert gendered perceptions of nurturing and responsibility. Throughout the video Hall is portrayed holding and playing with his son, while the boy's mother rarely appears in such a role. In the pivotal scene where Hall witnesses his wife's infidelity, he is seen walking into the house with groceries and flowers. While he is portrayed as the romantic devoted husband and father, the mother is depicted as calculating and irresponsible, having an extramarital affair with her son apparently present in the house. Sitting alone during the video's opening sequence, Hall says over the song's instrumental introduction, "My first son . . . isn't he beautiful. I'm not gonna let nothing, I mean nothing come between me and him." Hall continues, "God, I thank you for my seed, and for that, I'll raise him right." Again these lines help establish Hall's intention of being meaningfully involved in the parenting process, even to the exclusion of the child's mother. As in the aforementioned songs and videos, the invoking of God in the narrative endows Hall's desires with the power of religious expression, effectively protecting him from other failings—for instance, Hall has been accused of sexual battery in the past—because in God's eyes he is engaged in the more meaningful activity of being a good father and patriarch. Hall's reference to the fact that this is his first son is also rife with religious overtones, but also bespeaks the value and responsibility assigned to the firstborn male within the context of the family and by extension the larger community.

This notion of community within the spoken introduction is further articulated as Hall says that he is "representing for the fathers that can't see their seeds," which is followed by a reminder that "it'll be all right." In this regard, as in the Hollister song and video, Hall is aiming to connect his own personal narrative, as witnessed in the song, with similar experiences in the larger community, highlighting the notion that such conditions are a communitywide crisis. Much like the "Baby Mama Drama" video, the Guy video features a sequence in which the father and mother engage in a public dispute outside their home. In this case it is Aaron Hall's brother Damien who intervenes and prevents Aaron from striking his wife. Again the suggestion is that his wife's own actions are largely responsible for pushing Hall to the verge of striking her. Also, as in the "Baby Mama Drama" video, the entire exchange is witnessed by their young son, suggesting also that this will potentially serve as a wedge between the young boy and his father. Ultimately it is the mother's decision to leave the home and relocate with her new "boyfriend" and her son that proves the most significant challenge to Hall's desires to be a good father. Following the sequence in which the wife apparently sneaks out of the house, Hall is seen at various moments reminiscing about the times he played with his son when he was little and crying to himself because of the loss that he feels at not being able to fulfill his patriarchal duties. Because Hall's character has been "domesticated" in the video, the concept of father-lack is articulated across his body, as opposed to the mother's body. This further allows the mother to be displaced as a meaningful agent in the raising of their son. The wife's removal of their son from the domesticated space can be read as her endangering the child by separating him from his father and the modes of protection and nurturing that his father's patriarchal sensibilities afford. The mother's endangering of her son is powerfully reflected in the video's closing sequence. Hall's character, who apparently has been searching for his son over a two-year period, finally locates him. Hall sees his son leaving the house with his mother and her "new" man. The child's swagger, reminiscent of the swagger usually assigned to black male gang culture, is a subtle suggestion that with the absence of his father, the "street" has had an influence on the son's identity. Recognizing his father, who is standing across the street, the son runs to him, unaware of the oncoming traffic. Hall cradles his son, struck by an oncoming automobile, as the faces of onlookers and the child's mother all reflect the tragedy that has apparently just occurred.

The underlying narrative suggests that the mother's own irresponsibility was responsible for the tragedy. In this particular spin of the "baby mama drama," the mother eschews the tools of the state and illegally removes her son from her husband's house. Again this seemingly subtle change of strategy on the part of this particular baby mama is predicated on the fact that as the one who is domesticated, it was Hall, with the privilege assigned him via his status as a well-known recording artist, who would likely be supported by the state. The video's closing frame shows Hall cradling his son intimately as his son is miraculously brought back to life, as evident by his sudden motion as the video fades to black. The closing suggests that this father's love is so strong that it can bring the son back to life. In many ways the song and video give us a very refreshing view of the commitment of some black men to be engaged fathers. The director's willingness to present the father as domesticated is also appealing, suggesting as it does the ways in which some men have seriously considered a reevaluation of traditional gender roles. What makes the video so problematic is the suggestion that this newly empowered male domestic cannot coexist in the same domesticated sphere as the mother. There is not really so much of a reevaluation of gender roles within black families as a switch, one in which the mother takes on the negative characteristics that have historically been assigned to black men and fathers. Again, using the insights provided by Spillers and Holland, the condition of father-lack has been inverted into a condition of mother-lack, one in which black masculinity and patriarchy are empowered to contain those positive mothering attributes usually assigned to more traditional black mothers. Hence the baby mama has to "die," or at least be constructed as beyond the sensibilities of community, for the black patriarch to be fully empowered and the traditional black mother to be resurrected. In this process the mourning of father-lack has been accompanied by a very powerful and public mourning of the traditional black mother, a mourning process that resurrects traditional notions of black motherhood and the patriarchy that undergirds it, through memory and nostalgia.

In Memory of Big Mama: The Resurrection of Black Patriarchy

In 1973 the Spinners, one of the definitive practitioners of what has come to be known as the "Philadelphia sound," recorded one of their most memorable and moving recordings. "Sadie," which has become a Mother's Day staple on black radio, told the story of a dedicated mother and nurturer who sacrificed her own needs and desires in the interests of maintaining her family. Nearly two decades later, the track was rerecorded by R. Kelly as a tribute to his own mother Joann, who had passed away in 1993 after a bout with cancer. Though written by Thom Bell, "Sadie" captured the kind of family values that could also be found in songs written and produced by his more well-known Philadelphia counterparts Kenneth Gamble and Leon Huff, whose Philadelphia International Records (PIR) boasted a roster of the most visible soul artists of the 1970s, including Teddy Pendergrass, Harold Melvin and the Bluenotes, the Intruders, and the O'Jays. Some of the label's most memorable "family-oriented" recordings include "I'll Always Love My Mother" (also a Mother's Day staple on black radio), the last major hit recording for the Intruders, and "Family Reunion," the title track of one of the O'Jays' most accomplished recordings. At the time of its release in 1975, lyricist Kenneth Gamble wrote that "the generation gap is another evil plan. The result of which divided the family structure . . . being of truth and understanding of all things, we must recapture the family structure—Mother, Father, Sister and Brother."[49] Gamble's comments correctly assess the ways that the social paradigm shifts of the late 1960s and 1970s begin to challenge the very idea of black family or community—indeed, this was a common thread in Gamble and Huff compositions—but also suggest that the response to those challenges revolved around the reconstitution of traditional gender roles within the family.[50] In fact, during the song's "breakdown"—the spoken-word segment of some soul recordings in which the vocalist directly testifies to the listener—the lead vocalist explicitly describes the roles of family members.[51]

In 1997 Boyz II Men, one of the best-selling pop groups ever and the definitive "boy group" of the 1990s, released the track "A Song for Mama." Written and produced by Kenny "Babyface" Edmonds, the song was arguably the most visible celebration of black mothers in the history of American popular culture, countering in meaningful ways the imagery of welfare mothers and baby mamas prevalent in mass culture via network and local news, the print media, and film and television.[52] The recording was the main theme song of the film *Soul Food*, produced by Edmonds and his wife Tracy and written and directed by first-time filmmaker George Tillman Jr. The film examines the lives of three sisters, Maxine (Vivica A. Fox), Teri (Vanessa Williams), and Bird (Nia Long), and the family matriarch Big Mama Jo (Irma P. Hall), and their struggles to maintain a close-knit and stable family. At the time of its release, *Soul Food* was lauded by critics and pundits as an embrace of family values in black film, a tribute to Tillman's grandmother and the Sunday dinners she prepared for Tillman's family when Tillman was a youth in Milwaukee.

In a small booklet that accompanied the video release, Tillman explains that *Soul Food* embodies the "unity" missing in contemporary black life.[53] For Tillman the ritual of Sunday dinner was also an important acknowledgment that "the only thing slave families had was cooking and their family meals. There they were able to talk about their souls."[54] The film is representative of a cadre of films that nostalgically look at black life prior to or just after the great migration period, including Tim Reid's *Once upon a Time When We Were Colored*, based on the Clifton Taulbert book of the same title, and *Eve's Bayou*, written and directed by Kasi Lemmons.

In his critique of the Jim Crow nostalgia that pervades *Once upon a Time When We Were Colored*, Adolph Reed writes, "Class ideology, in fact, permeates and drives the current nostalgia. While it reflects a generic sentimentality about lost innocence . . . it's about the wish for a world that is simpler and more settled, to be sure, but simpler and more settled in ways that clarify and consolidate the status of the upper middle class as the social order's presumptive center."[55] Reed goes on to add, "This communitarian nostalgia propounds a political message that what an increasingly fractured black 'community' needs is to entrust itself to the loving care of its 'natural' leadership."[56] For my purposes I would like to suggest that in the context of the black family structure, particularly during the Jim Crow era, patriarchal privilege was a stand-in for a racial and class privilege generally unavailable to individual family members. This is not to suggest that there was no class privilege in the black community, or even race privilege, when viewed through the prism of the black community's color-caste system, itself often aligned to class interests; but in the absences of these dynamics, patriarchal privilege was viewed as a norm in black families. Thus the nostalgia that pervades Tillman's film is about the reinscription not necessarily of class privilege but of patriarchal privilege in the name of unifying the black family specifically and the black community broadly. Unlike the Million Man March, which called for black male atonement for a failure to be responsible patriarchs, *Soul Food* and recordings like "Sadie" suggest that black women also have a responsibility to allow for the flourishing of black patriarchy, often at the expense of their own needs and desires. It is my opinion that the romantic musings about "Big Mamas" and the dramatic mourning of their deaths are rooted less in an actual mourning of black mothers than in the symbolic mourning of the passing of the most potent symbol of patriarchy's power. In this regard, "Big Mama" has to be nostalgically recouped in death to allow the continued flourishing of patriarchy within the black community, particularly in an era in which the professional successes of black women outside the domestic sphere and the black community, and various forms of black feminist thought, have challenged the logic of the black community's continued embrace of patriarchal norms.

In Tillman's case nostalgic themes are achieved not via Jim Crow narratives, though they are used strategically in the film via Big Mama's stories and photographs, but rather via the narration of Big Mama's grandson Ahmad (Brandon Hammond). Ahmad is the son of Maxine (Vivica A. Fox) and Kenny (Jeffrey Sams). The narrator's youth and innocence are crucial to the film's theme because he is incapable of providing the critical insight necessary to challenge the patriarchal norms that the film largely attempts to champion. In this regard I am not arguing so much that Tillman actively sought to recoup black patriarchy, though that remains a possibility; rather, he unwittingly does so in his desire to re-create, in simplistic terms, I might add, a unified and stable black family in which patriarchy is presumed to be the normal mode of family leadership. The film opens with Boyz II Men singing the main theme while black-and-white snapshots of the city of Chicago and childhood photos of the film's major characters are shown on the screen. The film's opening nostalgically references the post–World War II black migration to cities like Chicago, invoking the struggles and sacrifices that many black families had to endure to build meaningful lives in the "Promised Land."[57] As Ahmad offers at the very beginning, "Families pulling together in times of need will make you strong." The quote was attributed to Big Mama Jo, whom Ahmad describes as never making "one enemy in her life." The film opens at Bird's wedding to Lem Davis (Mekhi Phifer). It is in this opening sequence that Big Mama's talent at "keeping the peace" is first witnessed as she intervenes on Bird's behalf to protect her from witnessing Lem dancing erotically with his ex-girlfriend, described by Teri and Maxine as a "hoochie mama." As the three sisters storm out of the rest room to beat down the "ho," they find Big Mama Jo instead dancing with Lem to the sounds of Blackstreet's "No Diggity."

The next sequence features the three sisters and Big Mama Jo preparing Sunday dinner in the kitchen. In an interview shortly before the film's release Tillman admitted that he wasn't allowed in his grandmother's kitchen as a youth and thus had not witnessed firsthand what took place in that space.[58] According to Tillman, "While the women were cooking, the men—my dad and uncles—would be in the living room watching the game."[59] In fact, Tillman requested that the film's food stylist, Freddie Petross, allow him to watch her cook actual Sunday dinners in her home so that he would know how to "break down the shots."[60] This is important, because Tillman really had little if any knowledge of the exchanges that took place among the women in his family behind the kitchen doors. Tillman attempts to shed some light on those experiences via the "catfight" that erupts between the sisters, which Big Mama Jo, of course, mediates by admonishing Maxine's attempts to "run down" her family and Teri's inattentiveness to her husband Miles. It is during this sequence that Big Mama Jo accidentally burns her arm on the stove, unaware that she is doing so until one of her daughters brings it to her attention. Big Mama's Jo's delayed reaction to her burn suggests she had a high tolerance for pain, if not a general insensitivity to pain, as if she has been conditioned to tolerate it. In line with Tillman's earlier comments about the kitchen being the space for the "women to cook," I would suggest that the kitchen is also the space where black women like Big Mama Jo salve their wounds and develop the level of tolerance for pain and disappointment needed to maintain patriarchal norms as they exist outside the kitchen. The argument between Teri and Maxine suggests that it is in the kitchen that these women do not have to hold their tongues and can be critically expressive of their conditions; but only behind the closed doors of the kitchen, in the absence of men. The one male privy to these conversations is Ahmad, buttressing his earlier claim that he has a "special connection" with Big Mama Jo.

The next scene features the family sitting around in the "classic" Sunday dinner setting, joined by the family's lascivious minister. Teri and Maxine continue their bickering in what is the one consistent element of the film excepting Ahmad's narration. At the base of this bickering is a competition for Big Mama Jo's affirmation. As the oldest daughter, Teri was pushed to achieve academically, culminating in a law degree and a potential partnership in a prestigious Chicago law firm. The film suggests that the price that Teri has paid for her ambition and public challenge to patriarchal norms in the professional world has been one failed marriage—her marriage to Miles quickly deteriorates during the course of the film—and no children. It is fairly clear throughout the film that with her professional success and financial support of the family—she finances Bird and Lem's wedding and provides seed money for Bird's beauty parlor—Teri is vying for the role of head of the family after the death of Joseph, the family patriarch. She attempts to claim this role on the basis of not only her position as elder daughter but the upper-middle-class status that she has attained professionally. In this regard, Teri is seen as taking on the attributes of a patriarch. In opposition to Teri, Maxine has chosen to be a dutiful housewife and mother of two, expecting a third child at the film's opening. Maxine relishes her role, in part, because it is perceived as closer to the role that Big Mama Jo has accepted as family matriarch. The second phase of her skirmish with Teri, in fact, was based on her assertion that her cooking skills—a talent, in Tillman's view, germane to keeping family together—are not unlike those of Big Mama and that Teri essentially has neither the skill nor the instinct to hold the family together. This notion is forcibly reiterated shortly thereafter when Teri goes into labor during the Sunday dinner. Bird, as the youngest of the sisters, is struggling to define her identity as a black woman, on the one hand accepting the role as dutiful wife and later expectant mother while also having professional desires, as witnessed by her entrepreneurial spirit in owning a business. Big Mama Jo's earlier censuring of her two eldest daughters was predicated on helping Maxine better understand the need to close ranks around family, and Teri, her role as a wife willing to defer to patriarchal privilege.

In an attempt to divert attention from the continued bickering between Teri and Maxine, Kenny asks questions about Lem's past as a felon and drug dealer. Bird's declaration of devotion to her new husband, despite his past, is the stimuli for Big Mama Jo's extended monologue regarding the power of unity within the family. Big Mama Jo begins by admitting, "My husband was gambling, and yeah, he was bad at it. In fact we almost lost this house. But I worked on my hands and knees, cleaning up after white folks, taking in laundry. You see, you do what you have to do to stay strong—save the family, even if you stumble trying." Here Big Mama Jo acknowledges that she had to ignore her husband's predilections for gambling to "save" the family and the house, even if that meant exposing herself to the indignities that black women domestics often faced during the Jim Crow era.[61] The commitment to maintain the house is driven by the need not only to have shelter but also to maintain the one province where a black patriarch can be autonomous. Big Mama Jo's sacrifices were as much about saving the place where a black man could truly be a "man" as they were about saving the house. Big Mama then moves on to further reiterate her earlier points about the power of family unity, stating, "Now, I'm gonna tell you something. One finger pointing the blame, don't make no impact. But you ball up all those fingers into a mighty fist, and you can strike a mighty blow. Now this family got to be that fist." Big Mama Jo's *Soul Food* "remix" of Knute Rockne's George Gipp speech ("Let's win this one for the gipper"), with its suggestion that family members should "accommodate" for the best interests of the family in lieu of holding on to personal agendas, is remarkably reminiscent of Booker T. Washington's "accommodation" speech at the Atlanta Exposition in 1895. In that speech Washington remarked that "in all things that are purely social" blacks and whites "can be as separate as the fingers, yet one as the hand in all things essential to mutual progress."[62] Here Washington essentially assured his largely white audience that he was not interested in blacks achieving social equality—thus accepting the social logic of segregation—but that blacks would naturally close ranks with whites, despite profound political differences, during times of crisis and on issues of common interest. Big Mama Jo's version of accommodation argues that it will be necessary for the black women in the family to eschew their natural desires for personal empowerment to allow for the function of black masculine privilege within the family, because the perception that this privilege truly exists is necessary for the stability and survival of the family. Her own experiences with accommodation are made symbolically clear, as the very fist that she shakes to acknowledge the power of unity is in fact the one burned earlier in the kitchen.[63] This speech will be the last major appearance for Big Mama Jo in the film, as she shortly goes into a coma and later dies. Ahmad is the last family member to see Big Mama Jo alive, as the youth believes that her final words to him include a charge that he keep the family together.

As Big Mama Jo's health deteriorates, Teri pushes hard to have the house sold to pay off debts and defray Big Mama's hospital costs. For many of the family members, the house is the very symbol of the family's unity. Maxine vigorously disagrees with Teri over several issues, beginning with an exchange over Big Mama's bed while she lies comatose. The argument is set off by Maxine's desire to continue to have Sunday dinner, despite Big Mama Jo's health. The rift remains between the two as Maxine gets an injunction to prevent the sale of Big Mama Jo's house after their mother's death. In the process, Teri's inability to act in the best interests of the family is witnessed by her desire to sell the house, her failure to be supportive of her husband Miles's desire to pursue a musical career, and, lastly, her role in a fight between Lem and one of the family's cousin's, whom Teri called after mistakenly believing that Lem had beaten Bird after an argument. The fight leads to Lem's arrest for weapons possession, thus separating him from his new wife. By contrast, Maxine is settling in with her third child, continuing her nurturing of Ahmad, and caring for Uncle Pete, who has lived in Big Mama Jo's house with his sister Big Mama Jo and Lem and Bird but suffers from some sort of emotional dysfunction that prevents his full integration into the family. Uncle Pete essentially stays in his room, watching TV and having his meals left in front of his door. In a crucial scene, Uncle Pete wanders down to the kitchen—the family had forgotten about the "damaged" patriarch during Big Mama Jo's travails—and mistakenly refers to Maxine as Jo. Again this reinforces the notion that Maxine is the daughter most likely to carry on the legacy of Big Mama Jo.

Under the pretext that Big Mama's final words to him contained information about money hidden in the house—money that most of the adult family members have long accepted as myth—Ahmad manages to bring the family back together at the house, including Lem, recently freed from prison with some assistance from Teri, and Teri's estranged husband Miles, whom she pulled a knife on earlier in the film after witnessing him having an affair with a cousin. As family members arrive at the house, they naturally fall back into the Sunday dinner ritual, again suggesting that the house, the province of black male privilege, is necessary to the maintenance of family unity. While sitting at Sunday dinner, Ahmad is forced to admit that he fabricated the story about the money to get the family together, as Big Mama Jo had instructed him to do at the time of her death. As he is being admonished by the adult family members, Ahmad runs into the kitchen and accidentally throws a dishcloth on the stove, starting a fire. As the male adults try to douse the fire, triggering the sprinkler system, Uncle Pete rushes downstairs into the kitchen with his TV, which is filled with the very money that the adults had accepted as mythical. In this regard, the "damaged" patriarch returns to the fold, cash in hand, to take his rightful place in the family. As the film ends, Uncle Pete is seen holding Bird's new baby, while Maxine and Teri are seen side by side, cultivating the garden outside the house, while the "men" look on. Ultimately it is Ahmad's faith in Big Mama Jo's power, even in death, that helps resurrect the "damaged" patriarch Uncle Pete and brings the family into a state of normalcy after her death. Tillman's film suggests that in the absence of legitimate patriarchal figures, the symbol of Big Mama in life, and her memory in death, is necessary for the emergence of a new family patriarch. Though the film focuses on the three sisters, ultimately it is a story about their own individual commitments to maintain patriarchal norms within their family. By the film's end, it is clear that Big Mama's memory is powerful enough to get all the sisters in line as matriarchs; Bird is seen as the new mother, and Teri is presented in a more nurturing role, cultivating flowers outside the house.

Perhaps a more truthful portrayal of "Big Mama," at least in the black male imagination, can be found in the work of stand-up comedian and actor Martin Lawrence. During the five-year run of his series *Martin*, the actor's character was often at odds with members of the opposite gender, two of which—his next-door neighbor Sheneneh and his mother—were in fact portrayed by Lawrence dressed in drag. These characters served the purpose of creating, in Lawrence's mind at least, a more authentic "round the way" girl and what Kristel Brent Zook suggests is a "legitimate matriarch" in Mrs. Payne.[64] One character who has a small recurring role is an elderly lady, "Ms. Gerry," whom Martin has physical altercations with on more than a few occasions. Lawrence's portrayal of women, particularly elderly women, be they Martin in drag or black actresses, are some of the most problematic aspects of the series. As Brent Zook writes, "One of the key contradictions of gender representation in *Martin* is that while Pam, Sheneneh, and Mama Payne are constructed as strong independent, 'authentic' black women, they are also represented as inherently unwomanly."[65] Lawrence's vision here is perhaps most blatantly articulated in the film, fittingly titled *Big Mama's House*, that solidified his position as a revenue-generating film star. The film centers on the activities of FBI undercover agent Malcolm Turner (Lawrence), who specializes in disguises. In the film Turner disguises himself as the grandmother or "Big Mama" of Sherry (Nia Long), a young woman suspected of being an accomplice to a bank thief, who has recently escaped incarceration. Much of the comedy of the film is focused on Turner's effort to maintain the facade that he is "Big Mama," who is away on a trip when Sherry arrives for a visit. In the body of Big Mama, Turner allows her to achieve feats naturally associated with male physicality, while Big Mama utterly fails at her more natural duties of cooking and serving as the community's midwife.

What is of interest to me about *Big Mama's House* is how the original

BABY MAMA (DRAMA) AND BABY DADDY (TRAUMA)

Big Mama is portrayed in the film, prior to Turner's appropriation of her body and persona. Speculating that Sherry will visit Big Mama after hearing that her former boyfriend Lester (Terrence Dashon Howard) has escaped from prison, Turner and his partner John (Paul Giamatti) set up surveillance in the house across the street. Turner attempts to install surveillance equipment in Big Mama's house while Big Mama, portrayed by Ella Mitchell, and the street's welcoming committee bring gifts to John. Big Mama returns home while Turner is still in the house. While Turner is hiding in the bathtub, Big Mama comes into the bathroom to defecate and then take a shower. The scene is significant because, as articulated by the title of the film, Big Mama has in effect created her own autonomous domain, where she does not have to negotiate with or acquiesce to forms of black patriarchy, a legitimate safe haven where she presides as the leader of the community. Thus this domain has to be "illegally" penetrated and Big Mama's privacy broached in order to provide a glimpse of this autonomous space. The seemingly gender-neutral surveillance equipment is rendered a distinct male gaze in that Turner physically witnesses Big Mama's activities in the bathroom. What Turner sees is a full-bodied, dare I say obese, naked, and flatulent senior citizen who is thus rendered an intensely grotesque object of disgust and humor. Turner's gaze serves to undermine the masquerade of Big Mama worship, revealing a distinct loathing of Big Mama, particularly in the absence of an evident and meaningful patriarchy.

The Post-Soul Intelligentsia
Mass Media, Popular Culture, and Social Praxis

The Negro movement is at an impasse precisely because it lacks a real functional corps of intellectuals able to confront and deal perceptively with American realities on a level that social conditions demand.

—Harold Cruse

The future of black culture demands that this generation bring forth a worldly-wise and stoopidfresh intelligentsia of radical bups who can get as ignant as James Brown with their wangs and stay in the black.

—Greg Tate

Educators, artists and cultural workers must address the challenge of developing educational approaches that teach kids how to use media as a mode of self-expression and social activism. We need to find new ways to translate pedagogy into an activist strategy that will expand the opportunities for young people to acquire the knowledge and skills that will help them extend their participation into, and control over, those cultural economic and social spheres that shape daily life.

—Henry Giroux

SOUL BABIES

My earliest musical recollection is of listening to what I would later learn was Junior Walker's "What Does It Take? (to Win Your Love)" while riding in my uncle's car with my Pops, driving down 168th Street in the Bronx. My father and uncle, who were both no more than thirty-five at the time, were definitively old-school, even by the standards of the day. The two were no more than ten years removed from their arrival at New York's Pennsylvania Station, having traveled from Thomson, Georgia, to begin new lives in the big city. The late Walker's tenor sax continues to resonate among a spate of childhood memories that are all cradled by the sounds of soul that dominated the era, a sound that allowed me to eavesdrop on the already blatant romanticism of the period. In truth I can barely imagine a world without Diana Ross's seven-minute epic "Ain't No Mountain High Enough" or the Spinners' "Mighty Love," though in fact this was the world that I faced as the soul tradition gave way to the unbridled nihilism of disco and the ragged emotion of funk in the mid-1970s, challenging my own investment in the fictive safety nets that the period's romanticism posited. Don't get me wrong; as a pubescent "soul baby," I got my original "groove on" listening to Funkadelic's "One Nation under a Groove," but somehow these were the sounds of a world slipping away into an uncertain and unfamiliar future. Given these dynamics, it seemed logical to ignore the rudimentary sounds of a musical genre I would a decade later embrace as my own and my generation's. If hip-hop was my music—was my future—it was noise that I wasn't willing to hear as the 1970s waned and Reagan's Roarin' 1980s dawned.

The house parties and park jams that figured so prominently in hip-hop's early development, and which represent perhaps the last hospitable social spaces afforded black youth in the burgeoning postindustrial city, were often outside my concerns. Having given up the "soul" and given up on funk a few years earlier, my impending maturity found refuge and its muse in the pressing political and social issues of the mid- to late 1980s. Fortunately, I was a part of an ever-maturing generation that was thankfully spared cosmic interpretations of our contemporary history via network miniseries—though we did have *Roots* and Oscar Brown Jr.'s *From Jump Street*—cinematic epics of the ilk of Spike Lee's *Malcolm X* or Mario Van Peebles's *Panther*, and multicultural school textbooks. Our history— the history of the modern civil rights movement and its brash and angry offspring, the Black Power and feminist movements—was shared with us via its dominant icons: the common, God-fearing, everyday black folks whose revolutionary charge was simply to transcend absurd and bizarre circumstances immediately and often. Yes, we would relive these moments in the living rooms, back porches, and church pews of our increasingly dispersed and mythical black nation, but these were not our moments . . . these were not our stories. Those stories were neatly packed away with the memories of Diana's shrill voice urging us to "touch some-body's hand" and brother James saying it loud and proud.

Yet we remained uniquely poised—this first post–civil rights, postna-tionalist, post–Black Power, post–Gary, Indiana, postintegration . . . post-soul generation—to interpret the political and cultural terrain of our own conflicted moment. Lacking many of the nostalgic ties that both defined and bound earlier generations of civil rights leaders and followers, we wit-nessed Jesse Jackson's two historic presidential campaigns, the rebirth and rise of the Nation of Islam, the first black Miss America, the child mur-ders in Atlanta, Spike Lee's *Do the Right Thing*, the liberation of Nelson Mandela, and the publication of Alice Walker's *Color Purple* as subjective strangers equally disdained by a young generation of whites, remorseful perhaps that they were the first generation who could not legally deny our freedom—or so we thought—and an Old Negro guard. But we were also a generation that would ultimately be politicized by the successful rise of the conservative right, its predominant icon Ronald Reagan, and the fail-ure of our leadership, elected and anointed, to adequately respond to the realities of black urban life in the 1980s and hazards posed by right-wing ideologues posing as legislators, presidential candidates, objective politi-cal pundits, members of the Hollywood elite, and on occasion race-bait-ing, "God-fearing" black ministers.

In his now classic critique of the black intelligentsia, Harold Cruse accused black intellectuals of failing to respond to the specific political, social, and most importantly cultural realities of the black masses. According to Cruse, "In the face of new trends, new voices, new issues, the content of Negro intellectuals never varies, never changes. Negro intellectuals are moved by the world, but they rarely move with the world."[1] Initially voiced in the mid-1960s, Cruse's criticisms were aimed specifically at those intellectuals he viewed as failing to provide adequate interpretations of the dynamics of American identity and culture, as many of those same intellectuals championed the coming integration of American society. In Cruse's view, integration would lead to "cultural negation" if black intellectuals were unwilling or unable to unravel the

African-American and thus multiethnic influences on American popular culture. In the artists and thinkers of the black arts movement, Cruse identified a cadre of "creative intellectuals" who could provide leadership in regard to deconstructing the myth(s) of American identity, particularly as constructed within mass media and popular culture. Their mission, Cruse asserts, was to "clear the way to cultural revolution by a critical assault on the methods and ideology of the old-guard Negro intellectual elite."[2]

Like the civil rights era that was the primary focus of Cruse's critique, the post–civil rights era has produced specific social and economic challenges foreign to the experiences of the traditional African-American intelligentsia. While this era was in part defined by the incidence of black middle-class flight, a substantial deterioration of black public life, structural transformations in the economy and the labor force, and the failure of post–civil rights strategies to respond adequately to any of these life-affecting threats, it is also defined by the increased proliferation of mass media, the corporate annexation of black popular expression, and the first substantial presence—both negative and positive, whatever those terms imply—of black images within mass media. This period also produces a post-soul intelligentsia, a generation of urban-bred black intellectuals born during the waning moments of the civil rights/Black Power movements, raised on the rhythms and harmonies of 1970s soul but having come to maturity during the mid- to late 1980s and embracing the oppositional possibilities of urban and hip-hop aesthetics, mass media, and popular culture as vehicles for mass social praxis. Though some of these thinkers can legitimately be called urbanites, a majority can more adequately be described as impacted by the urbanization of black popular culture. In many regards, this generation of thinkers personifies the intellectual vanguard of Harold Cruse's oft-cited essay "Role of the Negro Intellectual—Survey of a Dialogue Deferred." It is a generation of scholars who could rightfully be called the "children of Cruse."

I am specifically concerned with the generation of black thinkers who were born after the watershed moments of the traditional civil rights movement, in particular those born after the March on Washington in August 1963. Beginning with the bombing of the Sixteenth Street Baptist Church in Birmingham a scant three weeks after the march, the period ended the aura of expectation that grounded the traditional civil rights movement. Not only did the bombing represent a distinct threat to the nonviolent political paradigm that Martin Luther King Jr. advocated, it was an attack on the aura of innocence that pervaded black youth culture, as further witnessed by the subsequent attacks on black youth organizers within both civil rights and black nationalist organizations throughout the decade. What I am suggesting is that the generation(s) of black youth born after the early successes of the traditional civil rights movement are in fact divorced from the nostalgia associated with those successes and thus positioned to critically engage the movement's legacy from a state of objectivity that the traditional civil rights leadership is both unwilling and incapable of doing. Though writer/critic Nelson George first coined the term *post-soul* to delineate the cultural production of African Americans since the blaxploitation era of the 1970s, I have a very specific context in which to apply the post-soul theme.[3] While the end of the soul era could feasibly be documented with mainstream acceptance of disco music or any number of recordings released by Bobby Womack or the late Z. Z. Hill, politically the era ended with the Bakke challenge to affirmative action in 1978 and was further facilitated with the emergence of the Reagan Right after the 1980 presidential election. It is of course largely the policies of the Reagan Right, particularly its eroding of civil rights–era legislation aimed at addressing historic inequities experienced by blacks, that helped further instigate the advent of hip-hop music and culture as hip-hop became the most visible site of an oppositional urban youth culture.

Hip-hop's appeal as an aurally constructed site for the invisible, though ever-present, urban-determined youth that the genre has been so readily associated with has been invaluable to the development of these often symbolic, though still oppositional sensibilities. Examples include the reconstructed hypermasculinities that pervade hip-hop culture, with an attendant homophobia and misogyny, of course, or the liberatory uses of language and rhetoric that, while the product of popular vernaculars within the black community, became entities unto themselves, as witnessed by the very different connotations of the word *nigger* and its various incarnations such as *nigga* and *nigguh*. Hip-hop, whose early rhythms and cadences foreshadowed its oppositional potential a decade later, served as the ideal conduit for the inner rage of displaced, disadvantaged, and miseducated urban masses as well as the embryonic political musings of an urban-defined, college-age, burgeoning post-soul intelligentsia. In his work on black youth culture, critic Michael Eric Dyson suggests that the hip-hop generation has been viewed as "moral strangers" to the moral and cultural values that undergirded the civil rights movement.[4] In this regard, I believe the post-soul intelligentsia to be unique and transitional figures in the arena of African-American arts and letters. I identify this post-soul intelligentsia as a generation of black thinkers in large part distanced from the nostalgia that pervades the civil rights generation, but who as young adults and teens experienced the terror of the Reagan and Bush (Sr.) years armed with distinct social and cultural, albeit often nostalgic in their own right, memories of the traditional black public sphere. It is the critical musings of this generation of thinkers and creative artists, I believe, that will construct transitional social and political strategies for the twenty-first century, creating the necessary connections between our most recent political struggles and the struggles that will visit the generations that will immediately follow us. We are, perhaps, the black community's best intellectual hope to bridge the widening gap between yesterday's civil rights marcher and today's hip-hop thug.

Like the brash young thinkers of the early twentieth century, whose New Negro–ness continues to inform the traditions of African-American arts and letters, we are charged with navigating a new world defined by radical shifts in labor demographics, a bottom-to-top redistribution of wealth, and the development of computerized networks of communication that have redefined the very notions of communication, commerce, and public discourse. In our best moments we hope to eschew the "HNIC" (head negro/nigger in charge) elitism that perhaps defined and limited some New Negro thinkers, by critically interrogating the signs of "blackness" that define us and questioning our positioning to the black urban masses that we aspire to empower and the tradition of black intellectual thought that informs us. Where this earlier generation of thinkers often failed to equally relate to the Phi Beta Kappa and the Harlem Dandy, we have little choice but to engage the "thug-nigga," "chicken-head," "postmodern Negrotarian," "baby mama," "shuffling 'bama," and the many other diverse manifestations of black identity that continue to proliferate, particularly within the realm of mass culture. At the crux of this reality is to position ourselves beyond mere gatekeepers of some truncated, sanitized, and historically determined version of blackness, broadening the context of what are concurrently individualized, communal, and socially determined constructs.

Our status as intellectuals—broadly defined here as writers, visual artists, musicians, poets, independent scholars, and academics—demands some allegiance to the staid plaster of the ivory tower or the fourth estate and the middle-class lifestyles they afford. But the essence of our being—are some of us not the first and second generation of the most profound migration movement of the twentieth century?—often lies in the "ghetto-hoods" that we called home, be they the South Bronx or East St. Louis, to name a few, if only because those spaces represent the "other" against which we are sometimes defined, by ourselves and others. Gil Scott-Heron was right; home is often where the hatred is, but these homes, as Esther Phillips attested in her version of Scott-Heron's "Home Is Where the Hatred Is," have also been a place of love and sustenance, if not a living metaphor for human survival. Such realities can no longer be simply accepted as the dilemma that excuses our inability to adequately impact upon the social and political policies that most adversely affect our communities. This movement of "post-soul" intellectuals, or what writer Kevin Powell has defined as the "Word Movement,"[5] is poised to redefine the nature and purpose of traditional arts and letters, on the one hand blurring often oppositional discourses of popular and academic expression, and on the other positing, as did earlier generations of black scholars, the academy as a site to influence public policy and to critically confront the specter of race in American society. For academics specifically, this mission differs from earlier generations of black scholars in that the white academy of desegregated America has emerged as the primary site of our scholarly endeavors, providing the context to access valuable resources but also to confront our growing marginalization (as intellectuals) from the concentrated mass of young black minds that continue to emerge from historically black institutions. For nonacademic writers this has meant unprecedented access to mainstream print and on-line journals and for artists, corporate-subsidized grants and fellowships. Our abilities to counter the contradictions associated with these relationships will be witnessed in our commitment to critically engage public discourse, popular culture, political activism, and the belief that our theoretical groundings serve as viable models for mass social praxis.

The intellectual sensibilities of the post-soul intelligentsia are the dual product of America's segregated past and its failed attempts at an integrated present. Not simply "affirmative-action babies"—the realities of post–civil rights race relations are simply more expansive than debates about set-aside programs and quota systems—our access to predominately white institutional structures within academe, the arts, and the publishing and entertainment industries, perhaps, represents the most compelling example of the success of the civil rights movement. But in many regards, our political groundings were most notably influenced not by the traditional leadership of the civil rights movement, but by the largely urban intelligentsia that was locked out of the mainstream institutions during the 1940s, 1950s, and early 1960s because of segregation, and who perceived black institutions, particularly the Negro academy, as an increasingly limiting and inadequate paradigm to address the issues of black life. This cadre of thinkers, though not expressly defined by the rigors of traditional academic life, was nevertheless devoted to examining the philosophical issues surrounding black identity in a highly industrialized moment. More compellingly, their work highlighted an alarming paradox within the African-American diaspora. As the masses of blacks became increasingly urbanized as a corollary to mass migration, the Negro intelligentsia remained rooted in a social context that was distinctly southern and rural, rendering them incapable of adequately addressing the developing crises of black urban life. It is then not surprising that the first major work on the black urban condition, St. Clair Drake's *Black Metropolis*, is produced by one of the first black scholars to legitimately integrate a major urban university in the North.

Writers like Richard Wright, Ralph Ellison, Margaret Walker, Lorraine Hansberry, and Gwendolyn Brooks, whom Cruse refers to as "creative intellectuals" in an effort to distinguish them from black academics, represent an urban intelligentsia shaped by their experiences in the North and willing to use their texts as vehicles for social protest. Embracing a self-defined lifestyle that often existed beyond the Negro academy and mainstream American public life, as was the case with Wright and Chester Himes, this generation of thinkers and artists laid the foundations for an independent intellectual movement in the black community in the post–World War II era. Wright in particular carried this responsibility like a badge of honor and was highly skeptical of traditional black scholars, particularly those still fixated on black life in the rural South.[6] This is of course not to ignore valuable contributions by scholars like E. Franklin Frazier or Oliver Cox, but to recognize the reanimation of a third stream of black intellectual thought, not explicitly produced from the traditional white institutions or the historic sites of black intellectual discourse, and whose presence can be dated back to the work of nineteenth-century scholars like Frances Ellen Watkins Harper,

Martin Delany, Anna Julia Cooper, and Alexander Crummell. Wright's work, of which *Native Son* and the nonfiction pictorial essay *Twelve Million Voices* are most emblematic, details the deteriorating conditions of black urban life and the existentialist spirit inherent in it, even as the urban North continued to be championed as the promised land. Wright's efforts, like those of his contemporaries, inform the activist agendas of the young and often urban-based intellectuals of the 1960s like Amiri Baraka and Sonia Sanchez.

Representatives of the black arts movement and a school of black nationalist thought, artists and scholars like Baraka, Sanchez, Nikki Giovanni, and Haki Madhubuti, form some of the intellectual building blocks of the post-soul generation. The work of many of these scholars continues to resonate in the work of the post-soul intelligentsia, perhaps because they rightly understood that accessibility to the masses was not necessarily antithetical to high creativity, political activism, and intellectual acumen. My own intellectual awakening largely occurred as an undergraduate sitting in the E185 (black) section of my campus's library being introduced to many of these same artists. Many post-soul thinkers were also introduced to these scholars on mainstream college campuses during the 1980s in concert with the resurgence of black nationalism associated with the emergence of Louis Farrakhan during the decade. Controversies surrounding the efforts of various black student organizations to invite Farrakhan to their campuses helped define the concept of political and social agitation for some black college students during the era, particularly after protests against South African apartheid were no longer in vogue. It is this nationalist foothold on college campuses that often served to initially politicize the post-soul generation, especially when expressed via hip-hop icons like Public Enemy, KRS-One, and X-Clan. Despite a proclivity for problematic and ultimately confining constructions of nationalism and sexuality, the black arts thinkers, however briefly, established themselves as the most visible and independent stream of black scholars of the twentieth century, though many of their base sentiments were at profound odds with the largely middle-class and southern-based leadership of the civil rights movement. These scholars and artists, like their most influential political icon, Malcolm X, dared to imagine a "postcolonial" America and Africa that included their role as its dominant aestheticians.

In reality, once-revolutionary acts have been reduced to tenured faculty appointments and visiting lectureships on predominately white university campuses, where former intellectual revolutionaries increasingly appeared as faculty within the first generation of black studies programs and as regulars on the Black History Month/black student union lecture circuit of the 1970s and early 1980s.[7] While on one level emblematic of the limitations of diversity efforts within higher education, the presence of black artists and intellectuals on predominately white campuses represented the draining of intellectual resources from the black community, even if such resources had been formerly distributed largely within the parameters of a black academy bound to middle-class aspiration. With rare exceptions many black arts artists and scholars remained significantly marginalized from mainstream African-American life or frustrated and entrenched within a bevy of tenure battles, retrenchment initiatives, and university committees within the mainstream American academy, equally marginalized from the people and the policies that define contemporary African-American life. Interpreted within the larger context of American race relations, black intellectuals and artists have been effectively desegregated away from the very communities of blackness that produced them, while their presence tacitly validated America's claim to the realization of an integrated America.

In a broader sense the problematic conflation of intellectual and academic life exemplifies, as Russell Jacoby suggests, the demise of a vibrant bohemian culture in America's urban spaces.[8] Though contemporary academic life does afford a lifestyle supportive of America's elite intellectuals, too often the energies and the interests of the average academic remain aligned with the business of running the academy as opposed to the business of producing original and provocative scholarship. The most publicly affecting contemporary scholarship is rarely produced by intellectuals within the academy but rather by scholars supported by well-endowed conservative think tanks like the Hoover Institute and the Heritage Foundation, whose scholarship is produced in concert with the public policy initiatives of the right. The left in America has rarely been positioned to generate significant and consistent financial support, and the remnants of the left that continue to seek influence on matters of public policy have found the most accessible avenues of public debate—television and commercial print media—to be inaccessible to their financial and political means. In reality the demise of a vibrant intellectual culture within American bohemia—think here of the noncorporatized coffee-house and parlor spaces that defined New York's Greenwich Village, as well as San Francisco's Haight-Ashbury—has significantly affected the generally tenuous status of the American left. For the black community, often viewed as the left's poorer relations (was not Harlem simply New York bohemia's uptown annex during the first half of the twentieth century?), the changes in American public life have obviously had an adverse and unbalanced affect, as the cottage industry of African-American arts and letters has always required the patronage of the liberal bourgeois establishment or the strategic support of the right, when such scholarship helps valorize the public policy inclinations of the right.

Ironically, it was the remnants of bohemian culture in the Lower East Side and Greenwich Village of New York City that provided the impetus for one generation of cultural and social critics who directly precede the post-soul intelligentsia. Heavily concentrated in the urban underground of the 1980s that produced entities as varied as Greg Tate, Vernon Reid, the Black Rock Coalition, Jean-Michel Basquiat, George C. Wolfe, Darius James, Cassandra Wilson, and Geri Allen, these thinkers and artists are progeny of the generation of esoteric black intellectuals who inhabited New York's East Village during the 1960s, when self-styled black bohemians like Ellen Stewart, Steve Cannon, Ishmael Reed, and Archie Shepp purposely embraced the edges of marginalia to guarantee a hyperobjectivity toward a liberation movement gone awry. In one of Tate's seminal essays, an examination of the work of Basquiat, he suggests that "to read the tribe astutely you sometimes have to leave the tribe ambitiously, and should you come home again, it is not always to sing hosannas or a song the tribe necessarily wants to hear."[9] Tate articulates a vantage point that the East Village bohemians of the 1960s seemingly craved. Where Baraka left the confines of New York's bohemia, landing in Harlem as a nationalist, East Village bohemians maintained a cautious distance from the site of too many poorly conceived "Black to the Future" dreams. It is this same community in the East Village that was home to the Negro Ensemble Company, which under the direction of Douglas Turner Ward consistently and effectively presented complex and brilliant representations of African-American life that undermined acceptable depictions of African Americans.

Because of their presence at highly visible periodicals such as the *Village Voice* and *Billboard Magazine*, a collective of urban critics emerged in the late 1970s and early 1980s to give new meanings to the seemingly dispersed nature of black intellectual thought and the improvisation of black urban life. Championing hip-hop as the black arts critics had championed hard bop and be-bop, writers like Tate, Nelson George, and Harry Allen instigated an aggressive, oppositional criticism that embodied the sonic kinetics of hip-hop and black urban life as primarily defined by black male sensibilities. The early work of George and Allen, in particular, comprised the rudimentary elements of what was soon to become the burgeoning field of hip-hop journalism—a field largely responsible for the emergence of quintessential post-Soul voices like Kevin Powell, Scott Poulson-Bryant, Dream Hampton, and Toure. George is the only one of the trio who has achieved any real mainstream notoriety. With four non-fiction books to his credit, including *The Death of Rhythm and Blues*, and several books of fiction, George is the literary counterpart to a generation of (pre) post-soul entertainment icons like actor Eddie Murphy, film director Spike Lee, and mogul Russell Simmons, who all have translated marginal status into real material wealth and at least the perception of influence within their respective industries. More than anything their successes represent the kind of nonthreatening, capitalist-friendly cultural nationalism that has pervaded mainstream black culture and politics since the end of the civil rights era.

In comparison, Tate's willingness to engage forms of postmodern cultural theory usually reserved for scholars in the academy opened up possibilities for realization of a "popular post-structuralism—accessible writing bent on deconstructing the whole of black culture."[10] Crucial to his sensibilities was his distance, philosophically and generationally, from both petty bourgeois visions of the traditional civil rights leadership and the essentialist demanding ideology of some within the black nationalist wing of black intellectual and political thought. Beyond oppositional stances, Tate was devoted to redefining essentialist notions of black culture, a project in large part protected by a commitment to remain on the margins and thus to remain unbought and unbothered by the thought police and "soul patrol" alike. Tate's commitment was to present what he referred to as an "Anti-essentialist Essentialism." Acknowledging the artistry of George Clinton, Ntozake Shange, Samuel Delaney, Octavia Butler, and Richard Pryor, Tate argued at the time that "while black artists have opened up the entire 'text of blackness' for fun and games, not many black critics have produced writing as fecund, eclectic, and freaky-deke as the art, let alone the culture itself."[11] In many ways the only critic who came close to his own definition of a "popular poststructuralism" was Tate himself, though he did identify the work of Henry Louis Gates Jr., Clyde Taylor, and David Levering Lewis as emblematic of the kind of "critical aesthetic" that he desired. In that vein Tate mentored a group of critics and artists who were referred to as DNA: Dem Niggas Again. Given the seemingly esoteric nature of his project, it is not surprising that Tate's collection of essays, *Flyboy in the Buttermilk: Essays on Contemporary America,* is currently out of print.

Greg Tate personified the generation of artists and thinkers that author Trey Ellis chronicled in his controversial essay "The New Black Aesthetic."[12] Though less ambitious than Tate's work, the essay is generally regarded as his generation's manifesto. Beginning with commentary on the band Fishbone, Ellis writes, "I now know that I'm not the only black person who sees the black aesthetic as much more than just Africa and jazz. Finally finding a large body of the like-minded armors me with the nearly undampenable enthusiasm of the born-again. And my friends and I—a minority's minority mushrooming with the current black bourgeoisie boom—have inherited an open-minded New Black Aesthetic from a few seventies pioneers that shamelessly borrows and reassembles across both race and class lines."[13] With heavy allusion to a kind of black bourgeois renaissance, Ellis's essay encapsulates what Ronald A. T. Judy has identified as the traditions of "avant garde modernism" and "leftist vanguard agitprop,"[14] traditions that link the "New Black Aesthetic" (NBA) to both the "high Negro style" of the New Negro/Harlem Renaissance period and the provocative pop art of the black arts movement. At the crux of this New Black Aesthetic is a profound rearticulation of the sounds and signs of socially constructed notions of blackness as the praxis of obliterating "old definitions of blackness" that "show us the intricate, uncategorizeable folks we had always known ourselves to be."[15] Ellis describes the likely practitioners of the NBA as cultural mulattos "educated by a multi-racial mix of cultures," who "navigate" effectively within white cultural and educational spheres.

Instructive within the essay is Ellis's autobiographical admission that while growing up in predominately white working- and middle-class suburban communities in Michigan and Connecticut, "it wasn't unusual to be called 'oreo' and 'nigger' on the same day."[16] Effectively "queered" by both white and black communities for being inauthentically "black" or "white" simultaneously, Ellis acknowledges the ways in which the postintegration era allowed middle-class black youth access to suburban white sensibilities, but also exposed the added pressures of remaining "authentically black" in the eyes of the black community. This explains Ellis's failure to mention the ways that hip-hop artists, for instance, also borrow across race and class, despite some of them not being second-generation new black middle class; he is primarily interested in negotiating his own class sensibilities with those he has come to understand as black. With the intense commodification of black popular culture in the post–civil rights era and unprecedented access to it within mainstream commercial culture, young blacks were connected to mainstream commercial culture in ways that previous generations had not been. Many black youth who were not living in white suburban spaces could have just as easily been introduced to facsimiles of those environs while watching television shows like *The Brady Bunch, Eight Is Enough,* or *Family Ties.* Even the diverse musical tastes of the group Fishbone, which Ellis holds as being emblematic of the NBA, were likely cultivated listening to Top 40 radio in the 1970s, where it was not unusual to hear Led Zeppelin, the Spinners, Carole King, and Wilson Pickett in the same set. In this regard Ellis's championing of the NBA allows himself and presumably others like him the space to be simultaneously "seddity" like the New Negroes and as "ghetto-fab" as the "niggas," all the while traveling through white universities, publishing houses, corporate boardrooms, and art galleries as postmodern "Race Men." As Tera Hunter derisively (and rightfully so) queried at the time, "If one has to attend an elite, predominately white university to live among black people for the first time, to what extent is he talking about an aesthetic that is homegrown in black culture?"[17]

Ellis articulates his desires to open up blackness, while remaining in the "black," with his admission that while the NBA often lampoons the Black Power movement of the 1960s, "Nationalist Pride continues to be one of the strongest forces in the black community and the New Black Aesthetic stems straight from that tradition."[18] The NBA's own form of cultural nationalism, whether articulated in George's principled "protection" and reclamation of the black popular music tradition in *The Death of Rhythm and Blues* or in virtually every Spike Lee film from *She's Gotta Have It* to *Malcolm X*, is conscious of its own value in the markets where both popular perceptions and popular commodities are exchanged. Lee's pushing of "Spike Lee joints," be they films like *Mo Betta Blues*, the "X" caps that helped promote *Malcolm X*, or his own services as a video and commercial director for the likes of Tracy Chapman, Naughty by Nature, or the Nike Corporation, is the best example of this. But it is also a nationalism perhaps rife with guilt over the fact that NBA is deeply embedded with forms of corporate capitalism, leading Ronald A. T. Judy to suggest that the NBA is "certainly more of a flash of resistant subjectivity than it is a popular movement of resistance to transnational capitalism."[19] Tate's description of the New Black Aesthetic being a space where the "cult nats meet freaky-deke" captures the ways in which various signs of the NBA—Public Enemy's Flavor Flav, *Def Comedy Jam*, and the clothing line FUBU (for us by us)—are embraced within the context of contemporary black cultural nationalism. For the record, Flavor Flav (William Drayton) played "pomo step-'n-fetchit" sidekick to Chuck D's equally surreal "pomo race man as Gil Scott-Heron/Otis Sistrunk hybrid," while *Def Comedy Jam* was perceived by some as the black equivalent to the kind of lowbrow, dare I say vulgar, comedy that made Andrew Dice Clay and the late Sam Kenison household names in the late 1980s.

The political dressing aligned to much contemporary black popular culture, which has its roots in the beginnings of the NBA moment, helps to mask what is simply a desire for inclusion in the global marketplace. In this regard the creation of Def Jam or Bad Boy Entertainment is firmly in the spirit of the very "integrationist" desires that the reanimation of black nationalist icon and NBA staple Malcolm X has helped to obscure. Perhaps the most serviceable visual for this NBA reality are the images of Def Jam CEO Russell Simmons attending board meetings or, more recently, an audience with former attorney general Janet Reno, wearing a powder blue short set (dress shorts with a matching top) designed for his clothing line Phat Farm. Simmons, along with other black leaders such as Al Sharpton and Johnnie Cochran, met with the attorney general to discuss the escalation of police brutality in the black community. The issue, which even Simmons understands transcends class divisions in the black community, is one of the first public political stances that the forty-something mogul has taken. These best intentions aside, the mass commodification of the New Black Aesthetic did provide a context for rich and provocative constructions of blackness within mass culture. For example, despite perceptions of Flavor Flav's coonish antics, it is his "solo" effort, "911 Is a Joke," in which Chuck D is noticeably absent, that perhaps represents the group's ideology at its most lucid, critiquing the failure of law enforcement and emergency service agencies to respond adequately to the needs of black communities. Even *Def Comedy Jam* can be seen as the "chitlin' circuit" launching pad for the biting social commentary of comics like Eddie Griffith and Chris Rock. The NBA moment also engendered critiques of its own icons like *In Living Color's* and Tommy Davidson's lampooning of Spike Lee ("Mo Betta Butta") and *Def Comedy Jam*, including a parody of Russell Simmons's signature mumbled sign-off, "Good night and God bless."

It is these latter examples of the New Black Aesthetic that can link the aesthetic movement to the oppositional stances of black critics like Anna Julia Cooper, George Schuyler, Bayard Rustin, Audre Lorde, Ralph Ellison, and to a lesser extent James Baldwin, in that the New Black Aesthetic aimed to deconstruct popular assumptions of black identity—often through the process of parody/pastiche—and democratize black critical discourse. The work of the above critics and scholars, representative of the often hyperdemocratic tendencies related to black public discourse, has served to problematize simple constructions of black identity and black thought. Cooper, Rustin, and Lorde in particular have been instrumental in rearticulating notions of blackness along an axis of gender and sexual preference—constructions that remain at odds with dominant representations of blackness and challenge popular notions that increasingly posit patriarchy and heterosexuality as the foundations for acceptable social constructions of blackness. For instance, much black nationalist thought, particularly that which emerged during the 1960s and reanimated itself during the 1980s in the form of Louis Farrakhan, has silenced alternative and radical constructions of blackness by asserting heterosexual capitalist patriarchy as the primary vehicle for black empowerment, often to the detriment of maintaining real solidarity within the broader African-American community. Though the Million Man March cannot be reduced to a singular ideological viewpoint—to do so fails to acknowledge the broad interpretations the march holds for many—the acceptance of Louis Farrakhan as its figurehead is a tacit acceptance of heterosexist capitalist patriarchy within the black community. The New Black Aesthetic aimed to confront the increasingly oppositional nature of black identity within the context of a liberating creative process that embraced both the production and the subsequent criticism of contemporary art forms.

The New Black Aestheticians emerged almost simultaneously with the new face of the elite American academy. Twenty-five years after the historic emblems of segregated life had faded from the walls of the ivory tower and sixty years after the intellectual triad of W. E. B. Du Bois, Alain Locke, and Charles S. Johnson were emphatically denied access to the mainstream American academies of the North, a generation of young black intellectuals emerged from within the very confines that denied access to the best minds in the black community for much of the twentieth century. Many of these new intellectual voices would find institutional bases in African-American studies programs but also in the loosely defined cultural studies programs at elite universities, where ethnic studies and women's studies programs provided a relative safe haven for these often marginalized scholarly interests. To be sure, these folks had major skills. What most uniquely separated them from previous generations of black academics is that this contemporary group was produced primarily within the mainstream academy and would work almost exclusively within that same academy. What connects these thinkers to the broader examples of African-American intellectual thought is their devotion—a devotion that is arguably second nature—to public, political, and critical discourse, though much of this discourse is invariably linked to a white literate consumer public. As Robert S. Boynton suggests, "Theirs is scholarship with a social purpose. This generation of public-minded academics, while notable, is hardly the first to have straddled the worlds inside and outside the university. . . . What distinguishes these new public intellectuals from those of the past, is that their desire to transcend the academy was motivated almost exclusively by an interest in race."[20] It has been as the popular interpreters of race signs and race relations that this generation of scholars, both those linked to the left and to the right, has been most influential. In many regards they have served to validate the identity politics simultaneously articulated within the New Black Aesthetic.

The high visibility of many of these intellectuals has been largely due to the intense commodification of black popular culture during the past two decades, a process that demands articulate interpreters of a culture inherently exoticized and fetishized by mainstream consumers—particularly as black popular culture has framed and informed volatile and controversial events like the murder of Yusef Hawkins, the Clarence Thomas–Anita Hill debates, the Los Angeles riots of 1992, and the Million Man March. This prominence of black intellectuals within contemporary middle-brow and high-brow media culture has been unprecedented in American history and arguably bespeaks the significant presence of racial discourse within the same cultural parameters. With a striking inclination to popularize critical issues and debates within the black community, the visible presence of scholars like Molefi Assante, Patricia Williams, Derrick Bell, Henry Louis Gates Jr., Manning Marable, Michelle Wallace, bell hooks, Cornel West, Barbara Smith, and Michael Eric Dyson has had a significant impact in positing academic life as a viable pursuit for the post-soul generation. But this visibility has engendered its own criticisms, often from within those very communities of black academic elites. Ishmael Reed, for instance, has described Henry Louis Gates Jr. as the "intellectual entrepreneur and the capitalist who instructed black artists on how to become as rich as he," adding that the "formula seems to be one that one writes nothing that would heavily alienate white consumers, selling them guilt free products."[21] Reed's critique of Gates speaks to the ways that the latter has positioned himself as one of the most prominent gatekeepers of black intellectual property and the ways in which black intellectual thought and criticism are wed with the demands of the mainstream marketplace. No longer confined to "Negro" colleges and black-owned media, many prominent black intellectuals have created a niche in the marketplace that affords them a status historically denied many black intellectuals, and a fairly comfortable lifestyle, pursuing what Cornel West has called "a life of the mind." The high visibility of the "new" black intellectuals has arguably been one of the primary stimuli for the generation of blacks who have just emerged or will shortly emerge from doctoral programs within the humanities and social sciences, areas that have historically supported discourse and research on race and race relations.

It is within the context of this visibility that unprecedented volumes on race and the African-American experience have been produced by black intellectuals for academic and commercial presses alike—volumes that have ultimately served to "grandparent" the post-soul intelligentsia, with many of these scholars serving as distant and not so distant mentors to post-soul thinkers. The present emergence of a public class of black intellectuals, who ply their trade beyond the ivory tower and within the organs of mass culture, has had a particularly compelling impact in that contemporary black intellectuals have largely been framed and contextualized by their presence within mass media—arguably the dominant institution in the socialization process of the post-soul intelligentsia. Thus many in the post-soul era are familiar with the work of black intellectuals like bell hooks, Henry Louis Gates Jr., Cornel West, or Michael Eric Dyson through various trade publications such as the *New Yorker, Atlantic Monthly,* and even the hip-hop periodical *Vibe,* as well as through appearances on *Nightline, The Charlie Rose Show, C-Span, BET Tonight,* and even *The Chris Rock Show,* and through scholarly publications. The development of the post-soul intelligentsia is predicated on the explosion of mass consumer culture and the significant commodification of black popular culture. While the 1920s and 1950s also saw a significant expansion in the influence of mass consumer culture, the 1970s would witness the most significant incorporation of African-American culture within the discourse of mass consumer culture. Part and parcel of America's efforts to construct an integrated America that ironically was not wholly experienced by African Americans, the symbolic integration of American society via popular culture would offer the perception of full citizenship for a generation of young African Americans in the post–civil rights era. Furthermore, this last explosion is largely interpreted through the guise of "televisual" expression.

It is within this context of mass culture that contemporary black intellectuals, by extension, have posited the intellectual process and the lifestyle it affords as elements of what former Motown CEO Andre Harell has referred to as contemporary "Big Willie" or "High Negro" style. As the black arts movement blurred the historic boundaries between high art and black popular culture, contemporary black intellectuals have blurred the boundaries between academic and popular writing, in some regards reducing the critical process into accessible mass culture fodder like mainstream film reviews and reviews of popular fiction. Though the contemporary class of black public intellectuals is located firmly within the tradition of the so-called New York intellectuals of the 1940s and 1950s like Diana and Lionel Trilling, Dwight MacDonald, and Irving Howe—a generation of public intellectuals largely sustained by highbrow interests beyond the academy—much of their scholarship must be interpreted within the context of contemporary mass culture. For the budding post-soul intelligentsia the work of black public intellectuals has validated their own connections to mass culture, suggesting that there is value both in the study of "everyday life" and mass culture and in a middle-class lifestyle that could be sustained with it. While the accessibility of popular nonfiction on the African-American experience has been invaluable to a generation of black undergraduate and graduate students, the very essence of mass culture has demanded the dulling of the critical and theoretical edge of much of this scholarship. While this process clearly obstructs the nuanced realities of pursuing a life of the mind, there is perhaps no precedent to the access that young black scholars and writers have to the prominent thinkers within the community, excepting the dynamic web of historically black colleges and universities that nurtured the generation of black male intellectuals that dominate black intellectual life prior to the 1970s.

The power of their visibility notwithstanding, it is questionable whether this particular class of public intellectuals is truly engaged in the acts of resistance that defined previous eras of black thinkers and social activists—a legitimate doubt, given mass culture's ability to erode the political edges of art and literature. This watershed moment in the visibility of black intellectuals has arguably been accompanied by a general erosion of the quality of black leadership. Clearly, previous generations of black intellectuals didn't struggle at underfinanced and segregated institutions simply so that contemporary black scholars could have six-figure salaries, endowed professorships, and book contracts with commercial publishers. In this regard there is a clear connection to New Black Aesthetic icons and the black public intellectual. In his widely circulated essay "What Are the Drums Saying, Booker? The Curious Role of the Black Public Intellectual," Adolph Reed accuses black public intellectuals of "don't-worry-be-happy politics" in which they "make radical politics by climbing the tenure ladder" and feel good about themselves "through the pride of vicarious identification with the embedded theoretical sophistication of the folk."[22] However acerbic Reed's critiques, they do problematize the positioning of black public intellectuals as "certified world-class elite academics and as links to an extra academic blackness" who are able to "skirt the practical requirements of either role—to avoid both rigorous, careful intellectual and protracted, committed political action."[23] At root, is Reed's fear is of a dumbing down of the black intellectual tradition, a fear in part the product of earlier intellectual moments in which black intellectuals were wedded to certain notions of rigorous and even esoteric scholarship to challenge general perceptions that even the most gifted of black thinkers were intellectually inferior to whites. Todd Boyd has argued instead that "our goal is much like that of the country preachers I used to hear as a child who would be encouraged by a church member to 'make it plain.'"[24] Part of "making it plain" is to provide the kinds of critical readings of the popular signs of blackness as they are constructed and distributed in film, music video, literature, television, and music. Boyd's own commitment to more accessible intellectual endeavors that "make it plain" can be witnessed in the screenplay he cowrote with Rick Famuyiwa for the black male coming-of-age film *The Wood*.

Reed's critique neglects the fact that contemporary black public intellectuals are products of a world where market sensibilities pervade virtually every aspect of civic and private life. To resist the possibilities of the marketplace is to further render many black intellectuals in isolation. With unprecedented access to the engines of mass culture, black public intellectuals have helped create a model in which counter-hegemonic models of cultural and social criticism can be expressed and consumed within mass culture. One example has been the distribution of critiques of homophobia, sexism, and misogyny within the black community. The scholarship of Angela Davis, Hazel Carby, Kathy Cohen, Dwight McBride, Patricia Hill-Collins, Philip Brian Harper, Kimberlie Crenshaw, and Katie Cannon, to name a few, has arguably redefined gender and sexuality studies within the context of the African-American experience, though the marginal status of their scholarship to the canon of contemporary black thought is the obvious price they have paid for the patriarchy and homophobia that continue to inform black intellectual thought. Nevertheless their scholarship, particularly when considered alongside films such as Marlon Riggs's *Black Is, Black Ain't* or *Tongues Untied*, Julie Dash's *Daughters of the Dust*, Cheryl Dunye's *Watermelon Woman*, and even the cinematic treatments of the popular fiction of Terri McMillan, has allowed valuable public and popular commentary on the realities of gender oppression, sexual violence, and queer bashing, both physical and rhetorical, within the black community. Another instance of the ways black public intellectuals impact mass culture can also be recognized in bell hooks's conversation with gangsta rapper Ice Cube, which appeared in her book *Outlaw Culture*.[25] Hooks's willingness to sit down and "break bread" with Ice Cube, who at the time was notorious for homophobic and sexist lyrics on his recordings *Amerikkka's Most Wanted* and *Death Certificate*, represents both her own desires to have meaningful dialogue within the community and her perception that voices like Ice Cube's are as intellectually important to a reading of black life and culture as are those produced within the academy. Other examples include the lauding of the "poetry" of the late hip-hop artist Tupac Shakur and Rakim

(Allah) by poets Nikki Giovanni and Sonia Sanchez and cultural critic Michael Eric Dyson. This willingness to truly engage the various meta-identities present within black life and culture and the acceptance of broadened definitions of black intellectual thought by contemporary black intellectuals are particularly germane to the projects of the post-soul intelligentsia.

The post-soul imagination, if you will, has been fueled by three distinct critical desires, namely, the reconstitution of community, particularly one that is critically engaged with the cultural and political output of black communities; a rigorous form of self and communal critique; and the willingness to undermine or deconstruct the most negative symbols and stereotypes of black life via the use and distribution of those very same symbols and stereotypes. Perhaps no structural development delineates the emergence of the post-soul generation better than the postindustrial transformation of black urban spaces. Broadly interpreted as the "death of community," the transformation of urban centers from the sites of industrial production to the incubators of surplus labor and displaced humanity has provided the context for the emergence of the contemporary black underclass. Furthermore it continued to erode the already precarious status of the black working class, which, coupled with the incidence of black middle-class flight, provides the impetus for the radical transformation if not demise of the traditional black public sphere as represented in many segregated communities prior to the civil rights movement. While the transformation of the traditional black public sphere can be documented as early as the mid-1950s with the migration of white middle-class elements from urban centers into suburbia and later with the urban uprisings of the mid- to late 1960s, the structural transformation of the economy of the industrial city would have the most prodigious impact on black public life within these spaces. This would have a compelling impression on the post-soul generation in that the seminal institutions of the traditional black public sphere were largely responsible for the transmission and reproduction of communal values within even stratified black communities. The erosion of the black public sphere provides the chasm in which the post-soul generation is denied access to the bevy of communally derived social, aesthetic, cultural, and political sensibilities that have undergirded much of the success of the black community during the twentieth century, in part fracturing the post-soul generation and all those who followed from the real communal history of the African-American diaspora.

THE POST-SOUL INTELLIGENTSIA

Emblematic perhaps of the disconnectedness of contemporary American life, the post-soul generation is also marked by the hyperactivity of mass consumer culture and mass media, of which the commodification of contemporary black popular culture is a seminal enterprise. The post-soul generation becomes the first generation of African Americans who would perceive the significant presence of African-American iconography within mass consumer culture/mass media as a state of normalcy.[26] It is within this context that mass culture fills the void of both community and history for the post-soul generation, while producing a generation of consumers for which the iconography of blackness is consumed in lieu of personal relations, real experience, and historical knowledge. Furthermore the quest for individual satisfaction that undergirds contemporary acts of consumption has often rendered the concept of community and communal activities foreign to some within contemporary experiences. In her critique of contemporary examples of Harold Cruse's "creative intellectuals," Hortense Spillers writes, "Yielding apparently little resistance to the sound intrusion of market imperatives on the entire intellectual project . . . today's black creative intellectual lends herself/himself—like candy being taken from a child—to the mighty seductions of publicity and the 'pinup.'"[27] Thus it is not so ironic that hip-hop, a multibillion-dollar industry and arguably the most commodified form of popular black expression ever, provides the metaphoric inspiration through which the post-soul generation generates its critical and intellectual perspectives.

In its best moments, hip-hop has aimed to stimulate a dialogue across the chasm of silence that has engulfed black communal discourse in the post-soul era by popularizing the dominant issues within contemporary black urban life. While there is of course a fine line between celebrating the negative realities of black urban life and reporting the facts, nevertheless hip-hop has been largely responsible for presenting issues inherent to contemporary black urban life to broader audiences via mass culture, even if many of its constituents are simply constructed as consumers and aspects of black urban life are reduced to emblems of stylistic acumen for mainstream consumers. This aspect of hip-hop, which I believe is a quintessential trait of the post-soul intelligentsia, differs from aforementioned uses of mass culture by contemporary black intellectuals. Hip-hop posits mass culture not simply as a vessel of mainstream acceptance but as a conduit to introduce marginalia, on its own merit, into mainstream discourse, a process predicated in large part on the dominance of mass culture in

framing public opinion and the recognition of the role of mass production and distribution outlets to contemporary African-American culture.
The power that the post-soul intelligentsia finds within the marketplace
is also buoyed by Kevin Powell's assertion that hip-hop was the first form
of black music "where its originators could care less what white people
thought of them."[28] Afforded incredible access to the intellectual rum-
blings of thinkers among the current cadre of black public intellectuals
and informed by the sonic constructs of community and critique that
ground the best of hip-hop, the post-soul intelligentsia is poised to interpret the disparate energies and discourses of contemporary urban life and
to provide the critical and theoretical framework to best impact upon the
conditions of those within black urban and other spaces. While the projects of the post-soul intelligentsia will not markedly differ from those of
contemporary black intellectuals, the former have clearly been produced
within a context more organically connected to the realities that black
intellectuals are expected to interpret for both communal and mainstream
constituencies—particularly those realities in which urban life and mass
culture serve as clear pretexts and subtexts, as exemplified by the fact that
many of the post-soul generation were still in the 'hood when crack
rhetorically and physically transformed already-reeling black communities in the late 1980s.

Cruse declares in his critique of American society that "the most crucial requirement at this point is a complete democratization of the national cultural ethos. This requires a thorough, democratic overhauling of the
social functions of the American cultural apparatus."[29] What Cruse seems
to imply is that popular culture, and in this context black popular culture,
can serve to politicize and popularize national debates about race, class,
gender, sexual preference, and American identity. According to Cruse,
this endeavor is not solely limited to the content of popular art but "a
question of what methods of social change are necessary to achieve freedom of expression within a national culture whose aesthetic has been cultivated by a single, dominant ethnic group."[30] In that much of the modern
world for the post-soul generation has been interpreted by the guise of
mass media and culture, the post-soul intelligentsia's interpretations of
contemporary life will obviously use the iconography of mass culture to
frame and inform their critical insights. This is not simply an empty gesture to reach the "masses" of consumers, but a very real attempt, I believe,
to combat the growing marginalization of intellectuals from the everyday

realities of life in America. If we accept the premise that a majority of Americans are "plugged in," in one form or another, to the Time Warners, AOLs, and Sonys of the world, then it is perhaps incumbent upon intellectuals, be they social critics, political economists, or performance artists, also to be plugged in and capable of providing critical interventions in those spaces. Thus the use and critique of mass media and popular culture can serve as a viable mode of social and political praxis for the post-soul intelligentsia, as they seek to liberate dated tropes and stereotypes of blackness in ways that venture to decolonize contemporary African-American thought processes. The post-soul intelligentsia can then be seen, in Henry Giroux's words, as "taking the notion of leadership, criticism, struggle, and solidarity as a starting point, a politics in transit fueled not by the promise of celebrity but the possibility of revitalizing lost visions of social justice and future hopes of substantive democratic change."[31]

Central to this project is a rearticulation of notions of power as it relates to African Americans within the culture industry. As many within the black community decry the lack of positive images in popular culture, the lack of power to influence the corporate capitalist responsible for such imagery, and the hegemony of mass culture, the post-soul intelligentsia aims to endeavor beyond positive and negative interpretations of black popular culture to forge radical critical sensibilities that derive notions of subversion, resistance, and pleasure in a combined "meta-text" of text and critique. This mode of critique renders notions of powerlessness within the contemporary culture industry as meaningless or at least tangential by deriving power instead from the critical process. In this regard, popular culture will not be solely beholden to popular artists and the constraints often placed on them within the culture industry. One example of this is my read of the television series *The PJs*. The show's title is black urban slang for the "projects," the network of federally funded housing projects built during the mid-twentieth century. The series, which uses the Claymation technology that elevated the "California Raisins" to icon status in the 1980s, was the creation of Eddie Murphy and is produced by the Imagine production company led by director Ron Howard and Tony Krantz. In the late 1990s Imagine was responsible for several of Murphy's movie projects, including the hugely successful *Nutty Professor* franchise, *Dr. Doolittle*, and *Life*. The series focuses on the residents of the Hilton Jacobs housing project—the name a reference to actor Lawrence Hilton Jacobs and his popular Freddie "boom boom"

Washington character from the sitcom *Welcome Back, Kotter*—and its superintendent, Thurgood Stubbs, often simply referred to as "supa." As the "supa's" name—a surreal conflation of the late Supreme Court justice Thurgood Marshall and the lead singer of the Four Tops, Levi Stubbs—suggests, he is at once an antiquated reminder of a fictive black community where black folks struggled together amid detrimental and demeaning circumstances and a vivid caricature of a generation of black men who remain hopelessly sexist and vulgar, but who regularly redeem themselves in the name of community. In fact, as witnessed by the support for the Reverend Henry Lyons, Minister Benjamin Muhammad (formerly Chavis), and O. J. Simpson, the black community often closes ranks around the more prominent of these "characters." The show relies on distorted, alarming hypercaricatures of the black ghetto "underclass" that, while obviously problematic, do allow for a fairly vivid presentation of life in urban housing projects like the notorious Cabrini-Greene in Chicago or the Polo Grounds in upper Harlem, New York. Thurgood's regular confrontations with the receptionist (Jennifer Lewis) at the "Department of Housing and Urban Development," who appears behind a clouded glass window that obscures her real identity, particularly resonates among viewers familiar and often frustrated with the bureaucratic distance employed by "housing authorities" as a controlling mechanism against the residents of these spaces.

Shorty after the series premiere, filmmaker Spike Lee was quoted as saying that the show was "hateful towards black people" and "show[s] no love at all for black people."[32] Lee's comments were not surprising, given his middle-class background and position as an elite in the entertainment industry, where folks such as Lee have often voiced a displeasure with the proliferation of "negative" images of black folks in mass media. These concerns later became the focus of his film *Bamboozled*. But his comments also continued a long-standing feud between Lee and Murphy dating back to Murphy's status as a film icon in the 1980s and Lee's desires to become the dominant black film director. This conflict was publicly played out shortly before the release of Lee's *Do the Right Thing*, when talk show host and Murphy confidante Arsenio Hall browbeat Lee on his late-night show for publicly criticizing the proverbial "strong black man." Lee's comments are representative of the tensions associated with the construction of black identities in which the relative paltry presentation of "positive" black identities is viewed as a threat to the ability of some

African Americans to function effectively in the public sphere without negative stereotypes being read into their own identities. An alternative view, which I share, is that these blatant caricatures, dare I say stereotypes, allow for not only a rich critique of the obvious atrocities that take place in black urban spaces but also a contesting of the black community's own perceptions of black ghetto culture, if not of black identity itself. In my opinion the comedic nature of the series does not serve to downplay the harsh conditions of some black urban enclaves but allows for a popularization of these conditions, if not a form of catharsis for those folks who live this everyday reality. In response to Lee's criticisms, *The PJs'* executive producer, Larry Wilmore, suggested that the series made no attempt to represent the black community but instead focused on individual members of an urban community. He added that if actor Shawn Michael Howard, who provides the voice for Smokey, the local "crackhead," were playing the same character on a cop show such as *NYPD*, he would likely win an Emmy award for his portrayal.[33]

It is the character voiced by Howard that I specifically focus on in my reading of the series. In a series that is visually dominated by the urban grotesque—Ralph Bakshi's *Street Fight* (orignally titled *Coonskin*) immediately comes to mind as a comparison—Howard's Smokey is perhaps the most grotesque. As many of the show's characters are seen as marginal to mainstream society if not black life itself, Smokey the crackhead is the most marginal of those characters, literally living as homeless man outside the Hilton Jacobs houses. In "Smokey the Squatter," which was initially broadcast during the 1999–2000 season on the Fox channel, Smokey's marginal status is more fully critiqued, as Thurgood is forced by his wife and others residents to allow Smokey to stay in the apartment building because of "Hurricane OJ." The residents first become aware of Smokey's tenuous status during the storm when he is heard yelling for help in the distance. When Smokey is blown against Thurgood's window, the latter remarks, "There's a gremlin on the wing," a reference to the now classic *Twilight Zone* episode in which William Shatner is ironically spooked by a gremlin outside his airplane window. The reference serves to dramatize the stakes associated with Thurgood allowing the freakish Smokey access to the safe haven of the Hilton Jacobs houses, buoying his role as the building's benevolent patriarch. Thurgood allows Smokey to stay in his "secret apartment," for one night. When Thurgood returns the next morning to "evict" Smokey, the latter cites "Squatter's Law," which forbids Thurgood from evicting him for six months. Smoky is able to cite the law because he has read copies of Thurgood's *Modern Super Quarterly*, which Thurgood apparently failed to read closely if at all. The next day Thurgood returns to the secret apartment, only to find out that Smokey has burned his copies of the magazine because it is now being published on-line. Though the sequence is an obvious reference to the so-called digital divide in American society, where folks like Thurgood and his residents are unlikely to be subscribers to Worldnet or even free services such as Net-Zero or Juno, it is striking that the one character most likely to be unaware of the burgeoning cyberindustry is the one responsible for making its presence known to Thurgood. Later in the episode, when Thurgood orchestrates the residents to forcibly remove Smokey from the premises, the latter is seen sitting in the "breakfast nook," sipping on herbal tea and listening to classical music. When it is revealed that the apartment also has a water purifier, one of the tenants remarks that she doesn't have water, let alone a water purifier. As Thurgood attempts to defend the amenities in *his* secret apartment, Smokey informs residents, again citing *Modern Super Quarterly*, that by law Thurgood is responsible for fixing problems in their apartments like bad plumbing within six hours of notice. In the context of his presence in the apartment building, Smokey is revealed to be a fairly cultured, sophisticated, and literate critical thinker—in a later episode he takes an herbal wrap in a trash bin—that very much counters against perceptions of him as a crackhead, and raises questions about why Smokey either chose or was forced to live an existence marginal to the black urban community. It is my sense that Smokey serves as a metaphor for a frustrated intellectual within spaces in which critical thinking is neither valued nor cultivated and in opposition to leadership, as witnessed in Thurgood, naturally thought to serve the best interests of these communities.

I would like to briefly extend my critique of the series to Murphy himself, as it is not too difficult to speculate that negative criticism of the series was also informed by the black public's dissatisfaction and discomfort with Eddie Murphy. The series debuted less than two years after Murphy's well-publicized "queering." On the evening of May 2, 1997, Murphy was "detained" along with trangendered prostitute Atisone "Shalomar" Seluli. Murphy claimed at the time that his "pickup" of Seluli was little more than a "good Samaritan" act, in which he offered the woman a ride to her home. Though Seluli was arrested on an outstanding warrant for previous acts of prostitution, Murphy was not charged. At the time of the incident Murphy was quoted as saying, "I love my wife and I'm not gay. I'm married with three children. I'm not going to do anything to jeopardize my health."[34] Shortly thereafter Murphy filed a $5 million libel suit against the *National Enquirer*, after the tabloid published a story titled "Eddie Murphy's Secret Life: His Transvestite Hooker Tells All." As David Ehrenstein writes in his provocative book *Open Secret: Gay Hollywood, 1928–1998*, Murphy was "left with the much more delicate task of explaining, to a greatly amused press corps, why his 'good Samaritan' actions should be unfolding on a thoroughfare known to be trafficked by male prostitutes," particularly as Murphy had been dogged by rumors about his sexuality for more than a decade. Murphy had long been connected to queer issues largely because of his blatantly homophobic monologues in his concert films *Delirious* (1983) and *Raw* (1987); and his homophobia was the subject of some controversy in 1996 as gay and lesbian activists petitioned *The David Letterman Show* to withdraw an invitation to Murphy, at the time promoting his "comeback" film *The Nutty Professor*. Murphy ultimately issued a "when as a child, I spoke as a child" written apology for his remarks on the *Delirious* special, which was filmed when the comic actor was twenty-one years old.

Rumors aside, I have no interest in exploring Murphy's sexuality but would rather suggest that the incident with "Shalomar" and the premiere of *The PJs* occurred at a time when Murphy was exploring various "queer" themes in his work. I employ the term *queer* here not specifically as a reference to Murphy's or for that matter anybody else's sexuality, but as a description of themes in his film projects that suggest alternative and even "strange" or unique orientations that call into question the notion of stable black identities. My argument here is based on my acceptance that the characters from the *PJs*, particularly given their grotesque physicality, were queered via their marginal relationship to acceptable (safe) black identities. The most obvious example of these queer themes are within the films *Nutty Professor* and *Nutty Professor II: The Klumps*, which both feature Murphy playing multiple roles, suggesting a certain malleability of his identity, which is then written onto the identities of the Klump family members. Murphy had charted this territory earlier in his career in the film *Coming to America* and the brilliant film short "White Like Me" during his days as a cast member on *Saturday Night Live* in the early 1980s. "White Like Me" examined the issue of "passing," as Murphy in makeup is transformed into a white man. Perhaps less obvious are the queer themes that Murphy addresses in the films *Dr. Doolittle* and *Life. Dr. Doolittle* of course tells the story of a man who is "queered" because of his unique ability to "talk to the animals." In the Murphy version of the film, this ability is scorned by his parents, and as an adult, Doolittle finds it a burden. Much of the film deals with him trying to keep this ability a secret from his family. The "queer" sexuality theme is subtly examined in a scene where Murphy attempts mouth-to-mouth resuscitation of a rat, which is overseen by one of his colleagues, confirming suspicions that he is engaged in unusual activities. In fact, at one point in the film, Doolittle is institutionalized for his "queer" activities. I was struck how Doolittle is ostensibly "outed" in the full view of television cameras as he communicates with a tiger that he later operates on. The outing of Doolittle particularly resonates in a broader reading of Murphy's queerness as the film was released less than a year after his incident with "Shalomar."

Lastly, in the film *Life*, which traces the friendship of Rayford Gibson (Murphy) and Claude Banks (Martin Lawrence) over a fifty-year period, the two are unfairly incarcerated by a corrupt sheriff and eventually feign their deaths in order to escape the prison farm where they spent much of their adult life. Murphy blatantly address the issue of homosexuality via the relationship of Biscuit (Miguel Nunez Jr.) and Jangle Leg (Bernie Mac), two gay lovers who reside in the same prison camp. Shortly before his release Biscuit shares with Rayford his apprehension about returning to his "mama" as a queer. In an extraordinary moment in the film, Rayford consoles Biscuit by suggesting that his family will embrace him based on the fact that he is a member of the family. Biscuit is not swayed by Rayford's comments and purposely runs beyond the limits of the prison camp and is shot dead. Biscuit's choice of death over a return to his community is a strong indictment of the homophobia that exists in the black community; the sequence represents exceptional growth and sensitivity on Murphy's part, particularly given his earlier history as one of the most visibly homophobic entertainment icons and his own presumed queerness.

As my readings of Eddie Murphy and *The PJs* suggest, the post-soul intelligentsia is poised and, I believe, uniquely suited to equip contemporary black youth and others with the critical skills necessary to forge new definitions of social movement and identity that are not simply commodified and mediated by mass culture but instead appropriate mass culture to further cultivate both its audience and its goals. Harold Cruse suggests that this struggle transcends black intellectual concerns with the realities of black life, but instead should be engaged within the context of American identity. It is in this regard that Cruse finds limits in the black nationalist sensibilities of the civil rights era, stating that "American Negro Nationalism can never create its own values, find its revolutionary significance, define its political and economic goals, until Negro intellectuals take up the cudgels against the cultural imperialism practiced in all of its manifold ramifications on the Negro within American culture. But this kind of revolution would have to be predicated on the recognition that the cultural and artistic originality of the American nation is founded, historically, on the ingredients of a black aesthetic and artistic base."[35]

Cruse's comments, which echo C. L. R. James's assertion that popular arts reflect the "clearest ideological expression of the sentiments and deepest feelings of the American people,"[36] offer compelling support for the unique role of black intellectuals in excavating the profound influences that black popular culture has historically and contemporarily wielded on both American culture and American identity. S. Craig Watkins adds that "popular media culture is perhaps best understood as a perpetual theater of struggle in which the forces of containment and resistance remain in a constant state of negotiation."[37]

These processes are naturally suited for classroom instruction and are further facilitated by the expanded use of multimedia in classroom instruction, though the willingness of post-soul intellectuals to present their work to the audiences of popular organs like the *Source, Spin Magazine,* or *Vibe*—novelist Zadie Smith's deconstruction of the film adaptation of Dr. Seuss's *The Grinch Who Stole Christmas* in *Vibe* immediately comes to mind[38]—and to share their work with the cybercommunity via on-line journals and magazines will provide valuable alternatives to the classroom, particularly as the democratization of classroom space is continuously contested by those who aim to depoliticize instruction. According to Henry Giroux, "Erasing the political from the pedagogical . . . closes down the opportunities for teachers and students alike to engage and challenge the prevailing notions of authority and power" as they exist within the classroom and helps "rationalize the exclusions of specific histories, experiences, and ideologies."[39] Like the various counter public spheres historically constructed by ethnic and gender groups, the post-soul intelligentsia is perhaps naturally acclimated to the possibilities that cyberspace affords, given the centrality of advanced media technology to the basic socialization process of the generations of American youth who have come of age in the post–civil rights era. The post-soul intelligentsia faces the challenge of creating modes of critique that match the visibility and popularity of the very texts that it critiques in the first place. Examples of this are currently seen in the intense pubic debates over the style, content, image, and politics within various genres of hip-hop, as well as in the comedic routines of Chris Rock or the strips of cartoonist Aaron McGruder, who regularly problematize unsophisticated readings of black culture and identity. This willingness to venture beyond traditional educational spaces is particularly valuable as access to quality and affordable education and the emerging technologies is increasingly challenged. As many black scholars have helped legitimize the study of black popular culture by interpreting it via highly theoretical and academic language, it behooves the post-soul intelligentsia to rearticulate these highly theoretical ideas into language accessible to the very masses, black or otherwise, to which black popular culture is so crucial.

5

Native Tongues
Voices of the Post-Soul Intelligentsia

my hypothesis on this
is you niggas better come in terms of my vocabulary quick or get
    dissed
my brain bleeds mental complex feeds
bring it on kid I got exactly what you need
twisted metaphors to get your shit in star wars

—Keith Murray

Let's take a long walk around the park after dark
Find a spot for us to spark
Conversation, verbal elation, stimulation
Share our situation, temptations, education, relaxations, elevations . . .

—Jill Scott, "A Long Walk"

At a staff meeting with then new Washington, D.C., mayor Anthony
Williams, David Howard, the director of the public advocate's office, discussed the meager amount of money available for the constituent services office. Howard was quoted in the meeting as saying that he would have

to be "niggardly" with the office's budget. Howard's use of the word *niggardly*, which is defined in the Second College Edition of the American Heritage Dictionary as "stingy," instigated a controversy, offending other members of the mayor's staff, who perceived the word as too closely related to the racial epitaph *nigger*. Williams eventually forced Howard, who is white, to resign, largely in response to overwhelming public support for his removal and the mayor's own desires to challenge perceptions among some black residents in Washington, D.C., that he was not "black enough."[1] In the preface to his book *Losing the Race: Self-Sabotage in Black America*, John McWhorter presents black reaction to the controversy as evidence of the "Cult of Victimology, under which it has become a keystone of cultural blackness to treat victimhood not as a problem to be solved but as an identity to be nurtured."[2] According to the linguist, "Victimology determined the niggardly episode: the basic sentiment that racism still lurks in every corner led naturally to a sense that the use of a word that even sounds like nigger was a grievous insult."[3] While I concur with McWhorter's assessment that Howard should not have been forced to resign, I am interested in his critique of the incident and black public response to it for another reason. I contend that many blacks were in fact uncomfortable with the word not simply because it was perceived as a marker of racial difference but arguably, and more profoundly at this moment, as a marker of difference *within* the black community. No matter what the word *niggardly* actually means, I would submit that most black residents in the city and elsewhere heard the word *niggerish*, "acting like a nigger."

The use of the word *nigger* has been a source of some contention in the last decade because of its relative casual use by hip-hop artists and the kinds of "urban" comics who appeared regularly on Russell Simmons's *Def Comedy Jam* and Black Entertainment Television (BET)'s *Comic View*. I suspect that McWhorter used the "niggardly" episode as a focal point for his ideas on black victimology precisely because such casual use of the word by black youth both demystifies and obscures the racist overtones of its meaning. As witnessed in films like *Black and White* and the Danny Hoch/Marc Levin collaboration *Whiteboyz*, which both focused on white youth thoroughly immersed in "ghettocentric" culture, even white youth employ the term in its various guises as a term of endearment, community, and (racial) authenticity. I also suspect that both McWhorter and Mayor Williams clearly understood the connotations of difference, within the black community, that the word *niggerish* conveys and had likely employed the term to distinguish themselves from other blacks at various points in their careers. I make this latter point not out of any knowledge of the personal sensibilities of either man, nor to suggest that either believes that there is any endowed social privilege conveyed to them based on their status as black middle-class elites, but because such markers of difference do exist in the black community, and powerfully so. Comedian and actor Chris Rock suggested as much in his comedy film *Bring the Pain*, which was filmed, incidentally, at Washington, D.C.'s, Tacoma Theater in 1996. According to Rock, "There's a civil war going on with black people and there are two sides. Blacks and over there, niggers. And niggers have got to go. I love black people, but I hate niggers." While some black folks were likely offended by Rock's use of the word *nigger*, and likely more so because it was initially broadcast to subscribers of the Home Box Office (HBO) network, the fact is that Rock's performance was primarily attended by black audiences who were largely receptive to Rock's distinction between "niggers" and blacks. Rock went on to critique "nigger" literacy by suggesting that "books are like kryptonite for a nigger" and the celebration of one's welfare status as emblematic of "welfare carols" like "First of the Month" by the Cleveland based hip-hop group Bone, Thugs, and Harmony. During the well-attended performance, Rock publicly admitted to the tropes of difference that black people employ to distinguish themselves from each other, particularly along class lines. That these tropes exist was of course not surprising to some blacks, but Rock's willingness to air the dirty laundry was, and would come under some scrutiny as pundits began to politically align the comic to more conservative black writers and commentators like Armstrong Williams, Thomas Sowell, and the always entertaining Stanley Crouch. Rock's linkage to these figures is understandable, given his arguably gleeful assertion that he hates "niggers." Rock in fact parlayed the performance into *The Chris Rock Show*, a late-night show on HBO that ran for five years and allowed him to fully explore some of the tensions that he began to address in *Bring the Pain*. In one episode during the fall of 2000, Rock presented a chart of steps in which newsworthy items related to prominent blacks were judged as either steps forward or steps backward for the black community, highlighting general perceptions that the public fate of a few African Americans reflects on the larger black community. While Rock has been particularly deft at not providing any inkling of his ideological leanings—folks ranging from Jesse Jackson to New York City mayor

Rudolph Giuliani and hip-hop artist Jay-Z ("stab-a-nigga-jigga") have been regularly targeted by him—I would suggest that his humor is quintessential post-soul in nature. Rock has chosen to confront the contradictions inherent in contemporary black life in America, in the full view of the marketplace, often indicting himself, as he does in the *Bring the Pain* performance, allowing for an arguably fuller and more intense discussion of those contradictions. It is a role that Rock shares with many post-soul artists and critics, most notably novelist Paul Beatty, feminist critic Joan Morgan, vocalist Jill Scott, and cartoonist Aaron McGruder.

Can the Subaltern Signify? Paul Beatty as Ghetto-Fab Ethnographer and Cultural Critic

Having released two volumes of poetry, *Big Bank Take Little Bank* and *Joker, Joker, Deuce*, Paul Beatty was primarily known as a poet and spoken-word artist when his first novel, *The White Boy Shuffle*, was published in 1996. The coming-of-age narrative traces Gunner Kaufman's preteen years as the "cool black guy" who body-surfed in Santa Monica to his emergence as artistic icon after the publication of his book of poetry *Watermelanin*. As a preteen, Gunnar is often challenged by his own "queered" black identity and confused by the ways in which popular perceptions of black life and black popular culture are used to publicly judge and articulate black identity. When Gunner and his two sisters Christina and Nicole protest their mother Brenda's suggestion that they spend their summer at an all-black day camp ("because they're different from us"[4]), she decides to relocate the family to West Los Angeles in order to introduce her children to their blackness. Gunnar's move to West Los Angeles allows Beatty not only to examine conflicting constructions of black identity but also to use the character as a "ghetto-fab" ethnographer of black life and culture.[5] The term *ghetto-fab* can be best described as the way some black urban poor, particularly black youth, have elevated elements of their existence to a ghetto stylishness, contradicting claims that these are emblematic of the debilitating nature of their lives. At first look Gunnar, whose name is a reference to the Swedish ethnographer Gunnar Myrdal, who chronicled black life in *An American Dilemma: The Negro Problem and Modern Democracy*, seems to have enough distance from "community" to fit the "objective" role of the traditional ethnographer.

Beginning with the publication of W. E. B. Du Bois's *Philadelphia*

Negro, many black intellectuals—Elijah Anderson, William Julius Wilson, and Mary Patillo-McCoy are recent examples—have also been employed as ethnographers of black life within various social spaces.[6] Historically the distance that black ethnographers have maintained from their subject, despite sharing a racial heritage, one was thought to give them access to social spaces where whites might be deemed suspicious. This was supposedly made possible by their use of "objective" social science tools and presumably their status as middle-class black elites. In the past, it was generally regarded that such "training" was necessary for "Negro" ethnographers to be as objective as their white peers, who were thought to be more naturally endowed with a sense of objectivity, presumably because of their whiteness. Viewed in this context, Gunnar may seem ideal in this role, as reflected by his junior high school dossier, which suggests that "despite his race, subject possesses remarkable intelligence and excellent reasoning and analytical skills . . . with the proper patriotic encouragement Gunnar Kaufman will make an excellent undercover CIA agent. At a young age, he already shows a proclivity for making friends with domestic subversives and betraying them at the drop of a hat."[7] The dossier also represents the ways that students are tracked through institutions like public schools. Beatty later gives an example of how some students are tracked into metal shop classes to prepare them for license plate pressing when they become incarcerated.[8]

Gunnar's own objectivity in this role is initially undermined by the fact that he is victimized because of his "queered" (read: too white) identity. After a skirmish with two young girls and their cousin, Gunnar admits that the "ghetto intelligentsia had kindly provided the young Kaufmans a lesson in street smartology: never ever cry in public. . . . Since we sobbed like wailing refugee babies, we received a full-scale beatdown designed to toughen us up for the inevitable cataclysmic Italian opera ending in black tragedy."[9] In this regard Gunnar's initial read of what he calls a "ghetto hostage crisis" is largely informed by the fear and disdain he holds for the community because of his inability to be an ordinary "nigga." Gunnar's inability to be an objective "reader" of ghetto life is parallel to John H. McWhorter's intensely problematic diatribe *Losing the Race: Self-Sabotage in Black America*, in which McWhorter shares the story of how he was "beat down" by a group of black seven- and eight-year-olds—the specific culprit being the little sister of one of the group members—because he knew how to spell the word *concrete*. McWhorter uses the story to frame his opinions about what he calls a "cultural disconnect from learning" among black youth. My point here is not to quarrel specifically with McWhorter's opinions (and there are many to quarrel with) but to suggest that his critique raises obvious questions as to whether his position as a middle-class professor at Berkeley, who at times in his life and career has viewed the very idea of black community as a form of tyranny, provides him with the necessary connection to the community to render a legitimate read of it. It should be noted that the post-soul era has produced a wide range of political and social commentary on the black community, regardless of the social and political positions of the authors of these text. I am not suggesting that any clear-cut formula can determine which commentaries are more valid, but highlighting the difficulties that such an attempt would entail if connection or disconnection from the community were used as the primary criterion.[10]

Rather than questioning the validity of "foreign" ethnography, Beatty instead places the role of the traditional ethnographer in crisis by suggesting that the very presumption that he or she is studying authentic black culture is flawed in the first place. Beatty implies that most contemporary ethnography on "black" ghetto culture is faulty; that which is deemed authentic black popular culture is not only distorted by the process of commercialization but often repackaged to the very communities from which it was initially appropriated. For Beatty, black urban enclaves like West Los Angeles are little more than neocolonialist outposts where blacks and Latinos are stockpiled. Gunnar initially describes West Los Angeles as a community surrounded by "a great concrete wall that spans its entire curved perimeter save for an arched gateway at the southeast entrance. . . . At the bottom of this great wall live hordes of impoverished American Mongols."[11] In a later segment, Gunnar describes a local park as "an overgrown inner-city rainforest that some Brazilian lumber company needed to uproot."[12] What is mined and distributed from these ghetto enclaves is the language, music, and style that germinate from the everyday realities of black life. Gunner initially becomes aware of the "commercial" value of black urban style based on his inability to engage linguistically with the "natives"; as he states, "In a world where body and spoken language are currency, I was broke as hell."[13] In response to the physical threats posed by his inability to "speak" with the natives, Gunnar remakes himself into a postmodern Thoreau, who finds refuge in the camping section of the local Montgomery Ward. Beatty's allusion to Thoreau's rejection of the intrusions of industrialization and commercialization in the nineteenth century suggests the ways in which artists like himself have to create safe havens away from the glare of mass culture. The fact that Gunnar finds refuge in a large department store presumably located in a large mall implies that these artists can never escape the impositions of mass culture. Here Beatty also highlights the ways in which public space has eroded and become commercialized.[14] Beatty insinuates that the forms of black popular culture or "street culture" that were integral to the survival strategies of folks in the community are now controlled by large corporations that are insensitive to the role that popular culture(s) plays in their lives.

The relationship between the "ghetto as neocolonialist state" and the engines of corporate capitalism becomes clearer when the "Moribund Videoworks" company begins to film a rap video in front of Gunnar's house. For Beatty there is a clear connection between the music video industry and the genre of Tarzan/Jungle films that emerged in the 1930s and 1940s and reinforced popular perceptions of Africa as the "dark continent" whose natives needed to be tamed and civilized. In one scene the video's director is heard through a bullhorn: "Bwana wants to shoot this scene through an orange filter to make it seem like the sun's been stabbed and the heavens are bleeding onto the streets. Special effects can make the flames shoot farther out from the barrel of the Uzi."[15] The director's instructions suggest the ways that the violence in many hip-hop videos and films, such as *Menace II Society* and *Belly*, is stylized for audience consumption, rather than being representative of the true nature of ghetto violence. Beatty suggest that the "sybaritic rappers and hired concubines" are themselves aware of the nature of this relationship, as one actor later queries: "How was that, massa? Menacing enough for you?"[16]

Gunnar also observes the ways in which urban neocolonialism empowers local gatekeepers. Like the various politicians and entrepreneurs who directly profit from urban empowerment zones like the one that has facilitated the "Disneyfication" of Harlem, one local politician, named Pete "Hush Money" Brocklington, asserts that the video shoot will help pour loads of money into the community. What is more problematic for Beatty is the impact on Gunnar's community in the aftermath of the video's completion. As Beatty observes via Gunnar, "The Hollywood ethnographers were no longer examining the traditional native dances, and the dancers' hands slowly dropped down to their sides, their rumps stopped shaking. Like photogenic Riefenstahl Nubians watching the white god's helicopter pull away, the Hillside denizens watched the film crew coil the cables, load the trucks, and hustle off, leaving us to fight over the blessed remnants of Western civilization they left behind. My tribe wrestled for the rights to broken doughnuts and oily ham 'n' cheese croissants."[17]

The description of the film company as "ethnographers" is important because it highlights the ways rap videos and ghettocentric cinema attempt to translate the conditions of the 'hood to mainstream audiences for profit, but also how such products can affect public policy in relation to the inhabitants of those neighborhoods. Where the *Tarzan* series and others of that ilk helped desensitize audiences to the plight of the African continent and validated, in the public mind at least, continued efforts to colonize various African states, films such as *Boyz in the Hood* and *New Jack City* helped to heighten public desires for increasing the ranks of law enforcement officers and the reform of criminal law, like the various versions of "three strikes" legislation that cropped up in the late 1980s and 1990s. Furthermore, in the aftermath of corporate occupation of ghetto environments, the "natives" are left to struggle for the scraps left behind.

Throughout the text Beatty suggests that "immersion" within the enclaves of black and Latino ghetto life must be balanced by an active knowledge and understanding of mass culture. In Beatty's worldview, "organic" black life and culture, in its variant forms, is a product of not only the material conditions of black folk but also their engagement with the constructions of blackness currently existing within mass culture. As the author, Beatty, who earned a graduate degree in psychology from Boston University, becomes an ideal ethnographer because he is literate in both the dynamics of black urban life and the scholarly tools used to examine these spaces in traditional ways. Gunnar's struggle to understand his own "black" identity, often in opposition to those constructed via mass culture and further institutionalized within the educational system, the justice and penal systems, the film industry, and organized sports, forms the basis of his transition from "freak" to "organic" cultural critic. In the process Beatty and Gunnar morph into the kind of "intellectual" capable of producing cultural criticism rooted in the lived experiences of black urban dwellers, while also employing various discourses valuable in the ethnographic process. In this way Gunnar and Beatty are allowed to speak both with and for the post-soul generation, while serving as translator for the larger mainstream public. Gunnar admits to the duality of his (and

Beatty's) role in his "first" poem, "Negro Appropriation of Greek Mythology or I Know Niggers That'll Kick Hercules's Ass," as he writes:

> i have a notion
> that if i could translate
> the slobberin bellows of Ray-Ray
> the ubiquitous retarded boy's
> swollen-tongued incantations
> i'd find Melpomene reciting the day's obituaries
> anyone here speak Down syndrome or crack baby?[18]

Gunnar writes this poem after his first introduction to his next-door neighbor, Psycho Lobo, a local "gangsta" whose reputation has preceded him and who is home on parole for murdering a paramedic. Psycho Lobo and Gunnar initially bond when Psycho hears the latter singing the Edwin Hawkins classic, "Oh Happy Day," which he sang to pass time when he was serving time in the "Oliver Twist Institute for Little Wanderers and Wayward Minority Males." Psycho Lobo, as the leader of a local gang called "Gun Totin' Hooligans," is the alter ego of Juan Julio, a choirboy in the "First Ethiop Azatlan Catholic-Baptist Church"—a name emblematic of the creolized cultures that emerge in close spaces among various ethnic and racial communities.

The title of Gunnar's poem references the ways that black and Latino youth appropriate various "texts" to construct their identities, often distorting the appropriated texts in the process. The best examples of this are the ways that some contemporary hip-hop artists have used narratives from mainstream gangster films like *Scarface* (arguably a core text in the body of gangsta rap recordings), *Goodfellows*, and *Donnie Brasco*. One member of the Gun Totin' Hooligans, for instance, was a skinny black kid named Joe Shenanigans, who claimed familial relations with Sicilian mafiosi. The segment of the poem quoted above speaks to the ways that "ghetto" dwellers are naturally readers of the social and cultural dimensions of their experiences, but are unable or even unwilling to translate that reality to larger publics. This segment of the poem is reminiscent of the ways hip-hop has often been referred to as "noise" by blacks and whites alike, without any consideration of the ways that the genre's lyrics, in the best case, attempt to convey urban life to larger audiences. The poem is initially "published" on the wall that surrounds Gunnar's West

Los Angeles neighborhood, transcribed there by Gunnar's via the kind of spray paint cans synonymous with the graffiti art that accompanied the emergence of hip-hop culture in the early 1970s. This act places the poem in an obvious popular context in relation to Gunnar's community— arguably a counter-hegemonic act when considered alongside the graffiti tagging that took place in New York City in the 1970s[19]—but in that the poem also becomes the stimulus for Gunnar's later mainstream fame as the "unknown street poet," it highlights the duality of Gunnar's work.

Gunnar's relationships with his best friend Nicholas Scoby and later his mail-order bride Yoshiko allow Beatty to examine specific facets of the post-soul condition, while also marking Gunnar's transition to post-soul critic and unwilling "ghetto-fab" spokesperson or translator. Prior to his move to Hillside, Gunnar acknowledged that the only black folks that he knew by name were athletes and musicians such as Jimi Hendrix, Jackie Joyner-Kersee, and Valerie, the only black character in the cartoon series *Josie and the Pussycats*. The last example captures the way Saturday-morning programming geared to school-age children attempted to present a multicultural/ethnic world in the 1970s.[20] Gunnar's introduction to Nicholas Scoby serves as a catalyst to his acceptance within the community, as well as providing him with alternative concepts of black cultural expression. Gunnar initially describes Scoby as the "thuggish boy" and "autistic hoodlum" who sat in the back of their drama class, swaying back and forth to music funneled through his top-of-the-line headphones. Ironically, Scoby, while often oblivious to classroom instruction, is an exceptional and gifted student. Eschewing the R&B and hip-hop usually associated with young African Americans, Scoby instead listens to Julian "Cannonball" Adderley and other jazz performers. Scoby's knowledge and love of jazz music introduces Gunnar to alternative examples of black culture, particularly forms that are not as intensely commercialized as hip-hop. Gunnar's slow but conscious embrace of alternative or even highbrow forms of black cultural expression is witnessed in an exchange with a local "Afrocentric" group called NAPPY (New African Politicized Pedantic Yahoos). In response to continuous charges that he was a sellout, whose "fertile African mind" has been infested by white propaganda, Gunnar often flashes copies of books by Audre Lorde or Sterling Brown. Beatty's referencing of those authors, whose work actively celebrated forms of black folk culture, is a subtle response to charges among some Afrocentric thinkers that the folk culture of blacks is not representative of their "true" African identity. Gunnar further trumps the "true mathematics" theories—think here of Louis Farrakhan's "numerology" lesson during his speech at the Million Man March—expounded by groups like the Nation of Islam offshoot the Five Percent Nation by responding, "You niggers ain't hard—calculus is hard."[21]

Gunnar's friendship with Scoby (and the larger community of Hillside) is cemented, at least in Gunnar's mind, when the latter says, "Yeah, nigger, let's get together later this week." For Gunnar, that he has been embraced linguistically as a "nigger" and symbolically with his first soul shake ("My transitional slide into step two was a little stiff, but I made up for it with a loud finger snap as our hands parted"[22]) creates a context in which he views himself as part of the Hillside community. Scoby's acceptance of Gunnar is particularly important to Gunnar's sense of his own racial identity in that one of his friend's many "obscure" talents is being able to "smell a passing octoroon from a block away."[23] The fact that Scoby sees him as a "nigger" means that Gunnar's "blackness" is no longer placed in question. Gunnar's relationship with his new 'hood is further manifested when he accompanies Scoby to a pickup basketball game during school recess. As it is Gunnar's first game of basketball, a fact that heightens his queerness in his new environment, he literally learns the rules of the game minutes before he takes the court, particularly perplexed by in-game offenses like "double dribble," "foul," and "traveling." Given an explanation that one "travels" when attempting a jump shot and returning to the ground without releasing the ball, Gunnar derisively responds, "Traveled where?" In a comical moment during the game, Gunnar dunks his first basketball, largely because he is fearful of returning to the ground with the ball still in his possession. The dunk solidifies his position within "community," as fellow players are heard to utter, "Yo, that nigger had legs akimbo" and "Scoby, your boy's got like crazy hops."

Gunnar's acceptance is predicated on the fact that he proves proficient in the kind of informal activities where young black males are allowed to share in forms of masculine expression. For example, the connections between language and physical skills in the construction of black male peer groups, particularly in urban settings, can be witnessed in schoolyard pickup games like 21 (a rite of masculine passage), where masculinity is asserted by physical prowess, by rhetorical dexterity, or, in the most powerful instances, by both. In other words, it's incumbent on those who want to be considered part of the "crew" either to possess "mad skills" or be able to "talk shit." Gunnar's ability to excel physically gains him entrance to the space of

141

young black masculine expression, allowing him to differentiate that which is "lived" from that which is commercialized and consumed as products of black male vernacular expression. The later example is witnessed, for instance, in the clips of NBA and collegiate basketball players on cable sports channels like ESPN, CNN-SI, or Fox Sports, where single clips of spectacular dunks are often broadcast twenty times a day. Ultimately Beatty even undermines the presumption that basketball in urban spaces is solely the province of black males when Gunnar meets a group of "aging local legends," with last names like Morales and Ng and first names like Melissa.

Scoby himself is a schoolboy baller of some distinction, possessing a jump shot that never misses. Scoby's dual identities as schoolboy basketball star and gifted student show Gunnar how he could integrate his own seemingly disparate identities. Scoby's identity, however, is often still reduced to his prowess as a basketball player, despite his extraordinary intellect. That throughout the novel he is perceived as little more a jock by others is particularly ironic, given that he will later be followed and hounded by scientists and academics who want to study his "uncanny" ability to always put the ball in the hoop. The ensuing struggles that occur between the philosophy, African-American studies, biology, and other departments at Boston University over the right to examine Scoby highlight the fact that he has become a research object, a body to be claimed by "science" to fill the research coiffeurs of the university or by Afrocentric scholars, who would no doubt claim that Scoby's talents validate the higher capabilities of the "black man . . . the original man." Any serious considerations that Scoby's abilities might be a product more of his intellectual capabilities than of his physical gifts are rare, as the constant adulation and prodding become, in themselves, a form of incarceration for him. Echoing Charles Barkley's widely circulated assertion that he is "not a role model," Scoby admits to Gunnar, "I'm tired of these fanatics rubbing on me, pulling on my arms. . . . I'm not no fucking Tiki doll, no fucking icon. Don't folk have anything better to do with their lives than pay attention to what I'm doing?"[24] Through Scoby, Beatty alludes to the classic contradictions associated with being a black male icon, where star athletes are often held to such a high standard that if they fail to maintain the standard they themselves have set, the public may often attribute to them the same failings traditionally assigned to black men, such as laziness and shiftlessness.[25] For Scoby the heightened surveillance, in this case camouflaged as celebrity, and the hyperexpectations associated with his athletic skills are not much different from the challenges faced by black men during the antebellum period.

Gunnar's acerbic description of Scoby's plight—"Tote that barge, shoot that basketball, lift that bale, nigger ain't you ever heard of Dred Scott"[26]—is not simply a reduction of Scoby's plight to that of enslaved blacks but a commentary on how even the celebrity associated with Scoby's talents, or those of NBA players, does not allow them to transcend their positions as commodities to be bought, sold, owned, and exhibited. This way, the National Basketball Association can be seen as a postmodern "plantation," one in which up-and-coming "Dred Scotts" like Scoby and Gunnar are identified as early as junior high school. Because pre–Civil War chattel slavery has been reduced in the popular view to the mistreatment of blacks, the fact that the plantation functioned as an economic model is often obscured. Though Minnesota Timberwolves star Kevin Garnett may have a contract worth more than $100 million, his role as a laborer in relation to the ownership of capital has not dramatically changed—it has only been obscured by the high rate of his wages. It is not my intention to suggest that Garnett and others are being exploited the same way that hourly wage earners at McDonalds or the United Parcel Service are, or that they are, deserving of sympathy—clearly it is their choice to be exploited at $14 or $15 million a year—but there is a correlation between the exploitation of black male physical talents, be they on the plantations of the South in the 1840s or the postmodern plantations of the Fleet Center and Madison Square Garden, and high-level capital accumulation by corporate "plantation" owners. Not that black players are the only ones exploited in this system, but given the large black presence in the league—as high as 80 percent at the moment—black masculine expression on the basketball court is clearly the primary commodity consumed, even when that expression is recast in the "street" playing of white stars like Jayson "White Chocolate" Williams or Brent Barry. Ironically there is some extra value associated with whiteness in the NBA. Citing a 1999 study initially published in *Industrial Relations*, Kenneth Shropshire highlights the wage gap in the NBA that benefits white players and the fact that white players have 36 percent less chance of being cut, which translates into an average career expectancy two years longer than that of black players.[27]

Beatty is also conscious of this disparity, as he suggests that white "geniuses," such as chess player Bobby Fischer and novelist J. D. Salinger, have been allowed to retreat from the public eye. The key difference is that black male athletes are commodities in the heavily commercialized institution of professional sports, which transcends simple athletic competition and is intensely connected to the media and advertising industries in ways that Fischer's and Salinger's singular talents could never sustain. While television and movie stars are also hypercommodified, not often is their visibility and popularity tied to the element of genius. In this way, Beatty suggest that the kind of genius exhibited by black basketball players is often seen as solely the product of their sheer primitive physical skills, not their intellect or genius.[28] When Scoby is asked why he continues to play basketball, given the negative impact it has on him, Scoby responds, "Do what you do best. That's what I've heard my whole life."[29] Scoby's response recalls the classic black uplift narrative that I will paraphrase as, "If you have to be a street cleaner, be the best street cleaner you can be." An offshoot of the Booker T. Washington–dominated era of accommodation and the general investment in the "American Dream" by a wide range of American citizens, the phrase has helped generations of blacks take pride in their work, no matter how lowly, while also diverting attention from the real economic exploitation encompassed in the labor of those workers. Scoby's response addresses not only the ways that black males are tracked into athletic activities within the educational structure but also the constraints placed on young black men in terms of how they respond to their tracking and the very nature of that experience.

After his well-publicized attempt to choke his coach, Latrell Sprewell was suspended for sixty-eight games, which translated into $6.4 million of his annual $8.3 million yearly salary. According to Shropshire, the penalty, which was one of the most stringent in sports history, was a product of the "pervading sense that something had to be done to get the players back in line."[30] Sprewell punishment followed a series of less "violent" offenses by Nick Van Excel, Charles Barkley, Dennis Rodman, and Mahmud Abdul-Rauf (Chris Jackson), who refused to stand during the performance of the National Anthem during the 1995–96 season.[31] The perceived insolence of black basketball players infected public perceptions of the "lockout" of players by the league's owners prior to the 1998 season. At the crux of the disagreement between the players and the owners was the latter's desire to introduce a salary cap that would place limits on the players' earnings. Within the popular media the players were often portrayed as strikers who were demanding more money as opposed to laborers who were resisting having limitations placed on their earning potential within the league. It goes without saying that many fans and commentators, who often viewed the players' demands in the context of their own earnings, felt that the players should be happy for what they had. In the aftermath of the lockout and the subsequent retirement of the league's flagship product, Michael Jordan, the league has struggled to find players with the crossover image that Jordan cultivated into an industry unto itself. Many players, most notably Allen Iverson and Chris Webber, have been criticized for not living up to the sanitized and palatable image that Jordan parlayed into a cottage industry, regardless of their success on the court as ball players. Images that don't fit into the template that Jordan created, like Allen Iverson's "gangsta rap" recording and his corn-rows, have been viewed as a form of insolence.

Beatty examines perceptions of black male insolence during Gunnar's senior year at El Campesino high school, the "white" school Gunnar is transferred to after being caught stealing a safe from Montgomery Ward. Gunnar is one of a few black athletes—perpetually smiling scholastic lawn jockeys"—at the school.[32] Gunnar particularly resists the perception that he was the "Golden Child, white society's mercenary come to teach the pagans a lesson."[33] Gunnar's parents force him to transfer to El Campesino for just that reason; to sanitize him from elements within Hillside. Gunnar's use by the school as the "model negro" is parallel to the comparisons made between Iverson and Tim Duncan or Grant Hill, whose pedigree includes a former NFL player and Yale graduate as a father and a Washington-based lawyer for a mother. In a league that commercial-izes black male urban expression, players are defined via their class interests or failure to accept the "special" responsibilities and upper-middle-class sensibilities that being an elite athlete engenders. In his own effort to undermine these false distinctions, Gunnar embraces the role of the smil-ing "Sambo." Prior to the introductions of the starting five for an important play-off game between El Campesino and his old school, Phyllis Wheatley, Gunnar inserts fake middle names like "Rastus," "Aunt Jemima," "Nigger T." Gunner himself is announced to the crowd as "Gunnar 'Hambone, Hambone, Have You Heard'" as he speeds on court in full minstrel regalia: white gloves and white cold cream smeared on his face. After being berat-ed by his coach, Gunnar removes his uniform and chooses to sit next to his former coach from Phyllis Wheatley, which incidentally wins the game by sixty points. Gunnar has effectively undermined the distinctions made between himself and his former mates at the school, something that many NBA players, for instance, have been unwilling to do, as many of them were either indifferent to or critical of Abdul-Rauf's refusal to pledge allegiance to the American flag.[34]

Beatty is perhaps most provocative when critiquing Gunnar's later celebrity as "street poet," raising questions about his own celebrity in the process. Shortly after his graduation from El Campesino and his acceptance at Boston University, Psycho Loco shows his gratitude for Gunnar's friendship by buying him a male-order bride from Japan, Yoshiko Katso. Yoshiko is easily the most underdeveloped of the book's major characters, but her presence provides the springboard for Beatty's concerns over the globalization of black popular culture. Yoshiko's first words of English to Gunnar and his family are a recitation of the opening bars of Run-DMC's classic "Sucker MCs." Gunnar later finds out that Yoshiko became a mail-order bride largely to be able to attend an American university, chosing Gunnar after reading his poem "Your Problem Is" in a Japanese magazine. Gunnar's shock that his poem had been published abroad is not unlike the surprise felt by many hip-hop artists in the early 1990s that their music was being well received in Japan and other Asian and European nations. Gunnar will fully understand the intensity of his cult status during his first and only class at Boston University, in which Gunnar is made aware that he has become a cult figure, as various students and the instructor recite lines from his "published" poems. Particularly intriguing to Gunnar is the coffee-table book of photographs of his "graffitied" poems, entitled *Ghettotopia: An Anthropological Rending of the Ghetto through the Street Poems of an Unknown Street Poet Named Gunnar Kaufman.* The incredulous Gunnar responds, "What they mean by 'an unknown street poet named Gunnar Kaufman'? More to the point, what the hell is street poet?"[35] The title of the coffee-table book suggests that Gunnar's readings of the ghetto are authentic, but likely only so because he is literate in a language that is respected by literary critics, while remaining ensconced in the kind of "ghetto" culture that those same critics view as authentic. One of Gunnar's classmates, in fact, offers that the "urban piquancy" of Gunnar's work is so "resonant, so resplendent, so resounding" that he makes the "destitution" of his experiences "leap off the page."[36] Much like the happy singing Sambo that littered Hollywood screens in the 1930s and 1940s or the "ghetto-fab" day laborer who is thought to prefer to wear $150 Nike sneakers than buy a warm coat,

Gunnar is perceived as the poet of the urban downtrodden, who are amicably so, hence the title *Ghettotopia*. Gunnar's questioning of "street poet" exemplifies one of the ways mass culture, even elite highbrow mass culture—if such a concept is not a contradiction—appropriates various underground subcultures, ultimately having the power to name, market, and describe these subcultures in an effort to reach the widest audience possible.

But Gunnar remains absent in his own work—seemingly because "ghetto-fab" poets have no interest in such visibility—as his celebrity is largely the product of those who "spin" his work to catch the attention of the presumably savvy, chic readers who buy the fictional literary magazine *Locution* and who take creative writing courses at New England universities. In this regard, Beatty takes a subtle swipe at literary critics and the academic fields of critical theory and cultural studies, where star critics are born via the "deconstruction" of often obscure texts. It is also very much a criticism of black intellectuals and academics, including Beatty himself, who employ a significant amount of critical energy engaging forms of black popular culture, very often without any meaningful impact on the communities that generated those cultures. This is perhaps the most profound ambivalence experienced by post-soul critics, including myself, as many of us wonder if our success as popular critics comes at the expense of those we claim to best represent. As Beatty well knows, there are likely many black critics and intellectuals for which pimping the misery of black folks is solely a necessary corollary to their efforts to validate their presence at elite academic institutions or highbrow weekly and monthly journals. Prior to his decision to attend Boston University, Gunnar was recruited by a black "bespectacled public intellectual" who had set up a think tank in Los Angeles to study what he referred to as a "Petri dish for criminal vermin." Queried by Gunnar as to his real intentions, the Harvard intellectual admits that the "only reason I and others of my illustrious ilk pretend to help those folks is to reinforce the difference between them and us."[37] The black professor's interest in recruiting Gunnar to Harvard is very much an effort to buttress his reputation as a gatekeeper of black intellectual property, be it those folks aligned closely to him or the fields of knowledge that he can claim expertise in and thus control, as the title of his book *Antebellum Cerebellums: A History of Negro Super-Genius* insinuates. In this regard the black scholar is no different than Gunnar's writing instructor, Oscar Edelstein, though the latter is capable of delivering a publishing contract and advance to Gunnar. Beatty seems cognizant that no matter how visible black public intellectuals or, for the sake of argument, post-soul critics and intellectuals become, their power rarely transcends their own material spheres or the academic departments and programs they hold sway over; Gunnar admits as much when he suggests to the Harvard recruiter that the recruiter is "no Lionel Trilling."[38]

With Edelstein's intervention, Gunnar publishes his first book of poetry for Gatekeeper Press. The book's title, *Watermelanin,* represents a subtle clowning of racist whites who have seen blacks as little more than watermelon-eating "Sambos," and lay Afrocentrists who have endowed blacks with melanin-induced superpowers. Gunnar's fame is predicated on his ability not to take that fame seriously as he uses his five minutes of fame—selling over 126 million copies of a book of poetry in the process— to provide a necessary self-criticism of himself and black political movements. Invited to speak at a rally protesting Boston University's support of "M'm'mofo Gottobelizi," a South African tribal leader loosely based on Zulu chief Mangosuthu Buthelezi, whose willingness to cut side deals with the South African government in the 1980s helped to undermine the antiapartheid efforts of the African National Conference (ANC), Gunnar trumps the "righteous" consciousness that is often the inherent by-product of campus activism. By suggesting that such activism is the product of the superficial nature of college and university environments, Gunnar asserts that many of these activists are not "ready to die for black rule in South Africa." Gunnar admits his own complicity in this process by admitting, "I want them niggers to get theirs, but I'm not willing to die for South Africa."[39] Referencing the Notorious B.I.G. recording *Ready to Die,* Gunnar admits that he is not willing to die for anything, and thus serves no real social purpose. In the context of his political inertia, Gunnar admits to himself that "I ain't ready to die for anthing, so I guess I'm not fit to live. In other words I'm just ready to die."[40] In Gunnar's mind he and the larger black community are already dead.

Gunnar's self-criticism is then extended to contemporary black leadership. Clearly referencing media-savvy black political leaders like the Reverend Jesse Jackson, the Reverend Al Sharpton, NAACP head Kweisi Mfume, and even Minister Louis Farrakhan, Gunnar states, "That's why today's black leadership isn't worth shit, these telegenic niggers not willing to die. Back in the old days, if someone spoke up against the white man, he or she was willing to die. Today's housebroken niggers travel the country talking themselves hoarse about barbarous white devils, knowing that those devil aren't going to send them to a black hell. . . . What we need is some new leaders. Leaders who won't apostatize like cowards. Some niggers who are ready to die."[41]

Gunnar's critique of black leadership is notable because it speaks to the levels at which these leaders remain invested in a system in which they lobby for the ability to be administrators, gatekeepers, and brokers. An example of this is Jesse Jackson and other prominent black leaders brokering with founding Democratic Leadership Council (DLC) members Bill Clinton and Al Gore (postmodern Dixiecrats really) to deliver the "black vote," despite the general conservative nature of the organization—for the black masses. Given Gunnar's notion that the term *nigger* is a metaphor for community and authenticity, his assertion that black leadership needs "niggers who are willing to die" is tantamount to a call for a subaltern leadership that will emerge from within. On a subtle level, Gunner's use of the more traditional *nigger* as opposed to various forms of the phrase such as *nigga* or *nigguh* is evidence that he is not authentically "subaltern" enough to provide the kind of leadership needed for the black masses. Ironically, Gunnar's rejection of the concept of black leadership became the stimulus for his own ascendancy to the position of the leader of the masses, as his admission that he is ready to die, or rather already dead, leads to mass black suicides. Those suicides suggest that real empowerment among the ghetto masses can never be achieved unless leadership emerges from within, as imported leadership, be it the traditional civil rights leadership or Gunnar himself, does little more than administer over the "already dead."

In an interview, Beatty seems to directly address the differences between subaltern critic and "ghetto-fab" ethnographer, stating his annoyance when "people tell me that my work is 'street smart.' . . . I do research and scribble down observations, but just because I'm a black writer writing about these characters doesn't mean I'm producing autobiography. 'Street-smart' is one of those backhanded compliments, because it also implies lack of imagination."[42] The interview was done in support of his second novel, *Tuff*. In an attempt to address the concept of subaltern authenticity, the novel was originally titled *Nigger Tuff*. According to Beatty, editors at Knopf felt that the title was "bad-mouthing" the character. Beatty adds that "calling him a 'nigger' isn't necessarily bad-mouthing him. It's about getting inside a character's self-perception, self-definition, analyzing the way in which they interact with the world around them."[43] Specifically, the novel examines the ascendancy of

Winston "Tuff" Foshay from local 'hood rat and drug dealer to subaltern leader of the people. The character is transformed in this way when he decides to run for a seat on the city council, against a self-styled black elite who is not of the community. I would suggest that it does represent Beatty's effort to get at the construction and understanding of legitimate and "authentic" leadership within black urban enclaves, an issue that ultimately drives many post-soul critics and artists.

"A Feminism Brave Enough to Fuck with the Grays": The Around-the-Way Feminisms of Joan Morgan and Jill Scott

No one will ever accuse LL Cool J (James Smith) of being a feminist spokesperson. In 1990 the self-described king of hip-hop love songs embarked on a comeback of sorts with the release of his fourth recording, *Mama Said Knock You Out.* One of the highlights of that recording was "Round the Way Girl." The song was not only an articulation of LL's desire to remain rooted in the Queens, New York, communities that bred him but, more profoundly, an articulation of the affections that he held for the young women of those communities. LL was not just posturing; he eventually married a "round the way girl" after being linked publicly with many high-profile women, including Quincy Jones's daughter Kiadda. Years before those "round the way girls" had been recast within black popular culture as chickenheads, baby mamas, skeezers, and crack hos, LL gave praise to the "ghetto" girl next door; she of Sunday-morning Bible school, Now-or-Laters, double-dutch contests, jellies (low-end plastic shoes), and attitude for days and days.

However much LL gave praise to those "brown-skinned" woman-girls from around the way, he could not speak to their dreams, desires, and disappointments. Joan Morgan is one of those "round the way" girls. Growing up in the South Bronx and a product of the "young, gifted, and black" era of black uplift narratives (ask anyone who graduated from a Head Start program in the early 1970s), Morgan's first book, *When Chickenheads Come Home to Roost: My Life as a Hip-Hop Feminist,* gives a voice to that "round the way girl" who LL described as "a neighborhood jewel."[44] Morgan begins her book, in fact, by acknowledging her own desires to be a "round-the-way" girl while growing up in the Bronx in the 1970s:

It started with a dress. A hot little thing . . . in that shade of orange that black girls do the most justice. I bought it in La-La Land precisely because it reminded me of New York in the seventies, with its sexy sistas and those leotard and dance skirt sets they used to rock back in the day. This was back when I was a shorty with cherries for breast and absolutely no ass to speak of. I used to sit on our tenement stoop mesmerized by the way those flimsy little tops knew how to hug a tittie in all the right places, or the way a proper Bronx Girl Switch (two parts Switch to one part Bop) could make the skirt move like waves. Wide-eyed, I watched regla project girls transform into Black Moseses capable of parting seas of otherwise idle negroes. . . . And I couldn't wait to be one.[45]

For Morgan the femininity and sexuality of these women provided them with a power arguably fleeting at best, lasting only until the next ghetto conjure woman came round and switched just a little harder. Ironically the "dress" was bought to wear at the twentieth-anniversary celebration of Ntozake Shange's *For Colored Girls Who Have Considered Suicide/When the Rainbow Is Enuff.* Morgan is exhilarated both by her attendance at the event—she elaborates on her disappointment (she calls it a hissy fit) over her mother's decision to choose her father to accompany her to see the play during its original run in 1975 and not Joan—and by the black male passer-by who calls out, "Heey lady in orange." Here she is as consumed by the fact that she can finally express the kind of brown-girl sexuality that she witnessed as a young girl as she is by her own memories of how important Shange's work was to the generation of brown girls that came to maturity during the Reagan era. This segment introduces Morgan's ongoing ambivalence about the role of patriarchy in her life. She is conflicted between directly addressing the damaging aspects of black patriarchy, as Shange's play does, or holding out for a more benevolent patriarchy that she can hold in check via the employment of her sexuality.

In this opening chapter, "Dress Up," Morgan begins her book-length meditation on the contradictions of being a "round-the-way feminist," as she is challenged within the black community for a willingness to write publicly about sexism and misogyny and fearful that her legitimate critiques of black men can be seen as adding to the existing threats to black men posed by institutional structures like the prison industrial complex, the labor force, and so on. These broad contradictions accompany the more profound ones that Morgan herself confronts with regards to her feminist sensibilities, her natural heterosexual desires, and the seeming disconnect between the social cache she has earned as a highly visible member of the New York post-soul "niggeratti" and the humble Jamaica/South Bronx background that clearly fuels her intellectual sensibilities and remains central to her concerns. In Morgan these contradictions and disconnections are endemic to the post-soul era. It is this way that Morgan is able to recover, more or less, the value of hip-hop music and culture and hence her desire for a hip-hop feminism that is not afraid to "fuck with the grays."[46] Arguably, if hip-hop has done anything, it has been willing to confront and critique the gray areas of black identity, black community, black sexuality, and black material desires and attainment. As Morgan describes it, the willingness to deal with those "grays" guarantees the post-soul generation "a few trips to the terror-dome, forcing us to finally confront what we'd all rather hide from."[47]

What Morgan seemingly would rather hide from is the "chicken-head" that lurks within herself and many black women of her generation, and thus the book is an ongoing struggle between the chickenheads and the self-described "smart, successful, hard-working, educated, super-independent black girls."[48] For an analogy, imagine hip-hop artist Lil' Kim waging war with post-soul journalist Farai Chideya on MTV's *Celebrity Death Match,* with the winner impacting the future of black female representation in mass media. The undercard matches could be between stripper-turned-actress Lisa Raye (*The Player's Club*) and former deputy White House counsel Cheryl Mills, and an "old-school" match between Angela Davis and Millie Jackson.[49] The perceived antics of chickenheads aside, what Morgan really seems to struggle with is coming to terms with her own class interests and the contradiction that her middle-class status poses in relation to her working-class past. It is a contraction that defines many within the post-soul generation and has informed much of the writing of that generation's intelligentsia. Morgan is able to reaffirm her connection to community, ironically, by an investment in benevolent black patriarchy and black male (hetero) sexuality. Her investment in the latter is not unlike the road traveled by the group Salt 'N' Pepa. Buoyed by tracks like "Express Yourself" and "Let's Talk about Sex," the group cultivated an image of being hip-hop feminist. To counter perceptions that feminism was "antimale," the group began to record tracks and make videos in the mid-1990s that celebrated black masculinity and sexuality, such as "Shoop" and especially "Whatta Man," which featured vocals from En Vogue, themselves recovering from "antimale" backlash at their song "Never Gonna Get It," and a cameo by the "thug-nigga" of the moment, Tupac Shakur.

In the book's best chapter, "Hip-hop Feminist," Morgan examines her own feelings about the Million Man March. Unlike many prominent black feminists and more than a few progressive black male intellectuals, most notably Manning Marable, Morgan was not upset that black women were unofficially banished from the march.[50] According to Morgan, it is important to acknowledge the differences between male and female spaces. While I agree that such spaces are necessary and meaningful, as witnessed by the importance of barbershops and beauty parlors, for example, it is quite another thing when black male spaces are convened publicly in the name of speaking for and representing the totality of the community, whether those spaces be called the Million Man March, the National Basketball Association, or the national membership of One Hundred Black Men. Morgan's support of the march was in part stimulated by her belief that such a moment would never occur within the context of a black feminist movement. She argues that the failure of black feminist movements to take hold within the post-soul generation is rooted in a fracture between the issues that black women face and the general perception among black women about what exactly black feminism is. In response to assertions that black women don't have "time for all that shit," Morgan writes, "The shit that black women don't have time for is dying and suffering from exorbitant rates of solo parenting, domestic violence, drug abuse, incarceration, AIDS and cancer," all issues that a black feminist movement would likely address. Morgan suggests that these feelings about feminism are based on perceptions that feminism is driven by white "braless, butch-cut, anti-babes, who seemed to think the solution to sexism was reviling all things male and sleeping with each other."[51] She blames her own generation's ambivalence toward feminism on "black women's historic tendency to blindly defend any black man who seems to be under attack from white folks,"[52] hence the community's "principled" closing of ranks around problematic figures like former Washington, D.C., mayor Marion Berry, National Baptist Convention leader Henry Lyons, and O. J. Simpson.

For black feminism to work, Morgan suggests that it must be an apparatus responsive to issues that "explore who we are as women—not victims,"[53] not solely the role that black men play in making them victims. In an attempt to create such a feminism for herself, Morgan raises several critical questions: "Can you be a good feminist and admit out loud that there are things that you dig about patriarchy?" "Is it foul to say that imagining a world where you could paint your big brown lips in the most decadent of shades, pile your phat ass into your fave micromini . . . and not have one single man objectify you . . . is like a total drag to you?" and lastly, "How come no one ever admits that part of the reason women love hip-hop—as sexist as it is—is 'cuz all that in-yo-face testosterone makes our nipples hard?"[54] In some regards, Morgan's questions are juxtaposing the intellectual with the carnal, a comparison that is embodied in the smart "sista"/chickenhead dichotomy that is the central theme of the book. What Morgan "digs" about patriarchy is connected to the erotic pleasures and the feelings of safety that it generates for her. In Morgan's view, men with certain feminist sensibilities are outside the realm of the erotic; she admits that antisexist worldviews are interesting theoretical concepts that don't do a "damn thing for me erotically."[55] In the essay, Morgan willingly admits that she self-objectifies her body ("slip your freshly manicured toes into four-inch fuck-me sandals"[56]) because of the pleasure that heterosexual objectification brings her. Morgan's choice here is important because it points to the ways little brown girls turned black women are often confronted with disjointed messages about their beauty and physicality; thus the black man who roams "his eyes longingly over all the intended places" provides her with some affirmation of her self-image. Such affirmation is also important to Morgan in purely nonsexual and platonic terms as she seeks to recover a patriarchal figure that makes her "feel safe—like a li'l girl."

Morgan's honesty here is striking; she is willing to confront the hybridity of her own identity in ways that "good" feminists or "good" blacks might find offensive or even destructive—not just airing the proverbial dirty laundry, but also publicly engaging in forms of "friendly fire" that call into question the validity of positions of those ostensibly supportive of her own antiracist and antisexist goals. In the best examples, Morgan raises questions regarding the role of black women who willingly allow themselves to become "video-hos" in rap music videos or the fact that very rarely are the rights of fathers seriously considered in debates over a woman's right to choose. But her comments are also problematic on several levels. Morgan's admission that commodified images of black men in music videos and film make her "nipples hard," despite their sexist and misogynist connotations, suggests her own willingness to objectify black male sexuality. In some ways her celebration of black male sexuality in the context of their sexism and misogyny is no different from the ways that queer black men sexually objectify homophobic black male hip-hop artists,[57] but Morgan fails to acknowledge that the "violence" that black women face because they are sexually objectified also threatens black men, who often struggle to define their own sexuality and identity in comparison to the hypermasculine and hypersexual "thug-niggas" that populate mass culture.[58] Also, her honesty regarding her own erotic pleasures suggests that the choice to willingly objectify her own body is reserved for "smart black women," who presumably understand the limits and dangers of such decisions. At best this knowledge is only available to chickenheads when they are in pursuit of the material protections that black men can provide. For example, in her open letter to Ms. Chicken, Morgan writes, "For the record, none of us are buying that 'airhead' shit. Any fool that's seen you . . . knows you can be calculating, cunning, and savvy as hell."[59]

Morgan admits that the real reason that "smart" black women like herself are critical and even envious of chickenheads is connected to the question "why, with all those skills, your sole ambition in life seems to be the wife (or babymother) of somebody who makes enough chedda to satisfy your shopping jones."[60] Thus Morgan criticizes chickenheads for their investment in patriarchy's material possibilities, in contrast to "smart" black women like herself whose own intellectual talents provide materially and who need patriarchy only for the erotic pleasures and safe "fatherly" haven that it can provide. Morgan's nuanced distinction implies that patriarchy is most powerfully expressed in the ways that black women have been forced to rely on black men for economic support and stability, ultimately limiting the possibility that they may garner some "joy" and "pleasure," to echo Gina Dent's distinction, in their lives. But the distinction is ultimately faulty in Morgan's judgment, as she resolves that "in our loneliest and most vulnerable moments, we . . . wonder if chickenheads aren't the ones who have figured it all out. Is being alone the penalty we pay for doing it the 'right way'? Or is it the penalty we'll pay for seeing a bit of ourselves in you—and fronting like we didn't."[61] Morgan's admission is less a call for a fictitious or even romantic unity between diverse black women than an admission that hip-hop feminism is an activity of intense self-refection made necessarily so by her own hybrid identity as a "round-the-way girl" who has "come up" in the world. In this regard, the chickenhead is symbolic of the dangers posed by the 'hood to "brown girls," and thus Morgan desires a continuous connection to the chickenhead and the world that she inhabits, if only as a gesture predicated on her own conflict over her middle-class status.

Whereas Joan Morgan is often preoccupied with the 'hood that she left behind, vocalist and spoken word artist Jill Scott rarely ventures beyond "round the way." Scott's debut recording, *Who Is Jill Scott? Words and Sounds, Volume 1,* is at once an homage to the North Philly streets where she came of age and a collection of brown-girl narratives that aim less to change the world, or challenge patriarchy for that matter, than to take seriously the cultivation of those spaces, which, Morgan suggests, are necessary for the realization of a brown-girl feminism, if you will. The recording is the first to be released on the Hidden Beach label, which was founded by former Motown executive Steve McKeever via an investment by former NBA icon Michael Jordan and his wife Juanita. Sony/Epic is the label's distributor. The recording's title, *Who Is Jill Scott?* suggests an anonymity that is also reflected in the cover photo of Scott wearing a hat over her eyes, obscuring much of her face. While both convey a sense of mystery natural to the presentation of a new artist, I would like to suggest that the cover photo and title also represent the invisibility and silence of brown girls within the black community and the larger American society. For Scott, her North Philly neighborhood contained possibilities for a "poor black girl," as evidenced by the disc's rear photo, in which a preteen Scott is pictured with a joyous smile. Rarely have black women been allowed to publicly tell the stories of those little brown girls that Scott's childhood photo evokes, unless of course they are best-selling novelists or the beneficiary of the "one black woman public intellectual at a time" rule. The popular recording industry has historically preferred that black women appear, scantily clad, in music videos and promotional photos—particularly those women with the requisite "lite, brite, and lean" physicality—than share meaningful and endearing stories about their experiences that are not solely focused on heterosexual romance. Tricia Rose adds that at a time when "black popular culture has been able to center itself in unprecedented ways in American culture, young black women are generally facilitators in young men's efforts to attain status and display a burgeoning heterosexual masculinity."[62] The legacy of "brown girls" has been distorted and underpromoted within the popular recording industry, as former Arrested Development lead Dionne Farris, Sandra "Mack-Diva" St.

Victor, Carleen Anderson, Amel Larreiux, India Arie, and Angie Stone are perhaps the most visible of what has become an amorphous blob named "alternative" R&B.

What the paucity of brown-girl narratives implies is that within the entertainment industry in general, and the popular recording industry in particular, the voices of black women are largely valued in the service of black male uplift, as in Salt 'N' Pepa's "Shoop," or in the interests of male desire, as in Destiny's Child's video for the song "Bills, Bills, Bills." Though the latter is ostensibly an "independent" woman's critique of her shiftless and parasitic male partner, it is not very hard to imagine male viewers responding along the lines of, "Yeah baby, you can hate on me, but damn, you still look good." The prevalent thought within the industry is that the "sista-girl" narratives of black women are not bankable and thus not promotable, Erykah Badu and Lauryn Hill notwithstanding. In contrast to industry sensibilities, Scott's music is filled with the kind "sister-girlisms" that get exchanged on country porches, tenement stoops, and housing project lobbies along with jars of hair grease, straightening combs, and barbecue pork rinds. It is in these spaces that brown girls get to share their stories with each other and critique a world that often renders their sexuality, ambitions, and fears irrelevant and distorted. *Who Is Jill Scott? Words and Sounds, Volume 1* allows listeners to eavesdrop on those conversations. In this regard the recording is a clear attempt to counter the "champagne sipping, money faking"[63] narratives found in recordings like hip-hop artist Jay-Z's "Life and Times of Shawn Carter" trilogy, which supposedly authenticate the experience of the urban black male. For Scott, "keeping it real" is acknowledging things like the fact that a former lover kept her "wide open, wide loose, like bowels after collard greens," as she states on the track "Love Rain."[64]

Throughout the recording, Scott nostalgically invokes the city of Philadelphia and the musical tradition it has produced, appropriating that tradition to cultivate a distinct brown-girl landscape—a city of sisterly love, if you will. With the exception of the Motown recording company, Philadelphia International Records, which was founded over thirty years ago by the duo of Kenneth Gamble and Leon Huff, remains the most recognizable corporate icon of black popular music. The recording label, which included legendary performers like Teddy Pendergrass, Billy Paul, the O'Jays, the Jones Girls, Harold Melvin and the Bluenotes, and the late and tragically underappreciated "Diva-of-all-Divas," Phyllis Hyman, along with the songwriting duo of Thom Bell and the late Linda Creed, helped craft a sound synonymous with the city. In many ways the Philly sound was more distinguishable than the Motown sound. *Who Is Jill Scott?* is reminiscent of the early recordings of the Intruders, one of the first acts that Gamble and Huff produced in the late 1960s, whose music helped bridge the seemingly incongruent energies of Philly's doo-wop tradition and the slickly produced and glossy sound that defined much of 1970s soul. In this regard, Scott's recording melds her natural hip-hop sensibilities with a real love and respect for the old school—a school that ranges from Billie Holiday to Valerie Simpson—without pandering to "keeping it real" dictums and the "Jamming Oldies"–style nostalgia programmed on commercial radio stations. Scott is in fact one of the more visible artists associated with a resurgent Philly soul movement that has been cultivated by Ahmir "?uestlove" Thompson, drummer for the hip-hop band the Roots. This loose collective of artists includes artists as diverse as former Will Smith partner "Jazzy" Jeff Townes, jazz bassist Christian McBride, keyboardist James Poyser, vocalist Bilal, spoken word artist Ursala Rucker, producer Jay Dee (Slum Village), and adopted Philadelphians like D'Angelo, Erykah Badu, and Common. The collective recalls the groundbreaking "Native Tongues" collective of the late 1980s and early 1990s that included the Jungle Brothers, A Tribe Called Quest, Queen Latifah, Monie Love, and De La Soul.

Scott's black-woman-centered space is literally evidenced during the first line of the recording's first track, "Do You Remember." Scott twists, teases, and pierces the opening phrase, "Oh honey, w-h-y you got to be so mean," summoning the musical legacies of singers like Billie Holiday, Esther Phillips, Dinah Washington, and the elfin male vocalist Jimmy Scott. It is Scott's phrasing on the song and others, most notably "The Way" and "I Think It's Better," that distinguishes her from the pack of contemporary would-be divas. Among contemporary R&B vocalists the art of phrasing has been largely ignored, as many young singers instead focus on the practice of "riffing." An exaggerated form of melisma or note bending, riffing is perhaps best represented in black gospel vocalists in the post–World War II era who often held black church audiences captive with their vocal calisthenics "in the name of the Lawd." Sam Cooke and Aretha Franklin are perhaps the dominant examples of "riffers," the latter being inspired by the artistry of gospel singer Clara Ward. But Cooke and Franklin were equally adept at the art of phrasing, Franklin in this regard also being influenced by Dinah Washington. As Franklin, Cooke, and others like the late Johnnie Taylor began to pursue interests in the "secular" music industry, styles of riffing that were incubated in the black church became synonymous with soul music, marking the differences of presentation perceived between soul shouters like Patti Labelle and Wilson Pickett and song "stylists" like Nancy Wilson and Walter Jackson. The singular genius of artists like Franklin, Marvin Gaye, Al Green, and Donny Hathaway was a product, among other things, of their abilities to employ different vocal techniques—equally shouter and stylist. Among the most recent generations of soul and R&B vocalists, Whitney Houston and Luther Vandross, who has elevated riffing to a high art form, are the clear standouts. In the post-soul era, the soul vocalese styles prominent two decades ago have become empty clichés among contemporary soul and R&B vocalists, as evidenced particularly in the derivative styles of male R&B groups such as 112, Ruff Endzs, Jagged Edge, and Ideal. By contrast, Jill Scott recovers the song stylist within an industry only seemingly interested in marketing contemporary appropriations of the practice riffs of a second tier "Soul Man" like Gap Band lead Charlie Wilson.

In addition I would like to argue that Scott's phrasing on "Do You Remember" metaphorically manipulates accepted urban histories, recovering moments within those histories—including the aforementioned vocal stylists—in which "brown girls" were indeed visible and taken seriously. As she states in the verse to the song that is dedicated to the "fathers of us," "You and me you and me you and me/We build sand castles in the Serengeti . . . /You splashed my face with Nile water/daughter of the Diaspora you named me."[65] The lyric acknowledges a space where fathers and daughters create lasting and vibrant relationships around creative play and a shared African heritage, images too rarely present in contemporary black popular culture.[66] In her queer reading of "Cleopatra Jones," Tamara Dobson's blaxploitation heroine, Jennifer Devere Brody asserts that characters like Cleopatra Jones or Pam Grier's Coffy and Foxy Brown can "recall the fantasies of power many black women desired."[67] Brody argues that such readings, of these characters do not "simply replicate an always already known 'reality' but rather takes pain to read 'realness' in queer phantasmatic terms."[68] Brody's read of Cleopatra Jones is useful as a way of positing that Scott cultivates a "fantastic" space to reconstruct, or more likely reimagine, the positioning of black women in post–World War II urban histories. As the song's title implies, Scott nostalgically intervenes in response to the contentious nature of contemporary relations between black men and woman, particularly as they are framed within mass culture. Scott's assertion to the "brothers of us," that "I was there/Always been there," not only implants the voice of brown girls into the post-soul narratives but highlights a continued commitment to shared struggle within black urban spaces. Given the Philadelphia soul tradition so integral to Scott's artistry, her music counters the benevolent patriarchal voices that dominated Gamble and Huff recordings and have become a foci of the narratives of postindustrial nostalgia that permeate forms of black popular culture, particularly within the realms of gender relations, as presented, for example, in Spike Lee's *Crooklyn* or George Tillman Jr.'s *Soul Food.*[69]

Scott's privileging of "homegirl" spaces throughout the project is not simply an act of celebration but also an attempt to acknowledge and perhaps counter the antagonisms between black women. The track "Getting in the Way" finds Scott issuing a slow-drawl old-school challenge to her partner's former lover. Throughout the song, Scott attempts to find a commonality with her adversary by referring to her as "sista girl" and "suga honey girl." Vividly recalling my own memories of watching brown-girl fistfights, where all body parts were open for pummeling except the face, Scott's lyric, "Queens shouldn't swing (if you know what I mean), but I'm 'bout ta take my earrings off/Get me some Vaseline" (the Vaseline is used to protect her face from scratches), suggests a reluctance on her part to engage in violence, though she is prepared to protect herself.[70] The track that precedes "Getting in the Way" is the spoken-word poem "Exclusively," which tells the story of Scott hitting the local "bodega" after some "sweaty and sex funky" lovemaking and meeting a cashier girl who recognizes her partner's postsex scent. Both "Getting in the Way" and "Exclusively" highlight what Cherry Muhanji and Kesho Scott call the "tight spaces" that black women are forced to negotiate as they compete for the meager resources available to black women and their self-esteems. Young black women in particular are also forced to compete with the distorted hypersexual images prevalent in film, television, music videos, and urban periodicals like *XXL*, *Blaze*, and *Vibe* magazine. Ironically, the video for "Getting in the Way," which includes a sequence where Scott pulls off the ponytail hairpiece of her adversary, helped introduce Scott to a broader audience. Prior to the video's release, interest in Scott's recording was largely garnered via an impressive array of word-of-mouth networks, such as Lee Bailey's *Electronic Urban Report* (EUR), the on-line journal *Popmatters*, and most notably the black cybercommunity within OkayPlayer.Com, which serves as the primary on-line promotional and fan site for the Roots, Common, D'Angelo, and the Jazzyfatnastees.[71] Though the video for "Getting in the Way" clearly fostered a greater awareness of Scott's work, it is notable that the video reduces the complexity of the song's narrative to a street fight, where community members convene publicly to watch the two women fight. The video thus distorts the brown-girl spaces that the recording constructs by rendering these spaces little more than sites of spectacle and voyeurism.

"Getting in the Way" was the second single released from *Who Is Jill Scott?* The project's initial release, "Love Rain," was without the support of a video. While the lack of a video for the recording's lead release could legitimately be attributed to the paltry promotional budget of what is ostensibly an independent recording label, it also highlights the problems confronted by "plus-sized" vocalists in the era of music videos. The best example of the visual politics of contemporary popular music is the controversy surrounding C&C Music Factory's recording "Gonna Make You Sweat (Everybody Dance Now)." The group was the brainchild of dance music producers Robert Clivilles and the late David Cole. Though the group was visually fronted by rapper Freedom Williams and vocalist Zelma Davis, it was vocalist Martha Wash who sang (uncredited) the song's signature tag, "Everybody Dance Now." Figuring that her image would not successfully promote the recording and the image of the group, Wash was essentially erased from the project except for her vocals, as she was in a similar instance with the group Black Box. Wash first came to prominence as half of the duo Two Tons of Fun, serving with Izora Rhodes as the backing vocalists for the brilliant disco artist Sylvester. As the Weathergirls, the duo had a significant mainstream hit with the song "It's Raining Men," which became a classic in queer dance halls. Kelly Price, a contemporary of Scott, whose full figure and voice drew early comparisons to Jennifer Holiday, star of the Broadway musical *Dreamgirls,* faced similar difficulties with her debut recording *The Soul of a Woman.* The project's lead single was an R. Kelly remix of the cut "Friend of Mine." The remix and subsequent video for the song found Kelly and Price's mentor Ronald Isley reprising their roles as Kelly and Mr. Bigg, the characters who initially appeared in the video for R. Kelly's "Down Low." Kelly was brought into the project specifically for the remix, presumably because of the inability of Price's management, at the time headed by Isley, to market a full-figured black female vocalist. Thus in an industry often predicated on the selling of its performers as sexual icons, R. Kelly's more marketable sexual persona could compensate for Price's size, while his reputation as a producer could entice audiences to the project, even though the remix is the only track he produced. Ironically, Kelly's presence detracted from Price's own talents as a songwriter/producer, as she wrote or cowrote all of the tracks on *The Soul of a Woman* and produced seven of its thirteen tracks.

On the track "Watching Me," Scott addresses the heightened surveillance of black bodies, particularly in urban spaces. At one point on the track Scott states, "Video cameras locked on me/In every dressing room on every floor in every store/Damn can I get that democracy and equality and privacy/You busy watchin' me watchin' me."[72] Scott's lyrics juxtapose the hypervisibility of black bodies in mass culture—often seen as emblematic of a fully integrated and equal society—to state surveillance of perceived black criminality. The lyrics recall the Allen and Albert Hughes film *Menace II Society*, in which the videotape of O'Dog's murder of Korean grocery store owners serves as documentation of his "gangsta" status among the cadres of young men (in the film) who find value in such personas, while also serving as proof of his criminal activity. The video cameras that have become a fixture in retailer anticrime efforts are perhaps the most visible example of ongoing surveillance efforts, including the panoptic policing of black urban spaces, leading Mike Davis to suggest that the "obsession with physical security systems, and, collaterally, with the architectural policing of social boundaries, has become a zeitgeist of urban restructuring."[73] As Davis argues, such surveillance criminalizes the black urban poor, under the assumption that they are more likely to shoplift than other customers, even while the presence of retailers in these communities suggests a liberal commitment to the sustenance of those communities. Ironically the black urban poor are often criminalized attempting to consume the very clothing styles, beauty products, and entertainment products that are distributed in mass culture via black popular culture. Scott's critique of racial profiling and the condition of "SWB" (Shopping While Black) particularly resonates after the recent death of Fredrick Finley at the hands of a black security guard outside a Lord & Taylor store in suburban Detroit. Finley was choked to death after a confrontation with security officers who attempted to detain his daughter, under suspicion—courtesy of store surveillance cameras—of shoplifting a $4 plastic bracelet. The irony of acts of racial profiling can be found in Scott's assertion that "you're blind baybe/You neglect to see the drugs comin' into my community/Weapons comin' into my community/Dirty cops in my community and you keep sayin' that I'm free."[74] Scott's lyric "you're blind baybe" is a reference to the Public Enemy track "She Watch Channel Zero" in which Flavor Flav states, "You're blind baby, you're blind from the facts of who you are." While this song characterizes black women as disconnected from the insurgent political activity that Public Enemy's music attempted to inspire, Scott's echo counters those charges and acknowledges her voice within the relatively small group of contemporary black musical artists who have directly addressed issues of racial profiling.[75]

Both Jill Scott and Joan Morgan take seriously the cultivation of black-women-centered spaces within mass and popular culture that serve to address the concerns of not only black women but the larger black community. Unfortunately their work, as well as work by women like performance artist Sarah Jones or hip-hop artist Bahamadia, is challenged not only by an often rigorous rejection of feminism within black communities and the general devaluation of black women in American society but by narratives voiced by black women in which "ghetto fab" psychosis is masked as black feminist expression. In an era when acting "crazy" is in vogue, as witnessed on exploitative television shows like *The Jerry Springer Show* or *The Rikki Lake Show*, an artist like Kelis, for example, can be read as connected to a burgeoning post-soul feminist movement. Kelis's debut recording, *Kaleidoscope*, featured a song about infidelity, "Caught Out There," which includes the refrain "I hate you so much . . . right now." The rage in Kelis's voice in the chorus was only matched by her brandishing of a pistol during a performance of the song on *The Chris Rock Show* in the fall of 2000. That performance, after which Kelis stalked off the stage, refusing to engage Rock in postperformance banter, was an interesting and ultimately justified reaction to Rock's interview with Ananda Lewis, an MTV video host and former cohost of Black Entertainment Television's (BET) *Teen Summit*. During the interview, while Lewis tried to address the crisis faced by America's children, whom she incidentally helps to traumatize on MTV, Rock repeatedly objectified her by making reference to her "ass." Lewis's attempts to deflect Rock's "rhetorical groping," and Kelis's subsequent response, were undermined by Lewis's willingness to embrace the same imagery of "video-hos" she critiqued during the interview, in her role as a MTV host. When Kelis's taped appearance on MTV's *Jams* was broadcast several days later, presenting a subdued and demure persona, one was hard pressed to believe she was the same artist who appears in the song's video or who performed on Rock's show. In the larger universe of black popular culture Kelis's rage, while justifiable in some regards, reduces legitimate black women's issues to singular acts of violence. Kelis's performance also suggests that black women are disempowered solely by black male infidelity. As bell hooks argues in response to public perceptions that *Waiting to Exhale* was a "black feminist" film, "it's truly a testament to the power of the mainstream to co-opt progressive social movements and strip them of all political meaning through a series of contemptuous ridiculous representations."[76]

McGruder's Follies: Playa Hatin' BET in Public

For more than twenty years Black Entertainment Television (BET) has accepted the burden of televisually representing the concerns and emerging cultural practices of the black community. While the desire to cater to the entertainment, news, and cultural needs of African Americans has been laudable, it has also handicapped BET with the additional burden of accountability. For more than a decade, BET valiantly lived up to the expectations of a relatively small (by cable standards) but demanding base of subscribers, largely located in urban centers with significant black populations such as Washington, D.C., New Orleans, and Detroit. By late 1999 the company, founded by Princeton graduate Robert Johnson with start-up money acquired from the TCI corporation and then largely owned by Johnson, was lauded by *Forbes* magazine as one of the best small businesses in America. Supported with a base of over 55 million subscribers, BET Holdings boasted a burgeoning communications empire that included *Emerge* magazine, three separate cable channels, including *BET on Jazz*, a publishing company specializing in romance novels, several restaurants and soundstages, and the internet concern BET.Com, which debuted in the spring of 2000. While Johnson had clearly brought to fruition a corporate dream barely realized by Motown founder Berry Gordy two generations earlier, in the fall of 1999 he became embroiled in a bitter public debate with twenty-five-year-old cartoonist Aaron McGruder. Frequently referred to as the first hip-hop comic strip, McGruder's strip, *The Boondocks*, which initially appeared in a student magazine at the University of Maryland, is currently nationally syndicated in over 250 daily newspapers. The strip follows the travails of not-yet-teenage brothers Huey, a budding neocultural nationalist, and Riley, a "hoodrat" in training, as they confront the challenges of contemporary suburbia.

McGruder drew Johnson's attention when the former turned his satirical eye on BET in the fall of 1999. In one Sunday edition of the strip, Huey complains to his local cable provider about the litany of infomercials featured during BET's Sunday programming, quipping, "There seems to be a problem with my cable. I'm watching Black Entertainment Television, but I don't see anyone black and it's not entertaining."[77] Other than the immensely popular *Bobby Jones Gospel* and the solid news program *Lead Story*, which some tuned into solely to watch black neo-con Armstrong Williams and *USA Today* columnist Dwayne Wickham play the ideological "dozens," much of the network's Sunday programming was centered on an assortment of kitchen gadgets, which all seemed to be promoted by George Forman. These infomercials, which were shown during the channel's weakest daytime viewership, generated substantial cash for the company, hence the need for so many stations to use infomercials during off-peak hours, when traditional advertisers might not be as interested. It is these dynamics that led Huey, in a later strip, to question his adherence to the "economic philosophy of Black Nationalism" and the belief that companies like BET would "act in the best interest of Black America." Huey concludes, "Let's just say BET shot a few holes in that theory."[78]

But it was the network's peak-hour programming that raised the ire of some viewers and became the primary focus of McGruder's criticisms of the network. The stimulus for much of the criticism of BET was the utter disappointment among core audiences about the 1999–2000 programming schedule. After years of relying on throwaway sitcom reruns of *Sanford, Amen,* and *Thea,* consumer expectations were high that the station's immense growth would augment its music videos, which Johnson suggested accounted for 60 percent of the network's programming, with original and entertaining programming. Since the fall of 1996 the network had been compelled to chase the same audience demographic that supports MTV and has transformed black radio into little more than a babysitter for the jittery hormones of black youth aged twelve to twenty-five. As Nicole Johnson suggests, "booty and bling-bling" narratives have been the cornerstone of black video production since the release of the video for Wrecks-

N-Effects' "Rump Shaker" a little more than ten years ago, and BET has attempted to cultivate an audience via the distribution of these images.[79] One of the channel's new video shows for the season was *Jamm Zone*, later renamed *Cita's World* for the 2000–2001 season, hosted by a "cyber-hoochie" named 'Cita (apparently short for Mamacita), who relishes in her ebonically authentic language embodying some of the worst stereotypes associated with black women, including a requisite Venus Hottentot frame.

In one particular sequence broadcast during the 1999–2000 season, 'Cita provides commentary on the video for Avant's "Separation," which features a scorned female lover slashing the main character's car tires and physically harming herself, telling law enforcement officers that her former lover is responsible for her bruises. Addressing black women such as the one portrayed in the video, 'Cita states, "Some of those things we do as sisters, come on y'all, y'all know that stuff is just downright foul . . . but sisters, let us not contribute to the deterioration and the annihilation of the black man. I peeped that notion from this book, right, *Countering the Conspiracy to Destroy Black Boys*. It's serious out there y'all, using the system to get revenge is just plain wrong. Don't use the white man as a weapon." 'Cita's monologue at once undermines the legitimate forms of resistance that some black women employ in the face of black male violence, both physical and emotional, and reduces black feminist issues to a scorned lover's revenge. As a cyber-creation, 'Cita employs an "authentic" black femininity to reinforce patriarchal norms within black life and culture as represented within mass culture. This notion is underlined later in the aforementioned broadcast when 'Cita asserts, "I'm just trying to keep it real, 'cause that's what I do baby, I got to be true to myself and in being true to myself, I got to be true to you." BET's support of the objectification of black female sexuality has often transcended its musical video programming, in that black female presence on its news programs has often been obscured by the conscious promotion of authoritative black male icons, most notably Ed Gordon, whose postverdict interview with O. J. Simpson on BET in October 1995 led to a lucrative deal with MSNBC and author Tavis Smiley. For instance, in the early 1990s Madeline Wood, immortalized perhaps by Phife Dawg of A Tribe Called Quest on the track "Butter," was removed from her anchor position on the station's daily news program and literally reconstructed as the "video-ho" host of the program *Video LP*. Though journalist Cheryl Martin hosted the new program *Lead Story* during the 1999–2000 and 2000–2001 seasons, she was clearly subordinated by the black talking-head patriarchs who appear regularly on the program. In tribute to BET's programming strategy and Johnson's claim that BET has a "commitment to serve the interests of our African American viewers and stakeholders,"[80] McGruder published a strip that featured a black woman's gyrating ass with the caption, "And thank you, Bob Johnson, for shining your light for the rest of us to follow."[81]

The use of a cyberhost is very much in line with the kind of "plantation" logic that pervades BET's business strategy, which itself has been a target of ongoing criticism. In an October issue of *Newsweek* and a subsequent article in the *Washington Post*, the increasing dissatisfaction with BET was addressed—the airing of the proverbial dirty laundry—with concerns raised by everyone from comics paid below scale for their appearances on the highly rated *Comic View* to viewers concerned with the network's reliance on music videos. The network had been at odds with the performers' union the American Federation of Television and Radio Artists for its failure to deal with organized labor. In response to the network's labor practices, comedian Tommy Davidson was quoted as saying, "BET's attitude is like the fruit and vegetable companies in the Depression that said '[Expletive] anyone who won't work for 10 cents a day.'"[82] Playing the race card like a three-card monty game on 125th Street in Harlem, Johnson used the channel's *BET Talk with Tavis Smiley* (Smiley being mysteriously absent as host that evening) to respond to charges against him. A Johnson representative, former boxing promoter Butch Lewis, addressed the charges leveled in the *Newsweek* article by suggesting that black viewers should close ranks in support of BET and its embattled CEO, singling out former *Comic View* host and star of *The Hughleys* D. L. Hughley as ungrateful for the support the network gave him early in his career. Hughley was quoted in the *Newsweek* article as saying, "because it's black people mistreating black people, everyone's been hesitant to speak up"[83] against Johnson's labor practices. Given the monopoly that BET seemingly holds on the televisual presentation of black life and culture, many artists and commentators, including this one, have been reluctant to publicly critique BET for fear of losing access to the visibility that BET obviously affords. It is of course this very knee-jerk consumer nationalism that is at the core of many of McGruder's criticisms. In response to the *Washington Post* article, which included references to McGruder and *The Boondocks*, Johnson wrote an op-ed in the same periodical in which he accused the article's author, Paul Farhi, of elevating McGruder and "his irresponsible and simple-minded comments to a level of a bonafide critic."[84]

Nearly one year after the *Newsweek* and *Washington Post* articles and McGruder's public questioning of Bob Johnson's commitment to his black subscribers and the larger black community, Johnson finalized a deal with Viacom Inc. to acquire BET Holdings for nearly $3 billion dollars. Included in the purchase was 360HIPHOP.com, an urban site founded by entertainment mogul Russell Simmons and purchased by BET a month prior to the announcement of the Viacom deal. Johnson had translated his position as a gatekeeper of black cultural property into $2.5 billion in stock, which he will presumably use to finalize his creation of DC Air, a proposed black-owned regional airline based in Washington, D.C., that would buttress his position as the dominant business mogul within the black community.[85] The deal calls into serious question Johnson's assertion a year earlier that the 500 people who work at BET "represent a cross section of this country's finest African American talent with a myriad of expertise and career experience. It is inconceivable that these people would lend their services to BET without ensuring that BET has at the core a commitment to serve the interests of our African American viewers and stakeholders."[86] Months earlier Johnson presided over the dismantling of the publication *Emerge,* which was edited by George Curry. Though it was often uneven in its editorial content, Curry's commitment to have the magazine consistently present liberal political commentary was in striking contrast to other monthly periodicals with African-American themes like *Essence* and *Ebony.* As one example, *Emerge* was largely responsible for elevating the incarceration of Kemba Smith, incarcerated for drug trafficking largely on the basis of her relationship with a known drug trafficker, to national awareness. The *Emerge* cover story likely impacted then president Bill Clinton, who commuted her sentence in December 2000 as one of his last official acts as president. The relocation of the network's entertainment and news operations from Washington, D.C., to New York City led to the firing of over ninety staff members.[87]

McGruder's exchanges with Bob Johnson were only the most prominent of his ongoing efforts to elevate his strip to the level of social and cultural criticism, recalling the impact of Garry Trudeau's *Doonesbury* and Berke Breathed's *Bloom County* comic strips in the 1980s. The willingness of McGruder to publicly confront some of the basic assumptions of black identity and cultural practices while engaging in clear critique of post-soul race relations is emblematic of the balancing act that many post-soul critics are forced to become adept at. At the core of McGruder's balancing act are the personas of the strip's main characters, Huey and Riley, with whom he heavily invests the capacity to read the terrain of contemporary black culture and politics and to engage in forms of self-critique, relative to contemporary black youth culture. McGruder's narratives about emerging black middle-class life as experienced by black youth is likely his negotiation of that lifestyle as he experienced it, including the proliferation of "blackness" in the marketplace. But as Johnson's derisive description of him as simply a "twenty-five-year-old cartoonist" suggests, he also aims to take seriously the position of black youth as legitimate social critics, if not intellectuals in their own right. In this way McGruder naturally challenges general perceptions among older generations of blacks that a "mythical" vibrant and engaged black intellectual and moral life—which ironically was intimately connected to black youth culture during the civil rights movement—is consistently eroded by the post-soul and hip-hop generations. In his disparaging of "cultural politics," specifically surrounding the fetishization of Malcolm X (El-Hajj Malik El-Shabazz) in the late 1980s, Adolph Reed asserts that "treating youth as authentic bearers of a principle of opposition . . . confuses existential rebellion and political rebellion."[88] Trashing the legitimacy of hip-hop icons like Chuck D and KRS-One as intellectuals, even in the Gramscian sense, Reed questions the validity of considering black youth as an actual social class unto themselves. While I am not suggesting that black youth like those portrayed in McGruder's strip are now or will ever be the most prominent actors in an organized antiracist/antisexist movement, I do concur with S. Craig Watkins's concept that the "popular media productions created by black youth represent a distinct sphere of cultural production"[89] that "redefines the crisis scenarios that prominently figure young African Americans."[90]

Riley, the younger of the two brothers, is used by McGruder to comment on the considerable impact of contemporary black popular culture, particularly related to the construction of ghettocentric masculinities. This is witnessed during Riley's first day of school, where his white classmates and teacher sit terrified as he introduces himself as "Riley Escobar," the name mirroring the alternative personas that various hip-hop artists employ to integrate themselves into the largely white mafioso fantasies constructed in films like *Goodfellows* and the Brian De Palma version of *Scarface*.[91] As these alternative personas help to racialize illicit and underground economies as presented in film noir—Nas (Nassim Jones)'s transformation from minimalist black urban poet to Nas Escobar being a classic example—Riley's use of his gangsta persona is similarly connected to his desires to integrate into his new surroundings. McGruder fully understands that in such contexts, young black males engage in certain performative gestures as a mode of protection. Riley's assertion that he is "keeping it real" is his conscious embrace of the black male gangsta persona that he knows his fellow students derive some visceral pleasure in consuming via MTV or BET, but are largely fearful of when they actually meet it in their own community and school. For instance, in an earlier strip Riley is seen practicing his "thug mug" in front of the bathroom mirror, later lamenting to Huey that "keeping it real is hard work when you're cursed with cuteness."[92] Evidence that Riley is not wholly invested in the persona is also witnessed when his grandfather grabs Riley's headphones, expecting to hear that "awful gangsta rap music," only to find out that his grandson was listening to *The Miseducation of Lauryn Hill*.

As a repository and conduit for black popular culture, Riley is also utilized by McGruder to comment on how pervasive ghettocentric forms of black identity are within mass culture and society. In one panel Huey and his grandfather are playing with a Sony Playstation game. At various times in the strip McGruder has undermined the perception that black youth are naturally talented at playing video games, so it is no surprise that the grandfather is beating Huey at the game. When Huey suggests that Riley is responsible for his grandfather's ability to use Playstation and "talk a mountain of trash" in the process, the grandfather reveals his own understanding of ghettocentric slang as he responds, "Don't hate the playa, boy . . . hate the game."[93] In another daily strip the grandfather is pictured in full Fubu regalia. While the politically conscious Huey responds, "Black owned or not, gratuitous logo fashions are tacky," Riley is forced to admit, "man, I never realized how goofy these clothes looked."[94] Cindy, a young white girl in their neighborhood, also represents McGruder's ongoing critique of the commodification of black popular culture, as she aggressively pursues a "ghetto" authenticity. In her initial meeting with Huey, Cindy asks him for an autograph, thinking that he obviously had to be famous in order to move into her neighborhood. Later in the same conversation, she asks if he knows

Puffy (Sean Combs). In an extended story line in which Riley changes the name of street signs to reflect his ghettocentric sensibilities, Cindy accompanies him in his effort to change, for example, "Timid Dear Lane" to "Notorious B.I.G. Avenue." While Riley's vandalizing again reflects his desires to symbolically alter his new community—reminiscent of efforts by black college students to rename academic building on white campuses after black political and cultural icons—McGruder uses the story line to indict mass culture for its distorted views of black identity. As both Riley and Cindy are inevitably caught in their acts of vandalism, McGruder ends the story line with the announcement that Cindy's parents were suing the "Black Entertainment Network" for "contributing to the delinquency of Cindy McPherson."[95]

Perhaps because he more closely mirrors McGruder's own sensibilities, Huey is the more richly developed character; he is specifically utilized to challenge the limits of romantic political ideologies and affirm the possibility of seeing this generation of black youth, even as they thoroughly embrace mass culture, as potential social critics and intellectuals. While Huey consistently allows McGruder to address contemporary political issues, most notably during the 2000 presidential election, he is most profound in his critiques of black politics and culture. McGruder is perhaps his most adroit when he allows Huey's own political passions— extraordinary for a character ostensibly twelve year old—to undermine and destabilize romantic tropes of true "African" identity. In one sequence fairly early in the strip's run, Huey responds to his grandfather's query as to why he is standing outside in one-hundred-degree heat by asserting that "We have that as forgotten that as Africans we are a people of the heat. We are sun-drinkers."[96] As he begins to wilt in the sweltering heat, Huey finally quips to his grandfather, "Can a proud African get some Kool-Aid or something?" Though some readers have claimed that Huey's character is racist, many also fail to realize that he is himself a critique of certain antiquated forms of black nationalism, while still clearly remaining invested in a diasporic identity that is real and meaningful.

Another example of Huey's tenuous status to the very ideals that he espouses is the story line where he forgets to celebrate the African-American holiday Kwanza. Though he admits that he is more "radical socialist" than "cultural nationalist," Huey claims that forgetting Kwanza makes him a "poor excuse for a black revolutionary." McGruder is fully aware that the celebrating of Kwanza is itself not tantamount to a revolutionary identity; its thorough commercialization is witnessed in the line of Kwanza cards produced by a corporation like Hallmark or the postal service's selling of Kwanza stamps designed by African-American artist Sinthia St. James. I was struck during the Christmas season a few years ago by the presence of Kwanza candleholders at the affordable though stylish home furnishing chain Pier One and the rather detailed descriptions of Kwanza during holiday specials for children's programs like PBS's *Arthur* and the Disney Network's *Bear in the Big Blue House*, which not surprisingly conflated Kwanza with Christmas and Hanukkah. Huey in fact forgets about the now commercialized holiday because he is trying to "deconstruct" the real meaning of the Santa Claus myth.

Thoroughly ensconced in conspiracy theories about Santa Claus and the "illuminati," Huey eventually produces a full-length report that, among other things, suggests that Santa Claus is responsible for the crack cocaine epidemic. On the one hand, McGruder here takes a subtle swipe at the conspiracy theories running rampant in black communities—from my own youth I remember one about someone eating a fried rodent at a local fast-food restaurant—including the very public accusation that the CIA was responsible for the proliferation of crack cocaine in Los Angeles and the rather common belief among some black college students that blacks will lose their voting rights when the voting rights act expires in 2007. But McGruder doesn't use this merely as an indictment of black youth; as he writes "The Santa Conspiracy," Huey is also caught up in the largely media-driven conspiracies surrounding the end of the twentieth century and the "Y2K" bug that threatened to bring America's infrastructure to a halt. Like many Americans, Huey grapples with fully understanding the nature of American society, but as a twelve-year-old black youth who has always been skeptical of the Santa Claus myth, particularly given the realities of black urban poverty, a Santa Claus conspiracy is more intellectually tangible to him. Huey's assertion to his grandfather that Santa Claus is an "unseen power never to be challenged. He replaces God—diverting attention from spirituality to greed" is important because in the process of "deconstructing" Santa Claus, Huey constructs an alternative myth around the "real" Santa Claus, "Jolly Jenkins."[97] According to Huey's myth, Jolly Jenkins was a immortal black man who would "bring books and wisdom" on Christmas Eve, but he was unfairly incarcerated and placed on death row. On the one hand Huey's myth recovers the figure of Black Peter, whose presence in the Saint Nicolas myth has eroded since its import to the West, but the narrative of "Jolly Jenkins" can also serve to bring attention to real political prisoners such as Mumia Abu-Jamal, Herman Bell, and Leonard Peltier.[98]

Taken as a whole, McGruder's Jolly Jenkins story line is about perceiving black youth as committed to ongoing efforts to critically engage the world. In a particularly telling strip, Huey sits down at his computer to produce his first intellectual treatise, "Ward Connerly Should Be Beaten by Raekwon the Chef with a Spiked Bat: A Critical Look at the Black Conservatives," a "critical analysis of the black neoconservative movement." The project's title conveys Huey's ability to bring various discourses into conversation with each other, in this case the esoteric underground hip-hop of Wu Tang member Raekwon and the generations of black public intellectuals that would include a figure like Connerly, whose political views have been aimed at denying educational opportunity for black youth like Huey. As Huey grapples with his project, a voice-over raises the questions, "Will Huey alienate the masses with obscure references? Can he broaden the scope of his work without corrupting its cultural integrity and unyielding radical tone? Can he discover the elusive middle ground between Francis Cress Welsing and Henry Louis Gates Jr.?"[99] Though the two scholars are distanced by their political investments in Afrocentricity and mainstream liberalism, respectively, their signature works, Cress Welsing's "Cress Theory of Color-Confrontation and Racism"[100] and Gates's *Signifying Monkey: A Theory of African American Literary Criticism,* are two examples of attempts by black scholars to theorize about the meaning of racial symbols in American culture and literature. Cress Welsing's work, however problematic, can legitimately be considered as a precursor to the African-American cultural studies movement that now flourishes in academe. In an attempt to reach the broadest audiences possible, Huey renames his project "Ward Connerly Is a Bootlicking Uncle Tom," reanimating the vernacular styles of previous generations of race men. In response to Huey's new title, the voice-over states, "Way to Go Huey. . . . The ability to transcend cultural barriers is the mark of a great communicator. Keep this up and you'll be on 'Charlie Rose' in no time."[101] In many regards Huey is not unlike all of the post-soul critics identified above, in that even at such a young age he is conflicted by the desire to "keep it real," intellectually and politically, while remaining connected to the very engines of mass media that distort the images of black folks in general and black youth in particular. If a post-soul intelligentsia truly exists, and I obviously have faith in such a construction, Huey Freeman is a legitimate product of those efforts and an inkling of the possibilities for black intellectual thought as it germinates in black youth coming to terms with their place in the world.

Epilogue

A Soul Baby in Real Time
Encountering Generation Hip-Hop on Campus

"Andy Gibb? 'Shadow Dancing'? You listen to that shit?" So I was finally exposed. The little nappy-headed Negro boy from the projects had been outed. In the privacy of my own bedroom, I could live out my Top 40 crossover fantasies with Harry Harrison, Dan Ingram, Chuck Leonard, and the rest of the jocks on WABC while sitting on the floor playing Strat-O-Matic and enjoying the music of Seals and Croft, Elton John, and Neil Sedaka. It's not so much that I desired to be white. Rather, I desired to be normal. Brady Bunch normal. At age twelve I had experienced too many "Come Sunday" mornings of chitlins, grits, and the Mighty Clouds of Joy. The Brady Bunch kids never had to eat ham hocks and collard greens or listen to gospel music, and they were normal, so what exactly was wrong with my desiring to be like Greg or Peter? But in my Bronx neighborhood, such desires had to be controlled in public, lest your "ghetto pass" get revoked. Luckily, my friends were cool and allowed me to keep my pass, at least for another day. But that was not the end of having to "represent." I spent my high school years deflecting charges that I was an "oreo" and a "wannabe"— fitting charges, I guess, against someone who had eschewed the more ghetto-fabulous styles of Adidas hard shells, colored Lee jeans, Le Tigre knit shirts (that ghetto fabulous stand-in for Izod Lacoste), and, of course, the requisite Kangol headgear. I favored Sperry Topsiders, patched and faded jeans, and pink crewneck sweaters.

These charges reflected a belief that someone who doesn't toe the fashion line is rejecting not only the adornments of the group, the accessories of culture, but also its totems, and thus the group itself. And so it made sense that all through those years, I was haunted by the concern of whether I would continue to be perceived as authentically "black" to my crew of boyhood friends. I was faced with the quandary that many black young people face when their identities are torn between the need to "keep it real" and the desire to be themselves. "Keeping it real" meant keeping it black, or, for the real pubescent "playas," keeping it "ghetto." The problem, though, was that we hadn't a clue what it meant to be black. This preoccupation with black authenticity has hardly diminished over the years. As black life has become more complex and varied, as blacks have divided by class and moved into white environments, such issues have intensified. Nowhere are such identity negotiations more complex than among college students.

Today's black college students are the first generation to experience the explosion of black identities since the civil rights movement as practical opportunities. In the logic of integration, as long as blacks presented themselves in ways that were acceptable to whites, they would be protected from the most heinous forms of discrimination. Black nationalism expanded upon this identity. The sudden emphasis on Afro-puffs, dashikis, and the "cuss-in-prose for the sake of the movement" art of the Amiri Barakas and Don L. Lees of the world not only publicly articulated long-standing black resentment toward white supremacy but also helped legitimize black pride as a vehicle of protest and recovery. Yet it also added restrictions of its own; it often functioned to keep the various black identities within segregated black spaces, subsumed within the rubric of a common black identity. In both cases, blacks were denied the ability to fully explore their identities, both within and beyond the prism of blackness. The options today have expanded beyond these polarities. The possibilities are rich: racially proud crossovers like Oprah, Cosby, and Jordan; thug niggas and nigresses; lower-middle-class strivers concerned about crime and property values; New York lawyers rocking Cugi on the weekends; old-school nationalists and Baptists alike.

The title of Nelson George's *Buppies, B-Boys, Baps and Bohos* comically captured the range of these identities in the post–civil rights, post–Black Power era. There are enough of "my niggas," who are Brooks Brothers down, pushing everything from computer software to legal advice during the workweek, who don hooded sweatshirts made by Hilfiger, cross-training Nikes and NY Knick caps (requisite B-boy gear back in the day) on the weekend, as we stroll into the local CompUSA to buy rechargeable batteries for our laptops, dropping Ja Rule lyrics, alarming the customers and staff after our weekly racquetball games. We can't catch a cab either way. And neither can some of my BoHo (bohemian) brothers and sisters, whose dreadlocks, natural dos, and oversize plaids have them regularly mistaken as homeless. These are folks who have even been known to respond to such harassment by quoting Louis Althusser, Sun Ra, and poet Paul Beatty, to the surprise of no one. More than a few of them are completing graduate degrees and medical school and most likely will be buying houses in Scarsdale and driving to work in Volvos. While we embrace these identities as part of our being, we are also conscious of the fluidity of the communities to which we belong and the relative freedom to explore these identities, often playfully at the expense of white onlookers, in ways that our parents could never conceive. I don't know what I get off more on, wearing expensive suits while blasting the late Big Pun ("I'm not a playa, I just crush a lot") out of the car or showing up at the local Starbucks like a thug-nigga intellectual (in my neighborhood, all you got to do is be black and wear a faded baseball cap), asking for a pound of Sumatra and a French press while humming something by Miles.

This generational quest has been framed by broader forces. As the first generation born after desegregation, "Generation Hip-Hop" was endowed with a hope that eluded blacks before them. The most visible barriers to success were supposedly removed, and a more level terrain would allow them to flourish on a par with their white peers. But there was corollary: the generation born after *Bakke* also has a sense of possibility denied. The 1980s saw a lot of black folks standing on cheese lines and unemployment lines alike, while liberal politicians and black elected officials fronted as if white backlash was a necessary evil in the drive toward equality. Let's be real: crack was an equal-opportunity employer in my neighborhood those days. You didn't need affirmative-action legislation to slang rock. This atmosphere of racial tension takes a special form on college campuses. The presence of blacks elicits derisive responses among some white students who question college admission standards and resist sharing space with black students. Other whites see black students as valuable to the campus fabric but are put off by acts of black solidarity, like the formation of black student unions. Such organizations are often perceived as examples of Generation Hip-Hop's rejecting the integrationist ambitions of their parents. As if mixing together is not stressful enough, Generation Hip-Hop is moving out into white enclaves at a time of proliferating black images in mass media. Many within the entertainment industry continue to rely on decades-old, albeit updated, caricatures of black culture. The increased presence of black artists, writers, producers, and performers has not significantly altered reliance on these stereotypes. The more malign aspect of these images is the white association of blacks with the blaring menace of gangster rap.

As a result, a post-*Bakke* generation of blacks moves about mixed campuses aware of white scrutiny and the negative imagery of blacks in the popular media and white people's minds. This vigilance holds true even for blacks who are not eager to be accepted by whites, but simply concerned with survival. Some students even feel themselves forced into behaving like that "good Negro" of the civil rights movement. One of my students, a self-described loner from a working-class, single-mom background, who evinced no lack of pride in her blackness, precisely captured this experience: "I know that in the eyes of whites I am representing the whole black group, especially if there's only one or two black people in a class of thirty. I know I have to speak a certain way, my mannerisms have to be a particular way, so that they don't say 'Well, oh, she's ignorant.'" Finally, this generation of black students is under the censorious scrutiny not just of white folks but of its own black elders, who look askance at its baggy pants and puzzling music. Often Generation Hip-Hop's struggles and failures have been interpreted as a rejection of the moral foundations of the black community. This criticism is supposedly validated in the old school's mind by the escalation of black-on-black crime, crack cocaine addiction, and the violent narratives of gangsta rap.

In this difficult environment, black college students are trying to figure out what blackness means to them, so maybe the intensity with which black college students sometimes close ranks is not surprising. The feelings of exile are real, and very often my office (or the offices of my far-too-few brown-skinned colleagues) becomes the promised land, where the stares, whispers, and slights are put into some context. Despite differences among themselves and the cliquish nature of campus relationships, such efforts aim to ward off attacks, both real and imagined, on their intelligence, culture, and identities. I've seen enough avant-garde art elicit cries of racism on campuses. There have been students, and very often not those who wear their blackness the loudest, who simply pack up their clothes and leave, not willing to deal with the pressures of being "integration babies." At the very same time, some students have argued that one campus's yearly cross-burning is not something to be alarmed by. Lacking an appreciation of the nuances of black struggle and enveloped by the contrived realities of college life, many black students construct a strict code of blackness that attempts to buffer them from the dangers of predominantly white campuses even while building an even stricter code of community. And so some students find themselves rebuffed, for years sometimes, because they refuse to attend black student union meetings, although these meetings often serve as vehicles to plan parties, fashion shows, and the annual appearance of an African dance troupe. And God forbid if you just find your white roommate more interesting than most of the black folks you've met on campus.

In resolving this dilemma, black students are hardly all the same. Some of my African students—from places like Ghana and Nigeria, mind you—wear Anne Klein like regal kente cloth, while folks born in the South Bronx who can't name five African countries wear kente caps, socks, scarves, and earmuffs. These are the outer signs of more profound differences among black students, loosely summarized by the categories of activists, strivers, and crossovers. The activists are most aware of their racial heritage, generally as a response to their campus environment, the influence of their parents, or a genuine desire to know more about themselves. They range from those who seek to provide culturally specific activities to augment those provided by the campus to those attracted to more Afrocentric sensibilities and various forms of Islam. It is not unusual for these students to Africanize their names or at least choose names they perceive as nonwhite, like Mayisa or those old Five Percent Nation staples, "True Knowledge," "Born True," or "Mother Seed." They also choose hairstyles—locks, twists, mini–Don King naturals, short natural crops—and styles of dress that reflect more African-centered sensibilities. Though these students often respond most visibly to racial and cultural slights, the oft-chosen tag of campus militants can misrepresent them. They are more likely to be found on campus radio programming various hip-hop, old-school funk, and jazz shows, while also attending poetry slams like the Soul Kitchen series that is popular in Albany. Most use the opportunity to present work that affirms everything from black masculinity to monogamous heterosexual relations, though on occasion some real satire will be presented, like my man Jason Smith's tracing the lives of Fat Albert and the Cosby Kids to drug addiction and the penal system. Ironically, it is in these spaces that many connect with their white bohemian counterparts, who share an interest in jazz and progressive art. As Mojavi Wright, one of the Soul Kitchen organizers, reflected, "Some of the white guys will show up early and actually buy drinks and food. Some black folks will show up late, not buy a thing, and get mad because there are white folks in the audience!"

Students in these categories often play their self-assigned role of enforcing blackness, often in the most limiting ways. While lingo like wannabe, oreo, or even Uncle Tom is perhaps dated for this generation, those accused of not keeping it real are deemed "playa-hatas," or more economically "hatas," a term that covers a full range of cultural faux pas. Thus Calvin Butts and Bill Cosby can be said to "playa-hate" hip-hop culture, while those who are deemed foreign to their own culture ostensibly "hate" themselves and their heritage. A segment of students among the more Afrocentric activists have also generated the image of a generation of separatists, anti-Semites, and jury nullifiers who clapped for O. J. Simpson because they wanted to "let a brother go." But more often the impulse is the simpler one of indignation over injustice, a wish for self-sufficiency or comfort with one's own people and a desire not to have to worry about whites. One male student who described himself as an upper-middle-class activist but not an Afrocentrist, stated, "I really don't care what white people think. To hell with them. I care more about what other black people think. I think one of our biggest problems is that we are constantly looking at each other through white people's eyes."

Despite all the white agitation over the separatism of today's black youths, strivers probably make up the majority of black students on any given campus. These folks, who simply aspire to middle-class futures as lawyers, dentists, financial planners, and software designers, were once viewed as heirs to legitimate "Negrofied" bourgeois classes, blue veins and curly hair notwithstanding. But strivers are incredibly diversified themselves and hardly conform to some Frazier stereotype of self-hating, white-imitating Negroes. Though many of them are pressured to re-create middle-class lifestyles, some come from solid working-class and working poor environments. For the latter students, who are very often first-generation college students, the attainment of a college degree is a conduit into mainstream middle-class success. Race may matter to them, but not enough to jeopardize their academic and professional goals. When I was coming up, it was easy for student militants to deride these students for choosing schoolwork over the latest forum on South African apartheid, but one must remember that there are often vast parental investments, both emotional and financial, associated with their schooling. These ties are particularly apparent at historically black colleges. I once taught at one in Louisiana that specializes in preparing black students for the health professions. I was struck by the offense many of my students took at a mandatory course in black history: they simply they didn't see its connection to their desires to be medical doctors. Within the group of social strivers are a smaller group of students who are aligned with various black "Greek" organizations. With a true lineage to the Talented Tenth, the original social strivers of the early twentieth century, many of these fraternities and sororities unwittingly reproduce the color-caste politics that dominated the black community prior to the civil rights movement. For some of theses folks, skin tone and hair texture are still important matters when building the type of organizations that can put the race's best foot forward. In the worst cases, these groups exude a sense of difference toward other black students that parallels the sense of difference that many whites have toward blacks. While many of these fraternities and sororities include blacks of diverse socioeconomic backgrounds and physical features, it is clear that skin color, hair texture, and class continue to be major criteria. As one student suggested, "The Greek organizations are primarily responsible for the cliquish nature of black student relations with each other."

Finally there are the crossovers, whose numbers are probably higher than they seem, since many are on the "DL." The image of the black student listening to Poison on his or her Walkman, while wearing a pair of Wranglers and Converse cloth high-tops, holding hands with a white partner, is the all-too-obvious image of the social crossover. Most just look normal, like your average white kid or black kid for that matter, whatever that is—jeans, cotton shirts, tennis shoes, models in Eddie Bauer or L. L. Bean catalogs. But in reality many of these students are not so much rejecting their racial or ethnic heritage as they are trying to downplay the significance of race, to minimize the sense of difference from their white peers. At stake here is a campus experience not dominated by race. Some of these students may be the product of interracial parentage. Others may have been socially isolated from other blacks despite having two black parents and access to black extended family. Despite their desire to remain racially anonymous, if such a thing is possible, many crossovers are at the forefront of campus race politics. They are often lauded by their white peers for being model minorities. Meanwhile, black students, activists and strivers alike, often view the crossovers as examples of cultural ignorance and racial self-hatred. And so the black student who chooses to date or have friends outside of his or her racial group can expect to endure a certain exile—a double exile, if you will: as one male student related in a conversation about dating outside the race, "If someone is dating a white girl, because he feels more in touch with white people, I'd have to call him a sellout." Others may not be bold enough to step to anyone who dates outside the race, but their names and perceptions of their lifestyles often become part of the colloquial fodder where community is measured and defined.

Many within Generation Hip-Hop interpret such diversity as proof of the black community's lack of unity. In my courses, which over the past three years have been 90 percent black, my standard retort to such claims is, "Black unity was a myth and solidarity was a strategy." Rarely do their responses evoke the progressive thoughts on black community that I'm hell-bent on facilitating, and very often I have to defend my own right to a "ghetto pass." While few students will risk alienating a black professor by calling him a sellout or, even worse, gay, many students have queried other students and even faculty about my sexuality and racial preferences. There is that small sigh of relief when they come to my office and see the picture of my BLACK WIFE on the wall, as if the eighteen-by-twenty-four posters of John Coltrane, Malcolm X, Pete Rock, and C. L. Smooth, and of course the Louis Armstrong statue, are not more obvious markers. All these different possibilities find some expression in black popular culture, which seems fitting, given that the hip-hop generation has been especially socialized by mass media, particularly television. This is often forgotten by instructors who fail to consider that many of their young students experience the world via the cut-and-paste production techniques of television, video games, and the like.

Strivers, crossover types, and activists can find some reflection of themselves in the expanding range of black imagery. More than just matters of taste, such preferences often express students' poignant and ambivalent struggles over blackness. These conflicts exploded in a class I offer on black popular culture. To provoke discussion, I show Ralph

A SOUL BABY IN REAL TIME

Baskhi's mostly animated cult classic *Street Fight*. Released in 1975 to organized protest by civil rights organizations and largely based on the Brer tales that loom so large within African-American folk culture, Bashki's film challenges and offends the sensibilities of most of its viewers. My students' reactions to the movie didn't disappoint. As one student related, "That was some racist shit. Why'd he have to make black people look so nasty." In a class where critical free-for-alls often degenerate into critical beatdowns, their voices were remarkably in sync, questioning why someone would make a film that was so blatantly racist and what rock I turned over to find it. Of course virtually every character in the film is purposely drawn as grotesque, but given the general lack of "positive" images of blacks, the students were offended. Many of the students were not aware of the Brer tales and had never seen a film like Disney's *Song of the South*. I purposely show the film on the first day of class, for its obvious shock value, but at least three or four students didn't return for the next session, they were so offended.

Students even recoiled from the film's opening segments, which featured the late "Scatman" Crothers singing "I Got the Devil in Me," looking and sounding as if he had just walked off the set of an early 1930s plantation film. Of course Crothers was a remnant of an earlier era when black performers shucked, jived, cooned, and tapped for their two minutes of fame, but Bakshi used his performance in the film to evoke some of the nuances associated with social and political resistance during a time when so much of black expression was disregarded and silenced. My students didn't go for it. Their reactions were clear: no cooning allowed. Such cooning takes place regularly on weeknights on television networks like UPN (Paul Mooney once derisively called it the U-Pick-a-Nigga network) and the WB. Black performers like Shawn and Marlon Wayans, Eddie Griffith, and Jamie Foxx are contemporary examples of the rich black comedic tradition. But my students were unsparing in their rejection of shows like *Malcolm and Eddie*, *The Jamie Foxx Show*, *The Wayans Brothers*, and even *The Martin Lawrence Show*. They held them up to impossible communal standards in which they are expected to be front-line fighters in the war to construct "positive" black identity, in television sitcoms no less. This was common ground for the social activists and the social strivers, who often likened these comic images to those stock black images found on local news stations. As one female student responded, "They just had to go get the worst-looking person in the neighborhood.

The media just looks for people who look a certain way." What affected many students was that such comedians do not hold anything sacred; everything and everybody is open to their comic schemes. Caricatures of King, Mandela, and Farrakhan are tame compared to some other skits, like a Wayans Brothers episode that featured stock stereotypes of the African continent that could have been found in some of those Warner cartoons from the late 1930s and early 1940s. Still, many of these shows are widely watched by black audiences; *The Wayans Brothers* and *The Jamie Foxx Show* have often been the two highest-rated shows among black audiences. Truth is the shows are funny and often reinforce basic black sentiments about family and community. Even Cousin Pookie from the projects can be a part of the family.

These reactions have a defensive quality; they express a painful self-consciousness about how whites will react, a vulnerability to being shamed. But there is a less defensive strain evident in either a self-conscious pride in things black or a more natural embrace of a black presence. You can find this in black students' embrace of the ghetto noir cinema, in shows like *In Living Color*, in Spike Lee movies, in the efflorescence of black women's writers, in Chris Rock's comedy, in the love of professional basketball. For some students it's the element of having experiences and people that they know enlarged for their own consumption. What black woman, and a few black men for that matter, could have read Terri McMillan's *Disappearing Acts* or Saffire's *Push* and not felt that their truths were running through those pages? Like Ghostface Killer's lament about single motherhood and poverty on "All That I Got from You," in which roaches in the cereal box are not a commentary on sanitary lifestyles but a reality in which you didn't eat till the school lunch program—if you went to school—kicked in at noon. Who wouldn't want to celebrate somebody getting the Lex and the house and all the Tommy gear after such humble beginnings? When all is said and done, it's often about who got the skills and who is getting paid because of it, and that we often refuse to admit that these things cross both class and racial lines. So what if it seems the only thing that Jigga and JD ("Money Ain't a Thing") want to talk about?

Yet even the embrace of a black cultural world does not provide neat closure to the messy process of discovering identity. Some of these depictions enforce a ghettocentric solution to the question of blackness, and not only among the activists. Indeed, some black middle-class strivers are vulnerable to such accusations and self-accusations and find themselves impelled to show their black credentials. The classic example of this is the black middle-class student raised in isolation from black culture who embraces black popular identities as a way to fit in with the posse. These students often immerse themselves in hip-hop music and the popular slang of the day in order to be seen as authentic. In the worst-case scenario, this can end in tragedy. As a young adjunct instructor I was privy to a situation with a young black male who believed that the narratives of gangsta rap represented the essence of the black experience. He eventually became a local drug dealer as an emblem of his authentic black experience. But of course in Smalltown, USA, such activities among black students are more easily detected, and he suffered the consequences.

Like the collapse of blackness into the gangster persona, the limiting quality of unalloyed appeals to blackness takes less drastic but no less disheartening forms, such as homophobia. One student's comments about the late Marlon Riggs's examination of black identity in the film *Black Is, Black Ain't* were illuminating in this regard. He queried aloud as to whether the film should be renamed "Gay Is, Gay Ain't." Given the energy that I had spent trying to make my students less homophobic, such a statement could have been interpreted as an open challenge. But like most students in class, he was simply expressing a quandary over how sexuality plays a role in an identity that most have seen as primarily racial. In many of their worldviews, black identity can best be described as "black like me." Unfortunately, homeboy dropped the class after viewing the film—something about the class being too demanding and needing to graduate, but more likely a response to being "read" out loud by the one openly gay student in class and more than enough black women. A similar circumstance can be found in those who think crossover culture is simply betrayal, selling out: the long-standing criticisms of Bryant Gumbel, *The Cosby Show*, and at times Oprah Winfrey are good examples. Why does Gumbel talk that way? Why do Cosby be playa-hatin' hip-hop like he did Eddie Murphy back in the day? How come Oprah don't ever have any "black" experts on her show? In a world in which everything is supposed to be done for family and your peeps, many crossovers are seen generating their success because they cater to whites. In the mix, Gumbel's support of historically black universities and colleges, Cosby and wife's $20 million gift to Spelman, or Oprah's support for serious black literature are lost.

Nowhere are the tensions associated with black identity more apparent than in black popular music and in students' responses to it. Like hip-hop, the musical genre that has served as a sound track to their life experiences, contemporary black college students represent a disparate mix of tones, styles, colors, and preferences. But also like hip-hop, a form of expression that draws on many divergent musical styles while often disguising its radical borrowings, black college students often deny such diversity. At its inception hip-hop was unique as a form of black expressive culture because it was largely distilled from black youth culture itself. It was thus an ideal vehicle for black youth to affirm themselves, their lives, and their dreams. Yes, they could borrow from James Brown, Marvin Gaye, Curtis Mayfield, and the Isley Brothers, but no one was ever going to mistake hip-hop for classic soul. The entire complex of old-school hip-hop, with its mix of rap music, breakdancing, turntable scratching, and the mystique of the microphone, emerged as an alternative to fusion and crossover. This unleashing of the voice of the ghetto had a powerfully creative dimension. Groups like Public Enemy, NWA, and Boogie Down Productions challenged centuries-old notions of the uses and content of black political rhetoric, particularly for a generation of black youth who hadn't marched in Birmingham and had been given thirdhand descriptions of why such struggles were important. Generations-old staples like "We Shall Overcome" and "Say It Loud, I'm Black and I'm Proud" had given way to NWA's "Fuck the Police" and KRS-One's "Criminal Minded." Yeah, the Isleys talked about "Fight the Power" back in '74, but Public Enemy was down with Farrakhan, fighting the power with (fake) Uzis on stage and digging Malcolm and the Funk up from the grave and the crates. I have my own vivid memories of driving through the South Bronx, new college degree in hand, and hearing Public Enemy's "Don't Believe the Hype" for the first time. I thought *I* could change the world. The experience was no less enthralling for those of us who didn't have Ivy League pedigrees and corporate gigs downtown. Brothers I hadn't connected with in years because I was doing the college thing, I suddenly connected with as we bobbed our collective heads to joints like "My Philosophy" ("Yes, I think very deeply") and "Rebel without a Pause." While many of my students understandably find the music of Chuck D and KRS-One dated, clearly the L-Boogies and Jiggas ("It's a hard knock life for us") of the world do the same, if not more, for them as old-school hip-hop did for my partners.

Surely hip-hop has had its nasty ethnocentric moments. But we need to be careful not to overstate this. Case in point, many white students would love to have Will Smith as a friend, in that he embodies a hip-hop/ghetto-centric sensibility that is nonthreatening to mainstream society. Smith's own brilliant performance of urban identity in music, as well as his crossover alliances in films and TV shows like the *Fresh Prince of Bel Air*, *Men in Black*, and *Independence Day*, powerfully influences male students, both black and white, who are trying to negotiate acceptance within various campus cliques. Smith, more than any other black working icon, has found a way to balance his own working-class urban experiences with the buddy-next-door sensibility that is so comforting to folks in the mainstream. A cooler, sharper, easygoing Poitier for Generation X, Will can come home to dinner and save the universe, albeit with a white sidekick for dessert, all the while helping the nondancing, rhythmless masses get jiggy with it.

On the flip side, many of these students would reject hip-hop artist DMX as their role model. DMX is the latest in a line of what MC Lyte has described on her track "Ruffneck"—the "dirty, grimy" brothers that the sisters call sexy and other brothers—brothers who are clearly not trying to model for *GQ* or *Ebony Man*, for that matter, but more interested in being thuggish and serious MCs—give props to. Big Daddy Kane, the prototype, fell off because he hadn't figured out if his role model was Priest or Al Green. Naughty by Nature's Treach took the mantle from Kane, only to be challenged by Wu Tang's Method Man. While Meth may be still holding court, DMX is clearly in the wings. I have plenty of students who embrace DMX as a viable model, and not all of them hail from the ghetto or live the less savory side of life there that DMX and his lyrics embody. The natural question is, Why would working- and middle-class black college students embrace such a figure? It doesn't quite take away all the mystery to ask the parallel question: Why do so many white middle- and upper-middle-class students embrace the Smashing Pumpkins, Aerosmith, or Marilyn Manson? While racism, poverty, and police brutality are real, clear-cut resistance to them is not always so real. So why not embrace the fantastic outlaw who preys on lesser thans, having them "falling like white bitches in a scary movie," as DMX suggests in "Get at Me Dog"?

To some extent, for black students it's about possibilities. In *Enemy of the People*, Will Smith embodies the buppie dream. Smith may have all the fly clothes, the money, and maybe all the women (or at least a lawyer wife), and his kid has sleepovers with his white friend. Through it all, somehow, Smith manages to project a modicum of blackness too; he is no Erkle. But whose lifestyle is more attainable? Being black, however that is defined, is seen as more realistic to many black youth, especially if they do not come from elite backgrounds. As one student put it, many students feel that "if you don't have an attitude, if you don't act a certain way, if you aren't from the ghetto, the perception is that you are not black." So you playa-hate Will Smith because he chooses not to accept such limitations. But this isn't only a question of accessibility. Some of those who embrace DMX include relatively well-off middle-class black young people who may be bound for professional careers, but crave acceptance by their black peers and have also based their perceptions of blackness on hip-hop video and the "ghettocentric noir" cinema. As a result, whatever its salutory impulses, there is a cost to this ghettocentric romance, as if black urban youth somehow define the essence of the black experience. At core, these ghettocentric realities suggest a world that the middle-class student can only embody during the course of a four-minute music video or eighty-seven-minute film. As the frustrations of racism and police brutality cross class boundaries, these spaces open up a world where some folks can in fact resist these realities, without risking their material futures.

This romance takes many forms, in rap and in the students' lives. On the one hand you have Naughty by Nature's ditty "Hip-Hop Hooray," an anthem of community, culture, and youth, but no less celebratory was Nas swinging, "Whose world is this? It's mine, It's mine, It's mine." Once again, we're back to ownership: ownership of possibilities, language, and experiences, if not of blackness itself. This has had a dramatic impact not only on the self-image of some members of Generation Hip-Hop, but also how nonblacks perceive black youth. Given the broad popularity of black popular culture and the diversity of images within it, many black students embrace ghettocentric sensibilities as a mode of performance that gains white approval or acceptance by other black students. Consider all the regional and contextual uses of the word *nigger*, and on my campus no less. The hip-hop generation is clear: it now controls the meaning of a word once uniquely tied to African-American disempowerment, and it won't let an older generation's squeamishness or outrage turn it around. The word's use both endears African-American youth to each other and, ironically, defuses white youth's racial anxiety—so much so that many whites use the term as a marker of oppositional status in their own lives. The urging of groups like NWA that "real niggaz don't die" speaks volumes in a world in which AIDS, crack, police brutality, and poverty regularly accompany young death. So why wouldn't poor white youth want to be niggas too? And while it is true that many of these so-called acts of resistance—"I'm the nigga you love to hate"—rarely venture beyond performance, they are no less important to the performer.

The radical transformation of hip-hop over time, especially its crossing over into the market of white youth, has complicated its ability to proclaim black identity. It has come to symbolize the utter ambivalence of the black situation; on the one hand, serving up versions of a richly "black" identity, on the other showing an eagerness to join the American mainstream. In this respect, the omnipresent P. Diddy may be the most telling indicator of the contradictions of an entire generation intent at once on affirming some vision of blackness and on moving up and out into the economy, politics, and the culture at large. Like some of my ghettocentric students, P. Diddy, a college-boy dropout from Howard University, has associated himself with the voice of ghetto. That same multifaceted persona also provides powerful imagery, as Sean "P. Diddy" Combs and many of his artists, like Shyne or the late Notorious B.I.G., represent the faces of young black urban males, even if such imagery is more tied to selling units than furthering the art. P. Diddy's days at Howard, where he attended classes Mon–Wed, broke north to NYC to produce acts like Jodeci and Mary J. Blige on Thursday and Friday, and gave parties on the weekend, like the infamous City College New Year's debacle, are part of the lore that make P. Diddy, P. Diddy. As with the purported scholarship that Mase received to play Division 1 college hoops, P. Diddy chose the performance of ghetto identities over tried and true middle-class paths; and both were more successful than they could have ever been going the more traditional route.

As so-called gangsta rap has fallen out of vogue, it has been replaced with a kind of playa/pimp/baller/high-roller conflation that is the thematic foundation of Combs's music. Despite some of the gangsterish trappings and the vulgar language, these tracks are at their core classic black middle-class uplift narratives, where folks work hard and "handle their bizness," whether the game is the drug game, the NBA, or the recording industry. See P. Diddy running down the street in his "Victory" video, a postmodern *Logan's Run* in Technicolor blackface, talking about how he does it better than anyone and he's got the $2 million video, with cameos by Danny Devito and Dennis Hopper, to prove it. While it is just entertainment, P. Diddy, like the Berry Gordys and Melvin Van Peebles before him, is a legitimate success model. And for a generation that lacks the political focus of the civil rights era, for whom consumption of style is a central theme, P. Diddy's celebration of gaudy, unabashed hedonism and buying finds perfect realization in "It's All about the Benjamins" and in dozens of other tracks, to say nothing of all the status striving he embodies out in the Hamptons. Percy "Master P." Miller or Jay-Z are even more compelling, as drug dealers who "came up" by their bootstraps—er, Nike cross-trainers. On the real, though, wouldn't Booker T. be proud, trying to get P. Diddy to do the soundtrack for *Tuskegee*, the miniseries?

This other side of P. Diddy, despite the ghettocentric accessories, tracks with both the crossover possibilities mined by Michael Jordan and Oprah and with the more general emergence of hip-hop as simply American culture. For all the rhetoric, both positive and negative, that my students regurgitate about "keeping it real," fact is, most of them want to be solid middle-class citizens. P. Diddy or Jay-Z ain't never made a video talking about working in the criminal justice system or higher and secondary education, but these are the aspirations of a good many of my students. "My take is that he is a young black male who's doing it . . . that's the positive. On the negative, as a rapper he's terrible." Another quickly separated the authentic "hip-hop male" from the imagined one: "Mase and P. Diddy is what the media portrays as the typical black, down, hip-hop male . . . the one you want to be down with." Such sentiments were also reflected in an MTV special a few years ago, in which white girls aged eleven to fifteen years old described Mase as "cute" and P. Diddy as "hot." P. Diddy's commercial success as both an artist and a producer has led other artists to follow his path, as has been the case with Jay-Z, Wyclef Jean, and Jermaine Dupri. Again, my students display a certain ambivalence about it. Wyclef Jean in particular represents an alternative. In a nation where black folks are monolithically defined as African American, the Fugees broadened the ethnic landscape of hip-hop; while clearly products of East Coast hip-hop, they neatly interjected their Haitian heritage into the mix. It's not as if other Caribbean folks were trying to claim their "yards"—hell, Biggie claimed Brooklyn, not Jamaica. Wyclef's solo joint took it one step further, by saying that he's not just a Haitian hip-hop artist but a balladeer, dancehall artist, Soca artist, and so on. Thus all those folks who had to negotiate their ethnic identities with the "keeping it real" ethos found common ground in Wyclef.

But the meaning of the Fugees for my students is more than ethnic or aesthetic. More critically, the Fugees represent a more concrete example of folks willing to do for peeps. Their Refugee Camp project has shed serious light on the plight of Haitian immigrants, while the group has always been willing to give back via free concerts and lectures—all while still keeping the flow classic. The temptation to cross over puts all this at risk, but students, intriguingly, have a certain respect and certainly grudging tolerance for it. "I think Jay-Z has a lot of underlying messages in his music," suggested a female student. "I used to think the same about Wyclef, but since he became commercial," she added, "the artists realize that they are just part of a trend." While many of these students are critical of an "All about the Benjamins" mentality, they are not willing to deny many of these artists their ability to make the most money they can.

As with white rock-and-rollers in MTV videos, for the most part black men have controlled the dominant imagery of the hip-hop generation. And like the white male musicians, black men have been challenged by all manner of sisters. Even Erykah Badu, Queen Sister Mother Earth of the Hip-Hop Nation, a mantle she acquired from Queen Latifah, had to jump bad about infidelity and the general trifling behavior from her man in "Tyrone." For some of my students, "Tyrone" made Badu much more accessible and real. So were the images of the four women who adorned the film version of *Waiting to Exhale*; Generation Hip-Hop is no monolith, especially driven by powerful tensions of gender. Back in the day, I can remembers sisters complaining about their men, running to get their Janet on as they rewound to that joint, "What Have You Done for Me Lately?" Now my female students have group therapy sessions watching *Waiting to Exhale* and the Sparkle video "Be Careful" ("two years ago promises is all I heard . . . wait a minute, let me finish"). The relative explosion of black feminist fiction in the early 1970s, much of which challenged sexism and patriarchy in the black community, was perhaps the clearest example of these changes.

If there is a single aspect of black identity that strikes a strong chord in my students, it is the issue of black sexuality, especially black female sexuality. Sometimes their responses are humorous, as was the case when students referred to Janet Jackson's recent music video for "I Get So Lonely" as the "tittie" video. As one of the homosexual men in my class remarked, "Even I had to pay attention to them in that video." The same students who tolerated P. Diddy's contradictions were less forgiving of the depiction of black women, especially as parlayed by black women performers them-selves. One of my students reacted strongly to hip-hop artist Lil' Kim, who has often viewed her own sexuality as liberating black women from male-defined standards of sexuality. Kim, whose first single, "No Time," talked about running with all them other "rich bitches," is the type of woman that my mama would have beat my ass if I had brought her home as a teenager. Imagine mid-1980s Madonna, four feet high and black, and yes, with that same blond wig. Better yet, imagine hip-hop pimp of the decade Too Short in high heels, a blond wig, and a satin nightgown, and you have the Lil' Kim aesthetic.

In reaction to Kim's appearance in the recent video "Money, Power and Respect" by the Lox, one female student commented, "Maybe money, but you have no power and you never gonna get any respect. Who's gonna give you power or respect, walking around dressed like that!" Lil' Kim and Foxy Brown (named after the Pam Grier blaxploitation character) are the most visible contemporary black female artists who have gravitated to hypersexual personas to sell their craft, including Adina Howard, Total, Monifah, and even Toni Braxton. And to some extent, the negative appraisals of my black female students reflect a concern with white reac-tions. In the words of one student, "I think those images influence a lot, especially those who don't have regular contact with people of a certain group. Because with Foxy Brown and Lil' Kim, guys think you're sup-posed to be Foxy Brown or Lil' Kim. I'm sorry, honey, she's not real. She may be real on some level, but I'm sorry, all black women are not like that." Using much stronger language, another female student concurred: "The problem is more like society, being that throughout our history in this country, black women have been degraded as negative images, so why should black popular culture reinforce that if you're trying to get rid of those stereotypes." The same student was very clear about the implica-tions of these images. "It is a problem when white society uses black peo-ple like that in our forms of entertainment. You can have problems getting jobs. People in universities don't take you seriously, so if those stereotypes are already out there and our forms of entertainment are rein-forcing it, it causes problems."

And yet for many of the women, it is not white perceptions of blacks as much as implications for black women that are decisive. "This is a very sexual society, and being sexy . . . that's power," asserted one black female student. "If you can manipulate the opposite sex because of the way that you look, the way you dress, or your mannerisms . . . that's power. But is that a good thing and can you handle the consequence of that." Like the images of Puff Daddy and Mase, the images of black women influence in very powerful ways, but, as another student insisted, "It's not only on a white level that enhances this whole system; black people buy into that too."

At the moment, no one provides as resonant an alternative to the images of Lil' Kim and Foxy Brown within hip-hop as former Fugees front woman Lauryn "L-Boogie" Hill. L-Boogie's significance is at the core aesthetic; simply, very few hip-hop artists, men or women, can flow like she can. All you got to do is hear "Vocab" from the Fugees' first release or "Lost Ones" from her own joint to know that the sista is on some "best ever" shit. But it's more than that. Just checking out the cover art from her CD, which invokes the cover art of the Wailers' *Burnin'* and *Natty Dread* releases and the title film *The Education of Sonny Carson*, you get a sense of the traditions she is trying to bridge. Having Bob Marley's son Rohan as your "baby daddy" don't hurt either. Despite what we say about single moms in our culture, Hill is no victim, as she witnesses to on the track "To Zion." Some of my female students were strongly attracted to Hill's independence, something that many of them, particularly those with West Indian heritage, tied to the culture that produced their mothers, aunts, and grandmothers. While Kim and Foxy are supposedly having all the fun, L-Boogie is raising a family, taking care of her bizness (how many women artists ever get to self-produce their work, let alone a debut release, or produce Queen Aretha?), and upholding the mantle of contemporary black womanhood. These are things that are important to many of students the I talk to. Black men often identify Hill as the embodiment of a certain ideal hip-hop persona, but for black women, her significance is deeper still. "She expresses a lot of things as a black woman you want to hear and you want others to hear. Not Foxy Brown, not Lil' Kim. You don't want anybody to think about you like that. But Lauryn Hill, she's actually dignified, she has to represent more of a black woman."

While Generation Hip-Hop is clearly not a monolith, and the various analyses that have described it as such are unfair, there are some legitimate reasons to see this generation, despite its internal differences, as being collectively different from previous generations of blacks. Generation Hip-Hop is really a hybrid of past struggles, the need for self-determination, and a desire to simply succeed on America's terms, as virtually every other ethnic group strives to achieve. The challenge to "keep it real" and "still get paid" may seem crass to older generations, but it is the dominant ethos of Generation Hip-Hop. Despite tremendous insecurities about what "keeping it real" means and whether or not "getting paid" will buffer them from the tragedy of race and ethnicity in this country, they still forge forward, like some vanguard on new black futures, embracing whatever identities allow them to most effectively succeed in the mainstream and survive the margins. Old-schoolers can playa-hate all they want, but it's Generation Hip-Hop that has to live in the world that so many of their sensibilities and identities are responses to. But still, we're left this basic reality; as expressed by one of my students, "I'm all for diversity within our ranks. But the question comes down to whether or not you feel more comfortable with *your* people or the other people. If you don't like where you come from, then I have a problem with you."

Notes

Chapter One

1. Steven Best and Douglas Kellner, *Postmodern Theory: Critical Interrogations* (New York: Guildford Press, 1991), provide an excellent overview of the various postmodern factions.

2. bell hooks, "Postmodern Blackness," *Postmodern Culture* 1, no. 1 (October 1990).

3. Despite my concerns here, when I was shopping the manuscript to various presses, one African-American series editor offhandedly suggested that my work was "postmodern," a sentiment echoed at many African-American studies conferences where I presented early drafts of the manuscript. I mention this specifically because I have never explicitly used postmodern theory in my work.

4. S. Craig Watkins, *Representing: Hip-Hop Culture and the Production of Black Cinema* (Chicago: University of Chicago Press, 1998), 54.

5. Jurgen Habermas, "Modernity—-An Incomplete Project," in *The Anti-Aesthetic: Essays on Postmodern Culture*, ed. Hal Foster (Seattle: Bay Press, 1983), 5.

6. Scott Malcomson, *One Drop of Blood: The American Misadventure of Race* (New York: Farrar, Straus and Giroux, 2000), 174.

7. Ibid., 174.

8. Ibid., 150.

9. See Stuart Hall's essay, "What Is This Black in Black Popular Culture," in *Black Popular Culture*, ed. Gina Dent (Seattle: Bay Press, 1993).

10. Kimberly Benston, *Performing Blackness: Enactments of African-American Modernism* (New York: Routledge, 2000), 3.

11. I am conscious that the term *counter* suggests a naturally oppositional relationship between American modernity and African-American modernity. It is not my intention to suggest such an opposition, but rather to highlight an alternative mode as practiced by some African Americans. I am thankful to Ed Pavlic for his insights here.

12. Komozi Woodard, *A Nation within a Nation: Amiri Baraka (Leroi Jones) and Black Power Politics* (Raleigh: University of North Carolina Press, 1999), 261.

13. Perhaps the best example of this is the way that Bayard Rustin's homosexuality and Marxist leanings were conflated and used as a rationale for jettisoning him from Martin Luther King Jr.'s inner circle.

14. Quoted in Kobena Mercer, *Welcome to the Jungle: New Positions in Black Cultural Studies* (New York: Routledge, 1994), 131.

15. Huey P. Newton, "The Women's Liberation and the Gay Liberation Movements," in *Black Men on Race, Gender, and Sexuality*, ed. Devon Carbado (New York: New York University Press, 1999), 387.

16. See Cathy Cohen and Tamara Jones, "Fighting Homophobia versus Challenging Heterosexism: 'The Failure to Transform Revisited,'" in *Dangerous Liaisons: Blacks, Gays, and the Struggle for Equality*, ed. Eric Brandt (New York: New Press, 1999), 80–101.

17. Eldridge Cleaver's legendary diatribes against James Baldwin in *Soul on Ice* and the unofficial "banishing" of Bayard Rustin from the inner circle of civil rights leadership, both based on queer lifestyles, are two of the most well-known examples of such "violence."

18. hooks, "Postmodern Blackness."

19. Dwight McBride, "Can the Queen Speak? Racial Essentialism, Sexuality, and the Problem of Authority," *Callaloo* 21, no. 2 (1998): 377.

20. Joseph E. Holloway, ed., *Africanisms in American Culture (Blacks in the Diaspora)*. Bloomington: Indiana University Press, 1990).

21. See my conversation about the music of South Shore Commission in *What the Music Said: Black Popular Music and Black Public Culture* (New York: Routledge, 1998).

22. Hortense Spillers, "The Crisis of the Negro Intellectual: A Post-Date," *Boundary 2* (fall 1994): 106.

23. See E. Patrick Nelson, "Feeling the Spirit in the Dark: Expanding Notions of the sacred in the African-American Gay Community," *Callaloo* 21, no. 2 (1998): 399–416.

24. Robert Weems, *Desegregating the Dollar: African-American Consumerism in the Twentieth Century* (New York: New York University Press, 1998), 70.

25. At a conference a few years ago, I was struck by a presenter's assertion that the cover of *Vibe* magazine, which featured Percy Miller, Sean Combs, and Russell Simmons, represented the contemporary face of black capitalism.

26. Kali Tal, "Life behind the Screen," *Wired*, October 1996.

27. Robert George, quoted in "NAACP Hurting Image of African Americans, Group Says," *New York Voice*, August 17, 1994.

28. Michael Eric Dyson, *I May Not Get There with You: The True Martin Luther King Jr.* (New York: Free Press, 2000), 16.

29. David Lionel Smith, "What Is Black Culture?" in *The House that Race Built: Black Americans, U.S. Terrain*, ed. Wahneema Lubiano (New York: Vintage Books, 1998), 181.

30. Philip Brian Harper, *Framing the Margins: The Social Logic of Postmodern Culture* (New York: Oxford University Press, 1994), 29.

31. Lawrence Grosberg, *Dancing in Spite of Myself: Essays on Popular Culture* (Durham, N.C.: Duke University Press, 1997), 3.

32. Ibid., 164.

33. Stanley Aronowitz, *Dead Artists, Live Theories and Other Cultural Problems* (New York: Routledge, 1994), 7.

34. My comments regarding Bobby Brown recognize not only his consistent attempts to reference "the street" within New Edition, but how that stance was later appropriated by Danny Walberg, who was a member of the much more commercially successful New Kids on the Block. Both groups were founded and for a time managed by Maurice Starr, who is African American. Walberg and his brother Mark, who has made the crossover from rap star to Hollywood actor, were really the visual role models for contemporary "boy" groups like 98 Degrees, N'Sync, and the Backstreet Boys. The material for the latter two groups is, ironically, largely written and produced by Full Force, who were major figures in the early R&B/hip-hop hybrid sound in the 1980s.

NOTES

35. The song was initially featured in the Michael Jordan and Loony Toons vehicle *Space Jam.*

36. Quoted in Paul Ryan, "The Tortured Souls of Soul," *Weekly Journal*, January 26, 1995.

37. "You Remind Me of Something," *R. Kelly* (Jive/Zomba, 1995).

38. Quoted in Justin Onyeka, "A Special Lesson in Self-Love," *Weekly Journal*, November 16, 1995.

39. "Gotham City (remix)" (Jive/Zomba, 1997).

40. Al Green and David Seay, *Take Me to the River* (New York: Harper Entertainment, 2000), 6.

41. "Any Love: Silence, Theft, and Rumor in the Work of Luther Vandross," *Callaloo* 23, no. 1 (2000): 426.

42. See Arnold Shaw, *Honkers and Shouters* (New York: Schirmer Books, 1986); Brian Ward, *Just My Soul Responding* (Berkeley: University of California Press, 1998).

43. I am thankful to my assistant Nicole Johnson, a Chicago native, for this information.

44. "Down Low (Nobody Has to Know): The Motion Picture," *The Down Low: Top Secret Videos* (Jive/Zomba Video, 1996).

45. Andreas Huyssen, "Mass Culture as Woman: Modernism's Other," in *After the Great Divide: Modernism, Mass Culture, Postmodernism* (Bloomington: Indiana University Press, 1986), 44–61.

46. My thoughts about the "Ronald Isley" and "Mr. Biggs" dichotomy occurred after watching Isley's video for "Floating on Your Love," which featured cameos by hip-hop artists Lil' Kim, Sean "Puffy" Combs, and Isley's wife Angela Winbush, and hearing someone respond elatedly, "Oh, it's Mr. Biggs."

47. Green, *Take Me to the River*, 7.

48. Justin Onyeka, "A Special Lesson in Self-Love," *Weekly Journal*, November 16, 1995.

49. "Intro–The Sermon," *R. Kelly* (Jive/Zomba, 1995).

50. "Rosa Parks," *Aquemini* (LaFace, 1998).

51. David Ashenfelter, "Judge to Decide Parks' Name Claim," *Detroit Free Press*, November 5, 1999.

Chapter 2

1. Mark Reid, *Redefining Black Film* (Berkeley: University of California Press, 1993), 69.

2. Ibid., 77.

3. Also telling from these sequences is the faux-feminist construction of the white woman biker as the leader of her gang. The scene at once suggests the inability of these particular white men to sexually satisfy the woman, who is presumably a lesbian, and powerfully invests black male sexuality with the capability to both escape potential violence and reinscribe the heterosexist status quo.

4. Ed Guerrero, *Framing Blackness* (Philadelphia: Temple University Press, 1994), 91.

5. Quoted in ibid., 88.

6. Quoted in Reid, *Redefining Black Film*, 77.

7. Vincent Canby, "Film: Poitier in Two Roles," *New York Times*, June 17, 1975, 25.

8. WBLS was owned by Inner City Broadcasting, a corporation that was founded by then Manhattan borough president Percy Sutton, who was also the personal legal counsel of Malcolm X (El-Hajj Malik El-Shabazz).

9. Quoted in the *New York Times*, July 11, 1974.

10. Ibid.

11. Guerrero, *Framing Blackness*, 105.

12. Ibid., 110.

13. The much-ballyhooed 2000 opening of a "mega-multiplex" in Harlem, owned and operated by former NBA star Earvin "Magic" Johnson, is one example of how this trend finally began to address the absence of exhibition houses in largely black communities like Harlem.

14. See David Levering Lewis, *When Harlem Was in Vogue* (New York: Oxford University Press, 1989).

15. Reid, *Redefining Black Film*, 26.

16. Canby, "Film: Poitier in Two Roles."

17. Reid, *Redefining Black Film*, 31.

18. Joy James, *Shadowboxing: Representations of Black Feminist Politics* (New York: St. Martin's Press, 1999), 100.

19. Ibid., 101.

20. Ibid., 101.

21. See Robin D. G. Kelley's brilliant essay "Kickin' Reality, Kickin' Ballistics: 'Gangsta Rap' and Postindustrial Los Angeles," in her *Race Rebels: Culture, Politics, and the Black Working Class* (New York: Free Press, 1994).

22. Suzanne Smith, *Dancing in the Streets: Motown and the Cultural Politics of Detroit* (Cambridge: Harvard University Press, 2000), 34–35.

23. See Weems, *Desegregating the Dollar*.

24. I am thinking specifically of Randall Robinson's book *The Debt* (New York: E. P. Dutton, 2000).

25. My "chitlin' circuit" comment is a reference to popular traveling stage dramas like *Beauty Shop*, *Diary of a Black Man*, and *My Mama Prayed for Me*, which are probably closer to a religious revival than serious drama like that written and reduced by Douglas Turner Ward or August Wilson.

26. The term *moulie* is derived from the Italian word for eggplant, hence its use in describing African Americans.

27. See Kelley, Race Rebels; and Tera Hunter, *To Joy My Freedom: Southern Black Women's Lives and Labors after the Civil War* (Cambridge: Harvard University Press, 1998).

28. See *The Truly Disadvantaged* (Chicago: University of Chicago Press, 1998) and *When Work Disappears* (New York: Knopf, 1996).

29. See Kevin Gaines, *Uplifting the Race* (Chapel Hill: University of North Carolina Press, 1996).

30. While I am not privy to Cosby's particular taste in women, it is worth noting that the actor has had an affinity for light-skinned black women opposite his characters. Denise Nichols was cast as his opposite in both *Let's Do It Again* and *A Piece of the Action*, and Phylicia Rashad was cast as his wife in both of his televisions sitcoms, *The Cosby Show* and *Cosby*.

31. I was made more aware of this connection during an appearance by Morgan Freeman on *The Chris Rock Show* in the fall of 2000, when Freeman received an unusually warm and emotional greeting from the audience. While Freeman has clearly been one of most effective and brilliant actors of his generation, the applause caught me off guard, since such applause is usually reserved for Rock and the various music acts that appear on the show. As my assistant Nicole Johnson later reminded me, Freeman largely began his acting career as one of the ensemble members of the popular public television show *The Electric Company*, so many in audience could have likely remembered Freeman from their childhood.

32. Michael Eric Dyson, *Reflecting Black: African-American Cultural Criticism* (Minneapolis: University of Minnesota Press, 1993), 86.

33. Ibid., 84.

34. See Herman Gray, *Watching Race: Television and the Struggle for "Blackness"* (Minneapolis: University of Minnesota Press, 1994), 70–84.

NOTES

Chapter 3

1. Donald Bogle, *Toms, Coons, Mulattos, Mammies, and Bucks: An Interpretive History of Blacks in American Films*, 3d ed. (New York: Continuum, 1994), 211.
2. Ibid., 211.
3. Guerrero, *Framing Blackness*.
4. I am not suggesting that there were not other "family"-oriented popular programs that didn't feature traditional nuclear families. *Family Affair*, which starred Brian Keith and a "queered" Sebastian Cabot in the role of French the butler, is one example. Even *The Brady Bunch*, which more or less introduced the blended family to television audiences, was a departure from the tried-and-true formulas of the *Donna Reed Show*, *Father Knows Best*, and *Leave It to Beaver*, which presented the "natural" nuclear family and user-friendly patriarchy with a vengeance.
5. See Kristel Brent Zook's chapter "Sheneneh, Gender-fuck, and Romance: Martin's Thin Line between Love and Hate," in her *Color by Fox: The Fox Network and the Revolution in Black Television* (New York: Oxford University Press, 1999), 53–64.
6. Donna Franklin, *Ensuring Inequality: The Structural Transformation of the African-American Family*, (New York: Oxford University Press, 1997), 153–181.
7. Ibid., 165–166. See also Gerald Horne, *The Fire This Time: The Watts Uprisings and the 1960s* (New York: Da Capo Press, 1997).
8. Jimmie Reeves, "Re-Covering Racism: Crack Mothers, Reaganism, and the Network News," in *Living Color: Race and Television in the United States*, ed. Sasha Torres (Durham, N.C.: Duke University Press, 1998), 103.
9. See Marlon Riggs's film *Black Is, Black Ain't* (ITVS, 1995).
10. See *The Moynihan Report and the Politics of Controversy*, edited by Lee Rainwater and William Y. Yancy (Cambridge: MIT Press, 1967).
11. Franklin, *Ensuring Inequality*, 182–214.
12. Louie Robinson, "Bad Times on the 'Good Times' Set," *Ebony Magazine*, September 1975, 35.
13. See Jane Rhodes, "Fanning the Flames of Racial Discord: The National Press and the Black Panther Party," *Harvard International Journal of Press Politics* 4, no. 4 (1999): 95–118.
14. Louie Robinson, "Bad Times," 33–42.
15. Quoted in Margretta Browne, "John Amos: The First Dad of Black Life Telling it Like It Is." Blackfilm.com, May 2000. (http://www.blackfilm.com/0205/features/i-johnamos.shmtl)
16. *The E True Hollywood Story: Good Times*, broadcast September 2000.
17. Interview footage presented in *The E True Hollywood Story: Good Times*.
18. Les Brown, "'Good Times' Will Drop Male Parent; Black Media Coalition Protest Move," *New York Times*, June 7, 1976.
19. Ibid., 59.
20. Ibid., 59.
21. Hortense Spillers, "Mama's Baby, Papa's Maybe: An American Grammar Book," in *African American Literary Theory: A Reader*, ed. Winston Napier (New York: New York University Press, 2000), 277.
22. Sharon Patricia Holland, "Bill T. Jones, Tupac Shakur and the (Queer) Art of Death," *Callaloo* 23, no. 1 (2000): 387.
23. Ibid., 387.
24. Gray, *Watching Race*, 80.
25. See Dyson, *Reflecting Black*, and Gray, *Watching Race*.
26. Quoted in Browne, "John Amos."
27. Gray, *Watching Race*.

28. Ibid.

29. Patricia Hill-Collins, *Black Feminist Thought: Knowledge, Consciousness, and the Politics of Empowerment* (New York: Routledge, 1991), 71.

30. Ibid.

31. Ibid., 76.

32. Reeves, "Re-Covering Racism," 97–117.

33. Franklin, *Ensuring Inequality*, 198.

34. Ibid.

35. Karla F. Holloway, *Codes of Conduct: Race, Ethics, and the Color of Our Character* (New Brunswick: Rutgers University Press, 1995), 94.

36. See Joan Morgan, *When Chickenheads Come Home to Roost: My Life as a Hip Hop Feminist* (New York: Simon and Schuster, 1999), for a more detailed explanation of "chickenheads."

37. Juliane Malveaux, "Gladiators, Gazelles, and Groupies: Basketball Love and Loathing," in *Basketball Jones: America above the Rim*, ed. Todd Boyd and Ken Shropshire (New York: New York University Press, 2000), 56.

38. Rickie Solinger, *Wake Up Little Susie: Single Pregnancy and Race before Roe v. Wade* (New York: Routledge, 1992), 29–30.

39. Ibid., 29–34.

40. Dorothy Roberts, *Killing the Black Body: Race, Reproduction, and the Meaning of Liberty* (New York: Pantheon Books, 1997), 4–5.

41. Morgan, *When Chickenheads Come Home to Roost*, 217.

42. Holland, "Bill T. Jones," 387.

43. Dyson, *I May Not Get There with You*, 160.

44. Todd Boyd, *Am I Black Enough for You? Popular Culture from the 'Hood and Beyond* (Bloomington: Indiana University Press, 1997), 71.

45. Thembisa S. Mshaka, "Dave Hollister: Arrival and Revival, Ghetto Style," Launch Media, May 31, 1999. (http://www.launch.com/music/content/1,5850,158065,00.html?vo=)

46. The logic here is that if you shoot someone, they become "wet" with blood. I am further reminded of Dr. Dre's classic recording and video "Nothing but a G Thang," in which a female character is symbolically gang-raped when bottles of forty-ounce malt liquor, an extension of black male phallic power, are sprayed on her body.

47 See Charles Nero's essay "Towards a Black Gay Aesthetic: Signifying in Contemporary Black Gay Culture, in *Brother to Brother: New Writings by Black Gay Men*, ed. Essex Hemphill (Boston: Alyson, 1991), 229–52.

48. John Carmody, "The TV Column," *Washington Post*, February 5, 1987.

49. Liner notes for the O'Jays, *Family Reunion* (Philadelphia International Records, 1975).

50. See Nelson George, *The Death of Rhythm and Blues* (New York: Pantheon, 1988); Craig Werner's *A Change Is Gonna Come*, and my own *What the Music Said* for a more detailed discussion of the Gamble and Huff legacy.

51. The definitive examples of the breakdown segment include the introduction to the Isaac Hayes version of "I Stand Accused" and Lenny Williams's "Cause I Love You." Williams's signature "oh, oh, oh" riff from "'Cause I Love You" has been repeatedly appropriated by vocalist R. Kelly and was the subject of a comedy routine by Steve Harvey in the film *The Kings of Comedy*.

52. See Robert M. Entman and Andrew Rojecki's interesting study, *The Black Image in the White Mind: Media and Race in America* (Chicago: University of Chicago Press, 2000).

53. George Tillman Jr., *Soul Food Cookbook: Recipes of the Stars* [pamphlet inserted in video package], 3.

NOTES

54. Quoted in Carole Sugarman, "A Film to Feed the Soul: George Tillman Jr.'s Celebration of the Sunday Supper," *Washington Post*, September 24, 1997.

55. Adolph Reed, "Romancing Jim Crow," in *Class Notes: Posing as Politics and Other Thoughts on the American Scene* (New York: New Press, 2000) 19.

56. Ibid., 23.

57. See Nicholas Lehman, *Promised Land* (New York Knopf, 1991).

58. Sugarman, "A Film to Feed the Soul."

59. Tillman, "Soul Food Cookbook," 3.

60. Sugarman, "A Film to Feed the Soul."

61. See Tera Hunter's fascinating study of black women domestic workers, *To 'Joy My Freedom*.

62. Booker T. Washington, "The Atlanta Exposition Address," in *Up from Slavery*, (New York: Signet Classics, 2000), 154.

63. I'd like to acknowledge my graduate assistant David Curry for bringing some aspects of the film to my attention.

64. Brent Zook, "Sheneneh, Genderfuck, and Romance," 53–64.

65. Ibid., 58.

Chapter 4

1. Harold Cruse, *The Crisis of the Negro Intellectual* (New York: William Morrow, 1967), 468.

2. Ibid., 99.

3. Nelson George, *Buppies, B-Boys, Baps and Bohos: Notes on Post-Soul Black Culture* (New York: HarperCollins, 1992).

4. Michael Eric Dyson, "We Never Were What We Used to Be," in *Race Rules: Navigating the Color Line* (New York: Addison Wesley, 1996), 135.

5. Kevin Powell, "The Word Movement," in *Step into a World: A Global Anthology of the New Black Literature* (New York: John Wiley and Sons), 1–12.

6. Conversation with Madison Davis Lacy, who directed the documentary *Native Son* (1995).

7. Sanchez's presence at Temple University, Baraka's at SUNY–Stonybrook, and Nikki Giovanni's at Virginia Tech are prime examples of this trend.

8. Russel Jacoby, *The Last Intellectuals* (New York: Basic Books, 1987), offers a trenchant commentary on the demise of public discourse and the collapse of spaces for independent intellectuals not exclusively tied to the academy.

9. Greg Tate, "Nobody Loves a Genius Child: Jean Michel Basquiat, Flyboy in the Buttermilk," in *Fly Boy in the Buttermilk: Essays on Contemporary America* (New York: Simon and Schuster, 1992), 232.

10. Ibid., 198.

11. Ibid., 200.

12. Trey Ellis, "The New Black Aesthetic," *Callaloo* 12, no. 1 (winter 1989): 233–43.

13. Ibid., 234.

14. Ronald A.T. Judy, "The New Black Aesthetic and W. E. B. Du Bois, or Hephaestus, Limping," *Massachusetts Review*, spring 1995, 250.

15. Ellis, "New Black Aesthetic," 237.

16. Ibid., 235.

17. Tera Hunter, "'It's a Man's Man's Man's World'": Specters of the Old Renewed in Afro-American Culture and Criticism," *Callaloo* 12, no. 1 (winter 1989): 247.

18. Ellis, "New Black Aesthetic," 239.

19. Judy, "New Black Aesthetic and W. E. B. Du Bois," 251.

20. Robert S. Boynton, "The New Intellectuals," *Atlantic Monthly*, March 1995, 64.

21. Ishmael Reed, "Hoodwinked: Paul Beatty's Urban Nihilists," *Village Voice Literary Supplement*, April 2000.

22. Reed, *Class Notes*, 89.

23. Ibid., 85.

24. Boyd, *Am I Black Enough for You?* 7.

25. bell hooks, "Ice Cube Culture: A Shared Passion for Speaking the Truth," in *Outlaw Culture: Resisting Representations* (New York: Routledge, 1994), 125–43.

26. I am reminded here of my own experience as an eight-year-old watching the *Jackson Five* cartoon on Saturday-morning television.

27. Hortense Spillers, "The Crisis of the Negro Intellectual: A Post-Date," *Boundary 2*, 21, no. 3 (fall 1994): 73.

28. Kevin Powell, "The Word Movement," in *Step into a World: A Global Anthology of the New Black Literature* (New York: John Wiley and Sons, 2000), 4.

29. Cruse, *The Crisis of the Negro Intellectual*, 457.

30. Ibid., 464.

31. Henry Giroux, *Channel Surfing: Racism, the Media, and the Destruction of Today's Youth* (New York: St. Martin's Press, 1997), 153.

32. "Filmmaker Spike Lee Slams Fox's 'The PJs,'" *Washington Post*, January 18, 1999.

33. Ibid.

34. "People Watch," *Fort Worth Star-Telegram*, May 4, 1997.

35. Cruse, *The Crisis of the Negro Intellectual*, 189.

36. C. L. R. James, "Popular Arts and Modern Society," in *American Civilization* (Oxford: Blackwell, 1993), 119.

37. Watkins, *Representing*, 51.

38. Zadie Smith, "The Grinch Who Sold Out," *Vibe Magazine*, December 2000, 90–91.

39. Giroux, *Channel Surfing*, 148.

Chapter 5

1. "An Official's Vocabulary Lesson," *Washington Post*, January 28, 1999.

2. John McWhorter, *Losing the Race: Self-Sabotage in Black America* (New York: Free Press, 2000), xi.

3. Ibid., xi.

4. Paul Beatty, *The White Boy Shuffle* (New York: Henry Holt, 1996), 37.

5. One of the best examples of this is the stylish nature of poor urban blacks who use cell phones in lieu of having phones in their homes. When some folks, poor or otherwise, have their home phones turned off because of previously unpaid long distance bills, very often companies like Voice Stream offer alternatives by allowing folks to have cell phone service on a pay-as-you-go basis. The relative ease in which such accounts can be opened have led some, like the rap collective Mau Mau ("Blak iz Blak") and Jill Scott, to suggest that they allow the "authorities" better modes of surveillance.

6. I am thinking specifically here about Anderson's *Streetwise* (Chicago: University of Chicago Press, 1960), Wilson's *When Work Disappears* (New York: Knopf, 1996), and Patillo-McCoy's recent study of the black middle class in *White Pickett Fences* (Chicago: University of Chicago Press, 1999).

7. Beatty, *The White Boy Shuffle*, 61.

8. Ibid., 65.

NOTES

9. Ibid., 51.

10. A short list of these commentators would include Nathan McCall, Brent Staples, Debra Dickerson, Shelby Steele, Jill Nelson, bell hooks, and Henry Louis Gates Jr.

11. Beatty, *White Boy Shuffle*, 45.

12. Ibid., 49.

13. Ibid., 52.

14. For a more detailed discussion of shopping malls and public space, see Margaret Crawford's essay "The World in a Shopping Mall," in *Variations on a Theme Park: the New American City and the End of Public Space*, ed. Michael Sorkin (New York: Noonday Press, 1992), 3-30.

15. Beatty, *White Boy Shuffle*, 76.

16. Ibid., 77.

17. Ibid., 79.

18. Ibid., 86.

19. See Tricia Rose, *Black Noise* (Hanover: Wesleyan Press, 1996), and David Toop, *Rap Attack* (London: Serpent's Tail, 1991), for a more detailed explanation of the politial aspects of graffiti art in New York City in the late 1960s and 1970s.

20. See David Serlin's provocative essay, "From Sesame Street to Schoolhouse Rock: Urban Pedagogy and Soul Iconography in the 1970s," in *Soul: Black Power, Politics, and Pleasure*, ed. Monique Guillory and Richard C. Green (New York: New York University Press, 1998).

21. Beatty, *White Boy Shuffle*, 96.

22. Ibid., 67.

23. Ibid., 119.

24. Ibid., 118.

25. One of the most memorable examples of this in recent sports history was the criticism directed toward track and field star Carl Lewis during the 1984 Summer Olympics. Though Lewis achieved his stated goal of matching the legendary Jesse Owens's feat of winning four gold medals at a Summer Olympiad, both fans and commentators criticized Lewis for not breaking Bob Beamon's then-fifteen-year-old record in the long-jump competition. The criticism was heightened because Lewis chose not to try to break the record, although he had another jump left in competition. Having apparently already won on the basis of his first two jumps, Lewis chose instead to conserve his energy for another competition. In many ways the criticism of Lewis can be seen as displacing the more profound homophobic discomfort with Lewis's flamboyance, as expressed in of his bodysuits and Grace Jones–like high-top fade, which recalled the androgyny of early David Bowie and Michael Jackson.

26. Beatty, *White Boy Shuffle*, 119.

27. Kenneth Shropshire, "Deconstructing the NBA," in Boyd and Shropshire, *Basketball Jones: America Above the Rim*, 75–89.

28. See Michael Eric Dyson's provocative essay "Be Like Mike? Michael Jordan and the Pedagogy of Desire," in *Reflecting Black*, for a more detailed examination of the "genius" of Jordan's athletic prowess.

29. Beatty, *White Boy Shuffle*, 119.

30. Shropshire, "Deconstructing the NBA," 83.

31. See Sohail Daulatzai, "View the World from American Eyes: Ball, Islam, and Dissent in Post-race America," in Boyd and Shropshire, *Basketball Jones*, 198–214.

32. Beatty, *White Boy Shuffle*, 154.

33. Ibid., 163.

34. See Daulatzai, "View the World from American Eyes."

35. Beatty, *White Boy Shuffle*, 179.

36. Ibid., 179.

37. Ibid., 159.

38. Ibid., 160.

39. Ibid., 200.

40. Ibid., 200.

41. Ibid., 200.

42. "The Books Interview: Paul Beatty," *Independent-London*, July 22, 2000.

43. Ibid.

44. Morgan, *When Chickenheads Come Home to Roost*, 17.

45. Ibid.

46. Ibid., 59.

47. Ibid., 62.

48. Ibid., 185.

49. For a more masculine example, imagine congressman Jesse Jackson Jr., going toe to toe with Wu Tang Clan Member Old Dirty Bastard.

50. See Manning Marable, *Speaking Truth to Power: Essays on Race, Resistance, and Radicalism* (Boulder: Westview, 1998). The essay was originally published in the London-based journal *New Statesman and Society* on October 27, 1995.

51. Morgan, *When Chickenheads Come Home to Roost*, 35.

52. Ibid., 54.

53. Ibid., 56.

54. Ibid., 57–58.

55. Ibid., 58.

56. Ibid., 57.

57. I am thankful to Rinaldo Walcott for bringing this to my attention.

58. For an interesting example of how one artist strategically employs his "thug-nigga" status see D'Angelo's "Untitled" video.

59. *When Chickenheads Come Home to Roost*, 185–186.

60. Ibid.

61. Ibid., 188.

62. Tricia Rose, "Race, Class, and the Pleasure/Danger Dialectic: Rewriting Black Female Teenage Sexuality in the Popular Imagination," *Black Renaissance/Renaissance Noire* 1, no. 3 (spring/summer 1998): 175–77.

63. De La Soul, "The Bizness," *Stakes Is High* (Tommy Boy, 1996).

64. This line in "Love Rain" immediately reminded me of a commercial for a popular laxative in which a black mother and daughter (my former classmate Samaria Graham) talk frankly about constipation. I mention this to suggest that the commercial captures some of the private moments that black woman can share, like choices of laxatives, tampons, contraception devices, and so on, that rarely get played out in the popular media. Given the relative crisis in the black community surrounding teenage pregnancy, it is ironic that black popular culture has not contained more frank conversations about these choices.

65. "Do You Remember?" *Who Is Jill Scott?: Words and Sounds, Volume 1* (Hidden Beach Recordings, 2000).

66. For a particularly thoughtful exploration of black girls' play, see Kyra Gaunt, "Translating Double Dutch to Hip-hop: The Musical Vernacular of Black Girls' Play," in *Language, Rhythm, and Sound: Black Popular Culture into the Twenty-first Century*, ed. Joseph Adjaye and Adrianne Andrews (Pittsburgh: University of Pittsburgh Press, 1997), 146–63.

67. Jennifer Devere Brody, "The Return of Cleopatra Jones," *Signs*, August 1999, 100.

68. Ibid., 100.

69. See Neal, *What the Music Said*, for a more detailed discussion of postindustrial

nostalgia.

70. Scott, "Getting in the Way," on *Who Is Jill Scott?*.

71. Nicole Johnson's unpublished paper "Confessions of an Okayplayer: Cyberhoods and Net-ghettos" uses the Okayplayer site to examine the construction of black cyber-communities and the issue of passing.

72. Scott, "Watching Me," on *Who is Jill Scott?*

73. Mike Davis, *City of Quartz: Excavating the Future in Los Angeles* (London: Verso, 1990), 223.

74. Scott, "Watching Me."

75. Dwayne Wiggin's "What's Really Going On (Strange Fruit)" and the Mos Def–led supergroup Hip-hop for Respect are notable examples of these efforts.

76. bell hooks, *Reel to Real: Race, Sex, and Class at the Movies* (New York: Routledge, 1996), 54.

77. Aaron McGruder, *The Boondocks: Because I Know You Don't Read the Newspaper* (New York: Andrew Keel, 2000), 87.

78. Ibid., 93.

79. Nicole Johnson's paper, "Scrubs and Pigeons: The Commodification of Black Male and Female Relationships," was presented at the 2000 Mid-Atlantic Popular Culture/American Culture Association Annual Meeting.

80. "Clear Pictures at BET," *Washington Post*, December 11, 1999.

81. McGruder, *The Boondocks*, 129.

82. "For BET Some Static in the Picture," *Washington Post*, November 22, 1999.

83. "Bad Vibes at Cable's BET," *Newsweek*, October 25, 1999, 78.

84. "Clear Pictures at BET."

85. "Disbelief in the Air at BET," *Washington Post*, November 2, 2000.

86. "For BET Some Static in the Picture."

87. In the months following the sale of BET to Viacom, Tavis Smiley was fired from BET for selling a news story to a rival media outlet. See Mark Anthony Neal, "Big Pimpin' bourgeois Style: The Demise of Tavis Smiley's BET Tonight," Popmatters.com (http://www.popmatters.com/columns/criticalnoire/010329/html), March 29, 2001.

88. Adolph Reed, "The Allure of Malcolm X and the Changing Character of Black Politics," in *Malcolm X: In Our Own Image*, ed. Joe Wood (New York: St. Martin's Press, 1992), 228.

89. Watkins, *Representing*, 51.

90. Ibid., 61.

91. McGruder, *The Boondocks*, 68.

92. Ibid., 12.

93. Ibid., 42.

94. Ibid., 81.

95. Ibid., 92.

96. Ibid., 57.

97. Ibid., 107.

98. See Ishmael Reed's "Christmas novels" *The Terrible Twos* (Normal: Dalkey Archive Press, 1999) and *The Terrible Threes* (Normal: Dalkey Archive Press, 1999) for a more detailed exploration of the Santa Claus/Saint Nicholas myth as it relates to African Americans.

99. McGruder, *The Boondocks*, 69.

100. Cress Welsing, *The Isis Papers: Keys to the Colors* (Chicago: Third World Press, 1991), 1–16.

101. McGruder, *The Booddocks*, 69.

Selected Bibliography

Aronowitz, Stanley. *Dead Artists, Live Theories and Other Cultural Problems*. New York: Routledge, 1994.

Beatty, Paul. *The White Boy Shuffle*. New York: Henry Holt, 1996.

Bentson, Kim. *Performing Blackness: Enactments of African-American Modernism*. New York: Routledge, 2000.

Best, Steven, and Douglas Kellner, eds. *Postmodern Theory: Critical Interrogations*. New York: Guildford Press, 1991.

Bogle, Donald. *Toms, Coons, Mulattos, Mammies, and Bucks: An Interpretive History of Blacks in American Films*. 3d ed. New York: Continuum, 1994.

Boyd, Todd. *Am I Black Enough for You? Popular Culture from the 'Hood and Beyond*. Bloomington: Indiana University Press, 1997.

Boyd, Todd, and Ken Shropshire, eds. *Basketball Jones: America above the Rim*. New York: New York University Press, 2000.

Boynton, Robert. "The New Intellectuals." *Atlantic Monthly,* March 1995, 61–72.

Brandt, Eric, ed. *Dangerous Liaisons: Blacks, Gays, and the Struggle for Equality*. New York: New Press, 1999.

Carbado, Devon, ed. *Black Men on Race, Gender, and Sexuality*. New York: New York University Press, 1999.

Cruse, Harold. *The Crisis of the Negro Intellectual*. New York: William Morrow, 1967.

Dyson, Michael Eric. *I May Not Get There with You: The True Martin Luther King, Jr.* New York: Free Press, 2000.

———. *Reflecting Black: African-American Cultural Criticism*. Minneapolis: University of Minnesota Press, 1993.

Ellis, Trey. "The New Black Aesthetic." *Callaloo* 12, no. 1 (winter 1989): 233–43.

Franklin, Donna. *Ensuring Inequality: The Structural Transformation of the African-American Family*. New York: Oxford University Press, 1997.

Foster, Hal, ed. *The Anti-Aesthetic: Essays on Postmodern Culture*. Seattle: Bay Press, 1983.

George, Nelson. *Buppies, B-Boys, Baps and Bohos: Notes on Post-Soul Black Culture*. New York: HarperCollins, 1992.

Giroux, Henry. *Channel Surfing: Racism, the Media, and the Destruction of Today's Youth*. New York: St. Martin's Press, 1997.

Gray, Herman. *Watching Race: Television and the Struggle for Blackness*. Minneapolis: University of Minnesota Press, 1994.

Green, Al, and David Seay. *Take Me to the River*. New York: Harper Entertainment, 2000.

Grossberg, Lawrence. *Dancing in Spite of Myself: Essays on Popular Culture*. Durham, N.C.: Duke University Press, 1997.

Guerrero, Ed. *Framing Blackness*. Philadelphia: Temple University Press, 1994.

Guillory, Monique, and Richard C. Green, eds. *Soul: Black Power, Politics, and Pleasure*. New York: New York University Press, 1998.

Harper, Philip Brian. *Framing the Margins: The Social Logic of Postmodern Culture*. New York: Oxford University Press, 1994.

Hill-Collins, Patricia. *Black Feminist Thought: Knowledge, Consciousness, and the Politics of Empowerment*. New York: Routledge, 1991.

Holloway, Joseph E., ed. *Africanisms in American Culture (Blacks in the Diaspora)*. Bloomington: Indiana University Press, 1990.

hooks, bell. *Outlaw Culture: Resisting Representations*. New York: Routledge, 1994.

———. *Reel to Real: Race, Sex, and Class at the Movies*. New York: Routledge, 1996.

SELECTED BIBLIOGRAPHY

Hunter, Tera. *To 'Joy My Freedom: Southern Black Women's Lives and Labors after the Civil War.* Cambridge: Harvard University Press, 1998.

Huyssen, Andreas. *After the Great Divide: Modernism, Mass Culture, Postmodernism.* Bloomington: Indiana University Press, 1986.

Jacoby, Russell. *The Last Intellectuals.* New York: Basic Books, 1987.

James, Joy. *Shadowboxing: Representations of Black Feminist Politics.* New York: St. Martin's Press, 1999.

Judy, Ronald A. T. "The New Black Aesthetic and W. E. B. Du Bois, or Hephaestus, Limping." *Massachusetts Review,* spring 1995, 250.

Kelley, Robin. *Race Rebels: Culture, Politics, and the Black Working Class.* New York: Free Press, 1994.

Lewis, David Levering. *When Harlem Was in Vogue.* New York: Oxford University Press, 1989.

Lubiano, Wahneema, ed. *The House That Race Built: Black Americans, U.S. Terrain.* New York: Vintage Books, 1998.

Malcomson, Scott. *One Drop of Blood: The American Misadventure of Race.* New York: Farrar, Straus and Giroux, 2000.

McGruder, Aaron. *The Boondocks: Because I Know You Don't Read the Newspaper.* New York: Andrew Keel, 2000.

McWhorter, John. *Losing the Race: Self-Sabotage in Black America.* New York: Free Press, 2000.

Mercer, Kobena. *Welcome to the Jungle: New Positions in Black Cultural Studies.* New York: Routledge, 1994.

Morgan, Joan. *When Chickenheads Come Home to Roost: My Life as a Hip Hop Feminist.* New York: Simon and Schuster, 1999.

Powell, Kevin, ed. *Step into a World: A Global Anthology of the New Black Literature.* New York: John Wiley and Sons, 2000.

Reed, Adolph. *Class Notes: Posing as Politics and Other Thoughts on the American Scene.* New York: The New Press, 2000.

————. *Stirrings in the Jug: Black Politics in the Post–Segregation Era.* Minneapolis: University of Minnesota Press, 1999.

Reid, Mark. *Redefining Black Film.* Berkeley: University of California Press, 1993.

Smith, Suzanne. *Dancing in the Streets: Motown and the Cultural Politics of Detroit.* New York: Harvard University Press, 2000.

Spillers, Hortense. "Mama's Baby, Papa's Maybe: An American Grammar Book." In *African American Literary Theory: A Reader,* edited by Winston Napier. New York: New York University Press, 2000.

Solinger, Rickie. *Wake Up Little Susie: Single Pregnancy and Race before Roe v. Wade* (New York: Routledge, 1992).

Tate, Greg. *Fly Boy in the Buttermilk: Essays on Contemporary America.* New York: Simon and Schuster, 1992.

Torres, Sasha, ed. *Living Color: Race and Television in the United States.* Durham, N.C.: Duke University Press, 1998.

Watkins, S. Craig. *Representing: Hip-Hop Culture and the Production of Black Cinema.* Chicago: University of Chicago Press, 1998.

Weems, Robert. *Desegregating the Dollar: African American Consumerism in the Twentieth Century.* New York: New York University, 1998.

Woodard, Komozi. *A Nation within a Nation: Amiri Baraka (Leroi Jones) and Black Power Politics.* Raleigh: University of North Carolina Press, 1999.

Zook, Kristel Brent. *Color by Fox: The Fox Network and the Revolution in Black Television.* New York: Oxford University Press, 1999.

Index

INDEX

SOUL BABIES

New Black Aesthetic (NBA), 111–114, 118
New Edition, 11
New Jack City, 138
New jack swing, 85
"New" South, 33
New York intellectuals (1940s/1950s), 117
Newton, Huey, 5–6, 26
Nichols, Denise, 33, 49
Nichols, Harold, 36
Nike Corporation, 113
Notorious B.I.G., 14, 17, 52, 148, 189
N'Sync, 11
NWA (Niggas with Attitude), 72, 186

O'Jays, 16–17, 48, 89, 157
Once upon a Time When We Were Colored, 90
One Hundred Black Men, 153
"One Nation under a Groove," 100
Open Secret: Gay Hollywood, 1928-1998 (Ehrenstein), 127
Osborne, Jeffrey, 16
Out-of-wedlock fathers, 75
Outkast, 21–22, 62, 65
Outlaw Culture (hooks), 119

Page, Lawanda, 59
Panther, 100
Parks, Rosa, 21–22
Patillo-McCoy, Mary, 135
Patriarchy, 24, 26, 61, 64, 70–72, 84, 88–97, 114, 119, 151
 community and, 5
 feminism and, 154
 patriarchal-sexual-religious bond, 78–79
 privilege of, 90
Paul, Billy, 157
Payne, Allen, 81
Peeble, Melvin Van, 66
Peltier, Leonard, 173
Pendergrass, Teddy, 89, 157
Pentecostal tradition, 15–16
Pettigrew, Thomas, 61
Philadelphia International Records (PIR), 89
Philadelphia Negro (Du Bois), 135
"Philadelphia sound," 88
Phillips, Esther, 105

Physical skills
 black male athletes, 143–145
 economic "slavery" and, 143
 language and, 141
A Piece of the Action, 28, 37, 42–43, 46, 52–54
The PJs, 123–127
Plantation, as economic model, 143
The Players Club, 72
Poitier, Sidney, 28, 31, 33, 36–37, 42–43, 46, 49, 52, 58–58
Police brutality, 24, 27, 113
Popular culture; *see* Black popular culture
"Popular poststructuralism," 111
Portier, Sidney, 28–29
Post-soul aesthetic, 2–3, 11
 community reconstitution, 120
 deconstruction of negative symbols/stereotypes, 120
 familiarity component, 15, 17
 gender politics and, 57, 60, 73–88
 intelligentsia and, 11, 102, 104
 McGruder's social commentary, 168–169
 mass consumer culture/mass media and, 121–123
 self/communal critique, 120
 use of term, 103
 working vs. middle-class, 152
Postcolonialism, 107
Postmodernism, 110
 African-Americans vs. white European theorists, 1–2
 marginalized figures, 10
Poststructuralism, 111
Poulson-Bryant, Scott, 110
Poverty, feminization of, 62
Powell, Kevin, 105, 110, 122
Price, Kelly, 161–162
Prince, 11, 13, 18
Pryor, Richard, 30, 42, 52, 110
Public space, erosion/commercialization of, 137

Queer bashing, 24, 119
Queer themes, 127–128
"Quota queen," 74
Quota systems, 105

Racial profiling, 162–163

218

INDEX

Racial symbols, 173
Ralph, Sheryl Lee, 50
Raw, 127
Raye, Lisa, 152
Ready to Die, 148
Reagan administration, 14, 74, 101,
     103–104
Redefining Black Film (Reid), 25–26
Redford, Robert, 28
Reed, Adolph, 90, 118–119, 169
Reed, Ishmael, 109, 116
Reed, Tracy, 49
Reeves, Jimmie, 61
Regents of the University of California v.
     Bakke, 3
Reid, Mark, 25–26, 31–32
Reid, Tim, 90
Reid, Vernon, 109
Religious themes, 78–79; *see also* Black
     church
Reno, Janet, 113
Reproductive rights, 76
Resistance, 25
Retaliation, Revenge and Get Back, 77
"Riffing," 158–159
Riggs, Marlon, 61, 119, 185
Riley, Teddy, 80, 85–86
Roberts, Dorothy, 76
Rock, Chris, 114, 130, 133–134, 163,
     184
Rodman, Denis, 144
Roker, Roxie, 33
"Role of the Negro Intellectual-Survey
     of a Dialogue Deferred," 102
Rolle, Esther, 33, 62, 64–66
Roots: The Next Generation, 72
Roots (Haley), 67, 70–72, 100
"Rosa Parks," 21
Rose, Tricia, 156
Ross, Diana, 18, 100–101
"Round the Way Girl," 150
Roundtree, Richard, 33
Runaway slave, 24–25
Rustin, Bayard, 114

"Sadie," 88
Salinger, J. D., 143–144
Sanchez, Sonia, 107, 120
Sanford and Son, 58, 165
Sankofa, 25
Sartre, Jean-Paul, 2

Scarface, 139, 170
Schuyler, George, 114
Scott-Heron, Gil, 105
Scott, Jill, 131, 134, 150, 156–163
Seale, Bobby, 6
Segregation, 3, 106
Self-actualization of freedom, 24
"The Sermon," 84
Sermon, Erick, 80
Set-aside programs, 105
"Sex Me," 12
Sexism, 119, 151, 153
Sexual violence, 119
Sexuality
     black male and, 25, 155
     female sexuality, 27, 49, 191–192
     primitive sexuality, 25–26
Shakur, Tupac, 9, 68, 79, 119, 153
Shange, Ntozake, 110, 151
Sharpton, Al, 113, 148
Shepp, Archie, 109
She's Gotta Have It, 52, 112
Shropshire, Kenneth, 143–144
Sigel, Beanie, 14
Signifying Monkey: a Theory of African
     American Literary Criticism
     (Gates), 173
Simmons, Russell, 110, 113–114, 132,
     168
Simpson-Brown, Nicole, 72
Simpson, O. J., 24, 72, 124, 153, 166,
     180
Single mothers, 75–76
"Sista-girl" narratives, 157
Sixteenth Street Baptist Church
     bombing, 102
Smiley, Tavis, 166–167
Smith, Barbara, 116
Smith, David Lionel, 9
Smith, Kemba, 168
Smith, Suzanne, 38
Smith, Will, 187–188
Smith, Zadie, 129
Snoop Doggy Dogg, 79
Social criticism, in Kelly's music, 12
Social spaces, 135
     male vs. female, 153
Solinger, Rickie, 75–76
Some Kind of Hero, 30
Soul
     as black aesthetic, 4–5, 7

INDEX